Survival

GLOBAL POLITICS AND STRATEGY

Volume 58 Number 5 | October–November 201⁻

T0312744

'This public civic-nationalist conformism, however, did not reflect what a great many conservative white Americans were really thinking and saying to each other in private ... Trump has publicly articulated their fears and hatreds – and, in the process, severely damaged the civic-nationalist consensus on discourse in the United States, with potentially terrible results for race relations.'

Anatol Lieven, Clinton and Trump: Two Faces of American Nationalism, p. 17.

'Americans have lived so long without the prospect of conquest that voters consider all wars to be wars of choice. Internationalists need to make their case in terms that connect to people's interests, which means beginning by talking about the economy.'

Kori Schake, Republican Foreign Policy After Trump, p. 40.

'Leaders in Riyadh clearly have become convinced that high prices, however comfortable in the short term, have created a false sense of security by deepening the country's dependence on oil rents. In the face of credible threats to long-term oil demand, this poses a very serious risk to the country's economic security.'

Pierre Noël, The New Oil Regime, p. 79.

Survival
GLOBAL POLITICS AND STRATEGY
Volume 58 Number 5 | October–November 2016

Contents

Survival
GLOBAL POLITICS AND STRATEGY

The International Institute for Strategic Studies

2121 K Street, NW | Suite 801 | Washington DC 20037 | USA
Tel +1 202 659 1490   Fax +1 202 659 1499   E-mail survival@iiss.org   Web www.iiss.org

Arundel House | 13–15 Arundel Street | Temple Place | London | WC2R 3DX | UK
Tel +44 (0)20 7379 7676   Fax +44 (0)20 7836 3108   E-mail iiss@iiss.org

14th Floor, GBCorp Tower | Bahrain Financial Harbour | Manama | Kingdom of Bahrain
Tel +973 1718 1155   Fax +973 1710 0155   E-mail iiss-middleeast@iiss.org

9 Raffles Place | #51-01 Republic Plaza | Singapore 048619
Tel +65 6499 0055   Fax +65 6499 0059   E-mail iiss-asia@iiss.org

Survival Online www.tandfonline.com/survival and www.iiss.org/publications/survival

Aims and Scope *Survival* is one of the world's leading forums for analysis and debate of international and strategic affairs. Shaped by its editors to be both timely and forward thinking, the journal encourages writers to challenge conventional wisdom and bring fresh, often controversial, perspectives to bear on the strategic issues of the moment. With a diverse range of authors, *Survival* aims to be scholarly in depth while vivid, well written and policy-relevant in approach. Through commentary, analytical articles, case studies, forums, review essays, reviews and letters to the editor, the journal promotes lively, critical debate on issues of international politics and strategy.

Editor **Dana Allin**
Managing Editor **Matthew Harries**
Associate Editor **Carolyn West**
Editorial **Teresa Herzenberg**
Production and Cartography **John Buck, Kelly Verity**

Contributing Editors

Chris Alden	**Toby Dodge**	**Jeffrey Lewis**	**Teresita C. Schaffer**	**David C. Unger**
Gilles Andréani	**Bill Emmott**	**Hanns W. Maull**	**Steven Simon**	**Lanxin Xiang**
Ian Bremmer	**John L. Harper**	**Jeffrey Mazo**	**Angela Stent**	
David P. Calleo	**Pierre Hassner**	**H.R. McMaster**	**Jonathan Stevenson**	
Russell Crandall	**Erik Jones**	**Thomas Rid**	**Ray Takeyh**	

Published for the IISS by
Routledge Journals, an imprint of Taylor & Francis, an Informa business.

SUBMISSIONS

To submit an article, authors are advised to follow these guidelines:

- *Survival* articles are around 4,000–10,000 words long including endnotes. A word count should be included with a draft. Length is a consideration in the review process and shorter articles have an advantage.
- All text, including endnotes, should be double-spaced with wide margins.
- Any tables or artwork should be supplied in separate files, ideally not embedded in the document or linked to text around it.
- All *Survival* articles are expected to include endnote references. These should be complete and include first and last names of authors, titles of articles (even from newspapers), place of publication, publisher, exact publication dates, volume and issue number (if from a journal) and page numbers. Web sources should include complete URLs and DOIs if available.
- A summary of up to 150 words should be included with the article. The summary should state the main argument clearly and concisely, not simply say what the article is about.

- A short author's biography of one or two lines should also be included. This information will appear at the foot of the first page of the article.
- *Survival* has a strict policy of listing multiple authors in alphabetical order.

Submissions should be made by email, in Microsoft Word format, to the Managing Editor, Matthew Harries, survival@iiss.org. Alternatively, hard copies may be sent to *Survival*, IISS–US, 2121 K Street NW, Suite 801, Washington, DC 20037, USA. Please direct any queries to Matthew Harries.

The editorial review process can take up to three months. *Survival*'s acceptance rate for unsolicited manuscripts is less than 20%. *Survival* does not normally provide referees' comments in the event of rejection. Authors are permitted to submit simultaneously elsewhere so long as this is consistent with the policy of the other publication and the Editors of *Survival* are informed of the dual submission.

Readers are encouraged to comment on articles from the previous issue. Letters should be concise, no longer than 750 words and relate directly to the argument or points made in the original article.

ADVERTISING AND PERMISSIONS

For advertising rates and schedules

USA/Canada: The Advertising Manager, Taylor & Francis Inc., 530 Walnut Street, Suite 850, Philadelphia, PA 19106, USA Tel +1 (800) 354 1420 Fax +1 (215) 207 0050.

UK/Europe/Rest of World: The Advertising Manager, Routledge Journals, Taylor & Francis, 4 Park Square, Milton Park, Abingdon, Oxfordshire OX14 4RN, UK Tel +44 (0) 207 017 6000 Fax +44 (0) 207 017 6336.

SUBSCRIPTIONS

Survival is published bi-monthly in February, April, June, August, October and December by Routledge Journals, an imprint of Taylor & Francis, an Informa Business.

Annual Subscription 2016

Institution	$787	£449	€661
Individual	$216	£128	€175
Online only	$689	£393	€578

Taylor & Francis has a flexible approach to subscriptions, enabling us to match individual libraries' requirements. This journal is available via a traditional institutional subscription (either print with online access, or online only at a discount) or as part of our libraries, subject collections or archives. For more information on our sales packages please visit http://www.tandfonline.com/page/librarians.

All current institutional subscriptions include online access for any number of concurrent users across a local area network to the currently available backfile and articles posted online ahead of publication.

Subscriptions purchased at the personal rate are strictly for personal, non-commercial use only. The reselling of personal subscriptions is prohibited. Personal subscriptions must be purchased with a personal cheque or credit card. Proof of personal status may be requested.

Dollar rates apply to all subscribers outside Europe. Euro rates apply to all subscribers in Europe, except the UK and the Republic of Ireland where the pound sterling rate applies. If you are unsure which rate applies to you please contact Customer Services in the UK. All subscriptions are payable in advance and all rates include postage. Journals are sent by air to the USA, Canada, Mexico, India, Japan and Australasia. Subscriptions are entered on an annual basis, i.e. January to December. Payment may be made by sterling cheque, dollar cheque, euro cheque, international money order, National Giro or credit cards (Amex, Visa and Mastercard).

Survival (USPS 013095) is published bi-monthly (in Feb, Apr, Jun, Aug, Oct and Dec) by Routledge Journals, Taylor & Francis,

4 Park Square, Milton Park, Abingdon, OX14 4RN, United Kingdom.

The US annual subscription price is $787. Airfreight and mailing in the USA by agent named Air Business Ltd, c/o Worldnet Shipping Inc., 156-15, 146th Avenue, 2nd Floor, Jamaica, NY 11434, USA. Periodicals postage paid at Jamaica NY 11431.

US Postmaster: Send address changes to Survival, C/O Air Business Ltd / 156-15 146th Avenue, Jamaica, New York, NY11434.

Subscription records are maintained at Taylor & Francis Group, 4 Park Square, Milton Park, Abingdon, OX14 4RN, United Kingdom.

ORDERING INFORMATION

Please contact your local Customer Service Department to take out a subscription to the Journal: **USA, Canada:** Taylor & Francis, Inc., 530 Walnut Street, Suite 850, Philadelphia, PA 19106, USA. Tel: +1 800 354 1420; Fax: +1 215 207 0050. **UK/Europe/Rest of World:** T&F Customer Services, Informa UK Ltd, Sheepen Place, Colchester, Essex, CO3 3LP, United Kingdom. Tel: +44 (0) 20 7017 5544; Fax: +44 (0) 20 7017 5198; Email: subscriptions@tandf.co.uk.

Back issues: Taylor & Francis retains a two-year back issue stock of journals. Older volumes are held by our official stockists: Periodicals Service Company, 351 Fairview Ave., Suite 300, Hudson, New York 12534, USA to whom all orders and enquiries should be addressed. *Tel* +1 518 537 4700 *Fax* +1 518 537 5899 *e-mail* psc@periodicals.com *web* http://www.periodicals.com/tandf.html.

The International Institute for Strategic Studies (IISS) and our publisher Taylor & Francis make every effort to ensure the accuracy of all the information (the "Content") contained in our publications. However, the IISS and our publisher Taylor & Francis, our agents, and our licensors make no representations or warranties whatsoever as to the accuracy, completeness, or suitability for any purpose of the Content. Any opinions and views expressed in this publication are the opinions and views of the authors, and are not the views of or endorsed by the IISS and our publisher Taylor & Francis. The accuracy of the Content should not be relied upon and should be independently verified with primary sources of information. The IISS and our publisher Taylor & Francis shall not be liable for any losses, actions, claims, proceedings, demands, costs, expenses, damages, and other liabilities whatsoever or howsoever caused arising directly or indirectly in connection with, in relation to or arising out of the use of the Content. Terms & Conditions of access and use can be found at http://www.tandfonline.com/page/terms-and-conditions.

The issue date is October–November 2016.

The print edition of this journal is printed on ANSI conforming acid free paper.

Clinton and Trump: Two Faces of American Nationalism

Anatol Lieven

Hillary Clinton and Donald Trump exemplify – in Trump's case, to the point of caricature – contemporary versions of what I have previously called the thesis and antithesis of American nationalism.[1] Both of these traditions have undergone important changes over the years in response to social, cultural and demographic shifts. Nevertheless, both also embody very old strains of American political culture, stretching back, in some cases, to the foundation of the republic and beyond. The contest between the new forms of these old traditions is likely to define politics in the United States for many years to come.

In terms of overall ideology, the two strands of nationalism in the US resemble similar divides in France and India. Both countries have long possessed one nationalist tradition which stresses the country's identity as a bearer of universal values, and demands loyalty to the state and to those values as the test of being French or Indian; and opposing traditions which define a particular set of religious, racial or cultural characteristics as the test of belonging.

In US foreign-policy terms, this divide corresponds, to some extent, to what Walter Russell Mead has called the 'Wilsonian' and 'Hamiltonian' traditions, on the one hand, and the 'Jacksonian' tradition on the other. (Mead describes a fourth, 'Jeffersonian' tradition that is somewhat more complicated in these terms.[2]) The two traditions can also be defined as

Anatol Lieven is a professor at Georgetown University in Qatar, and the author, among other books, of *America Right or Wrong: An Anatomy of American Nationalism* (Oxford University Press, second edition 2011). He was formerly editor of *Strategic Comments* at the IISS.

Survival | vol. 58 no. 5 | October–November 2016 | pp. 7–22   DOI 10.1080/00396338.2016.1231526

expansionist and defensive (while keeping in mind the old adage about the best method of defence being attack). In cultural and psychological terms, they represent optimistic and pessimistic versions of American nationalism, and it is therefore natural that their respective supporters today correspond roughly to those who feel that, on balance, they have benefited from some aspect of the economic, cultural and social changes of the past half-century (or that they will in future), and those who feel that, on balance, they have lost. Because of their rootedness in American history, and because they are being fed by powerful and ongoing economic, demographic and cultural developments, these opposing nationalist positions will not disappear in the years to come, though both are likely to undergo important modifications.

The likelihood of the enduring power and influence of Trump's ideology in the United States is underlined by the fact that, as David Brooks has acutely observed, while the followers of Democratic challenger Bernie Sanders differ bitterly from Trump's on issues of social and economic justice, the role of the state, race, inclusivity and cultural diversity, they are in some ways very similar when it comes to economic nationalism and their support for a reduction in American commitments and engagements abroad (attitudes, fairly or unfairly, dubbed by the bipartisan US foreign- and security-policy establishment as 'isolationism').[3]

Thesis

I have called the mixture now represented by Hillary Clinton 'the American nationalist thesis' because in recent decades – and in important respects for much longer – its central elements have been propagated by policy elites in Washington DC and by the US school system, and adhered to in public by a large majority of the American people, to the point where dissent (notably on racial issues) has had to be coded, and outright opposition has led to public vilification and serious political and professional harm.

The tremendous strength of this nationalist thesis lies in the fact that it is solidly based on what has been called the 'American creed'. In the words of the Swedish economist Gunnar Myrdal, 'Americans of all national origins, classes, religions, creeds, and colors, have something in common: a social ethos, a political creed.'[4] The religious overtones of the word 'creed' are deliberately intended to suggest a kind of quasi-religious faith and doctrinal conformism among its adherents. The term 'American creed' was first coined by the English Catholic thinker G.K. Chesterton, but has since been used by many American scholars, including Richard Hofstadter, Louis Hartz and C. Vann Woodward. The importance and intensity of the creed in American political culture was summed up by Hofstadter: 'It has been our fate as a nation not to have ideologies but to *be* one.'[5]

The essential elements of the American creed and American civic nationalism are faith in liberty, constitutionalism, the law, democracy, individualism, and cultural and political egalitarianism, and have remained in essence the same ever since they were described by Alexis de Tocqueville in the 1830s.[6] They are chiefly rooted in the Enlightenment, and are derived in turn from English roots: the liberal philosophy of John Locke, and much older beliefs in the law and in the ancient English popular and political battle cry 'the rights of free-born Englishmen'.

In recent decades, racial tolerance and equality have also widely come to be seen as essential components of the creed, and Hillary Clinton and her supporters have added the rights of women and homosexuals – though these rights have been contested by considerable numbers of Americans, to whose sentiments Trump has heavily appealed. Informally, as reflected both in popular culture and in works by authors from Herman Melville to Francis Fukuyama, another important part of the creed is the belief that America embodies and exemplifies the only model of successful modernity in general. 'Americans', observed Frances FitzGerald, 'see history as a straight line and themselves standing at the cutting edge of it as representatives for all mankind.'[7] According to Samuel Huntington,

> It is possible to speak of a body of political ideas that constitutes 'Americanism' in a sense in which one can never speak of 'Britishism', 'Frenchism', 'Germanism', or 'Japaneseism'. Americanism in this sense is comparable to other ideologies and religions … To reject the central ideas of that doctrine is to be un-American … This identification of nationality with political creed or values makes the United States virtually unique.[8]

Both the power of the creed and its overpowering grip on the American mind were noted as long ago as the 1830s by Tocqueville, who wrote that the Americans 'are unanimous upon the general principles that ought to rule human society'.[9] Many of the iconic creedal statements and symbols emerged from the Union side during the Civil War. Between approximately 1890 and 1920, however, two new elements emerged which are of tremendous importance to the political identity and strategies of Clinton and her supporters.

The first was a deliberate rethinking and formulation of creedal civic nationalism as a force to integrate the immense masses of new immigrants to the United States – from ethnic, cultural and religious backgrounds very different indeed from the English, Scots–Irish and Germans who had made up the overwhelming majority of Americans until the mid-nineteenth century – and turn them into loyal American citizens. It was in this sense, and with this purpose, that American progressive thinkers propagated American nationalism in the years before 1914 (which makes it ironic that their descendants are wont to announce that there is no such thing as American nationalism). Clinton and the Democratic Party have introduced or accepted an emphasis on diversity which was not there previously – on which more later – but otherwise are at one with this tradition in emphasising that loyalty to American political and civic values allows anyone to become an American, regardless of their religious, racial or ethnic origin.

The second new element has been summed up in the term 'Wilsonianism', and refers to President Woodrow Wilson's attempt to use American power to expand American values to ever wider parts of humanity, albeit largely through new international organisations such as the League of Nations. Together with this attempt came a new belief that authoritarian states were in some sense natural enemies of the United States, or at least could not be wholly natural allies; and that US power in the world was closely associated with the spread of democracy.

This belief became closely associated with what was later called democratic peace theory, the belief that democracies are less aggressive than other states and, above all, do not fight each other. The foundations for these beliefs were old ones (summed up in the famous phrases 'a city on a hill' and 'the last best hope of earth') but, in foreign-policy terms, Wilson gave them a radical turn from the exemplary to the expansionist. This shift was associated with America's transition from a continental to a global power, and was entrenched in the United States' establishment and much of its political culture by the ideological aspects of the struggle against Nazi Germany and the USSR. As Russell Nye has observed, 'All nations ... have long agreed that they are chosen peoples; the idea of special destiny is as old as nationalism itself. However, no nation in modern history has been quite so consistently dominated as the United States by the belief that it has a particular mission in the world.'[10]

Temporarily damaged by the defeat and shame of the Vietnam War, these beliefs were restored under Ronald Reagan, and appeared triumphantly vindicated by victory in the Cold War, the collapse of communism and the emergence of the United States as the sole global superpower. This national-ist ideology was central to the Bill Clinton administration from 1992–2000, and was exemplified by secretary of state Madeleine Albright. They form a central and recurrent theme both of Hillary Clinton's pronouncements as secretary of state under Barack Obama, and of her memoir of that period, *Hard Choices*, in which she echoed Albright: 'Everything that I have done and seen has convinced me that America remains the "indispensable nation".'[11] As Joseph Lelyveld wrote in his review of that book,

> No opponent will ever get away with accusing her of not embracing the doctrine of American exceptionalism, a civil religion to which every recent president, including Barack Obama, has had to pay homage.[12]

'American exceptionalism' is just another way of saying American civic nationalism without using the word nationalism. It is important to note, as Lelyveld did, that beliefs such as these have in recent decades been com-pletely bipartisan ones, and have been expressed in iconic statements by Republican presidents. Take, for example, George W. Bush's speech at West Point on 1 June 2002, which also ushered in the doctrine of preventive war:

> Wherever we carry it, the American flag will stand not only for our power, but for freedom. Our nation's cause has always been larger than

our nation's defense. We fight, as we always fight, for a just peace – a peace that favors human liberty ... The 20th Century ended with a single surviving model of human progress, based on non-negotiable demands of human dignity, the rule of law, limits on the power of the state, respect for women and private property and free speech and equal justice and religious tolerance.[13]

Similarly, in Hillary Clinton's words, 'We've made a lot of mistakes. But I think if you look at the entire historical record, the entire historical record shows we've been on the side of freedom, we've been on the side of human rights.'[14] Her support for the Bush administration's invasion of Iraq in the name of a mixture of promoting US security and spreading 'freedom' was therefore in no sense accidental, but rather looked forward to her own role in the US intervention in Libya and her demands for US intervention in Syria and elsewhere.

As Lelyveld wrote, 'Faced with a thorny choice – on Afghanistan, Iran, Syria, Libya – [Clinton's] own instinct is usually to act in furtherance of America's "global leadership" role, not abstain.'[15] The closeness of her positions to those of the neoconservatives was demonstrated both by some of her appointments when secretary of state, such as Victoria Nuland's, and by the support for her campaign against Trump by certain neoconservatives, led by Robert Kagan.

This is an almost precise reversal of the process, involving the same families, whereby in the 1970s leading 'Scoop Jackson Democrats' (named after the ideological and strategic Democratic hawk Senator Henry 'Scoop' Jackson) gravitated to the Republicans. The Clinton Democrats prefer to work with allies and international organisations 'whenever possible', and take unilateral US action only 'when necessary'. In practice, however, like George W. Bush, hawkish Democrats have been willing to take unilateral action when backed only by a handful of European states and US dependencies.

Antithesis

If this set of beliefs and attitudes represents the American thesis, what is the antithesis? David Brooks has summed up its central theme as 'we take care of our own'.[16] As Trump declared in his first major foreign-policy speech on 20 April 2016, '"America First" will be the major and overriding theme of my administration.'[17] This tradition does not reject the formal democratic and civic values of the American creed. On the contrary – as exemplified by the Tea Party – it has a passionate and even quasi-religious belief in them. However, it also embodies a strong belief that only white Americans sincerely hold these beliefs and are capable of putting them into political practice. An extreme version of this view was stated by the Christian conservative activist Phyllis Schlafly:

> Global treaties and conferences are a direct threat to every American citizen … Our Declaration of Independence and Constitution are the fountainhead of the freedom and prosperity Americans enjoy. We Americans have a constitutional republic so unique, so precious, so successful that it would be total folly to put our necks in a yoke with any other nation. St Paul warns us (II Corinthians 6.14): 'Be ye not unequally yoked together with unbelievers, for what fellowship hath righteousness with unrighteousness? And what communion hath light with darkness?' The principles of life, liberty and property must not be joined with the principles of genocide, totalitarianism, socialism and religious persecution. We cannot trust agreements or treaties with infidels.[18]

This tradition has its origins and natural home in what Thomas Jefferson called, and what the inhabitants of these regions believe to be, 'the honester South and West'.[19] It has been profoundly shaped by the historical racial politics and conflicts of these regions. Its emblematic historical figure is President Andrew Jackson, who, as a commander of frontier volunteers, defeated and crushed the Native Americans and expelled the British and Spanish from what became the deep-southern states of the United States. Jackson's code was said to embody 'toughness, whiteness and maleness'.[20]

This tradition is obviously deeply militarist, but is limited by its belief that wars should be waged only for the clear benefit of the United States, or in response to attacks on the United States. In Trump's words, 'We will never enter into any conflict unless it makes us safer as a nation.'[21] It has no truck with wars for idealistic motives, since the people these wars are meant to help will be neither grateful nor capable of benefiting from the help America has brought them. It is strongly hostile to foreign alliances, except when they are of unquestionable benefit to the United States, and the United States is in absolute control of them.

Thus while both Trump's and Sanders's supporters are deeply hostile to overseas interventions and military sacrifices that they regard as unnecessary, in the case of Sanders's supporters this is mainly because they distrust the wisdom and benevolence of American power, while in the case of Trump it is because they distrust the foreigners whom such interventions are supposed to help. Both camps, however, unite in a deep distrust of American foreign- and security-policy elites.[22]

Indeed, the Jacksonian tradition's hostility to overseas entanglements is closely tied to its profound hostility to elites, or at least those of the East Coast, California and, especially, Washington. These elites, it is believed, lead America into foreign adventures for their own ideological or personal interests, which have nothing to do with the interests of ordinary Americans. This anti-elitist strain in politics (strongly associated with anti-intellectualism) has run throughout American history, though its moments of dominance have been fortunately rare, and have only occurred when the US has suffered economic depression or the white conservative population has felt either the US or itself to be under particular threat.

The underlying sentiment is, however, perennial. In Walter Russell Mead's words,

> Jacksonian realism is based on the very sharp distinction in popular feeling between the inside of the folk community and the dark world without. Jacksonian patriotism is an emotion, like love of one's family, not a doctrine. The nation is an extension of the family. Members of the American folk are bound together by history, culture and a common morality. At a very basic level a feeling of kinship exists among Americans. We have one set of rules for dealing with one another; very different rules apply in the outside world.[23]

The sense of external and internal threat to America, its democracy, and (white) civilisation has been fundamental to this tradition since the beginning, leading to what Hofstadter called 'the paranoid style in American politics'.[24] In the South and West, this was largely rooted in a fear of blacks and Native Americans.

More generally, however, this fear was produced by the radical and continuous changes stemming from America's success as a capitalist economy and leader of modernisation – from demographic change as a result of immigration, and from cultural change as a result of the undermining of the Protestant cultures on the basis of which American society was formed. Over time, this tradition ingested many immigrants to whom it had previously been bitterly hostile (the most notorious representative of the paranoid style, Senator Joseph McCarthy, was an Irish Catholic by origin), combining with them in hostility to new immigrants, to the existing black minority, and – especially since the 1960s – to cultural changes seen as profoundly threatening to white conservative identities in general. Trump's threats to build a wall to prevent illegal Mexican migration, and provisionally to bar all Muslims (later amended to Muslims from specific countries) from entering the United States, are entirely in tune with this tradition.

Since this reactionary tradition was fuelled by economic change even when globalisation was working overwhelmingly to the advantage of the United States as a whole, it is hardly surprising that it should have flared up in a particularly acute form when the tides of globalisation have turned decisively against a great many ordinary Americans. For the first time in US history, the middle and working classes have seen their incomes stagnate or decline not during a relatively brief depression, but over two generations.

Meanwhile, immigration means that, by mid-century, whites in the United States will have been reduced from a majority to a plurality. The great majority of the new immigrants are Latinos, leading to impending Latino pluralities – and presumably, sooner or later, majorities – in California, Arizona, New Mexico and Texas. Recent Latino immigration has also been extremely unsettling to the old South, which previously experienced very little of the mass migration which transformed other parts of the US, and until the 1990s remained solidly Anglo-Saxon or Scots–Irish (or, of course, black) in origin.

All over the world and throughout modern history, the negative effects of globalisation have produced radical conservative and nativist reactions. Mack Walker attributed the origins of radical chauvinist feeling in nineteenth-century Germany to the shock that modern capitalist economic development (even, in this case, *successful* economic development) brought to the traditional middle classes of Germany's old free cities.[25] This took a sinister turn to modern anti-Semitism in the 1870s and 1880s, when economic depression coincided with the first mass migration of East European Jews to Central and Western Europe. In his own particular American way, Trump fits solidly into this pattern.

The novelty of Trump

If Trump is part of such an old tradition, why has his emergence caused such astonishment and horror among the Republican elites, and American policy elites more widely? Much is due, of course, to his extremely questionable personal character, and the fact that he came into the Republican Party via television, without any background at all in the party or in elected office. His anti-elitism, however, has been the stuff of Republican electoral politics for several decades, and was shared by his main Republican rival, Ted Cruz.

There are two ways in which Trump has sought to shatter the civic-nationalist consensus which has existed now for several decades. The first is his explicit racism. Republicans have exploited racism ever since Richard Nixon adopted the strategy of appealing to Southern whites angered and unsettled by the Democrats' advocacy of civil rights for blacks. For many years, however, Republican racist appeals have been overwhelmingly of the so-called 'dog-whistle' variety, subliminal or coded messages that make their chauvinist point while avoiding overtly racist language or imagery. The particularly feral hatred directed at President Obama (described to the author as an 'Eisenhower Republican' in his policies by a descendent of that president) by Republicans was largely, and obviously, inspired by racism. But this sentiment was publicly expressed through questioning his religion and whether he was really a US citizen.

Politicians who crossed the line into open public racism paid a heavy price. Moreover, Republicans (and some of the conservative Evangelical churches which back them) have also made a genuine effort to present themselves as multiracial, pointing to appointments such as those of Clarence Thomas, Colin Powell and Condoleezza Rice. Conservative organisations such as Fox News have also made symbolic bows in the direction of racial diversity. Concerning Latinos, Republican public attitudes, and policies on migration, have been heavily influenced by the belief that if Republicans conclusively alienated this growing population, they would sooner or later make themselves unelectable to the presidency.

This public civic-nationalist conformism, however, did not reflect what a great many conservative white Americans were really thinking and saying to each other in private. This used to be a matter of anecdotal evidence (such as my own experiences when a student in Alabama in 1978–79) but in recent years the anonymity of the internet and social media has created a massive public arena for white-racist sentiments.[26] Trump has publicly articulated their fears and hatreds – and, in the process, severely damaged the civic-nationalist consensus on discourse in the United States, with potentially terrible results for race relations. The new openness of racism is also reflected in the savage response of many white conservatives to the Black Lives Matter movement, organised to protest police shootings of blacks.[27]

Even more radical have been Trump's 'America First' positions on foreign policy.[28] If, as stated, these are thoroughly in line with an old and powerful strand of the US tradition, it is a strand which has been rigorously suppressed among American elites since Pearl Harbor. In Washington, the charge of isolationism stifles debate and damages careers. One explanation for this, of course, is enduring memories of the catastrophes into which US isolationism (strategic and economic) led the world between 1920 and 1941. Trump has been strongly condemned by leading Republican former officials and experts for his views.[29] But there have also always been American critics who have believed that the particular interests of the Washington elites in US global power have played a key role, and have led them to take up positions that have little to do with the interests of the United States, let alone of ordinary Americans.

In the wake of the disastrous invasion of Iraq (and intervention in Libya), and the failure in Afghanistan, an aversion to new overseas commitments now dominates US public opinion. After the shock of Pearl Harbor and the Second World War, and the subsequent Soviet threat, establishment isolationism of the kind reflected in the America First Committee of 1940–41 disappeared or went underground. Hostility to foreign military entanglements, however, remained a recurrent theme in American popular culture. This can be found in American country music, a tradition deeply entwined with that of Jacksonianism. Thus, country singers of explicit and indubitable patriotism, such as Johnny Cash and Merle Haggard, have also issued iconic statements of America First sentiment. Indeed, this was the title of a Haggard song of 2005, one of the first signals of conservative America's disillusionment with the wars in Iraq and Afghanistan, and with the expansionist strategies of the Bush administration in general.

For even longer, there has been widespread anger both at 'free riding' allies and at US concessions over trade. The charge of free riding against European allies – or, more diplomatically put, criticism for their failure to meet commitments on defence spending – is not of course the preserve only of isolationists. It has been made repeatedly by US officials over the years.[30] Some of the remarks made in 2011 by Robert Gates, secretary of defense under both Bush and Clinton, could have been Trump's:

> The blunt reality is that there will be dwindling appetite and patience in the U.S. Congress — and in the American body politic writ large — to expend increasingly precious funds on behalf of nations that are apparently unwilling to devote the necessary resources or make the necessary changes to be serious and capable partners in their own defense.

Gates warned of a 'two-tiered' membership structure, 'between those willing and able to pay the price and bear the burdens of commitments, and those who enjoy the benefits of NATO membership but don't want to share the risks and the costs'.[31] Trump is, however, the first presidential candidate from one of the leading parties since Pearl Harbor to have criticised the US alliance system as such and threatened to dismantle it if necessary. In an interview with the *New York Times*, Trump questioned the United States' treaty commitments: 'if we cannot be properly reimbursed for the tremendous cost of our military defending other countries … Then yes, I would be absolutely prepared to tell those countries, "Congratulations, you will be defending yourself."' Challenged with the observation that US military commitments around the world had defended international trade and so helped the US economy, Trump replied:

> How is it helping us? How has it helped us? We have massive trade deficits. I could see that, if instead of having a trade deficit worldwide of $800 billion, we had a trade positive of $100 billion, $200 billion, $800 billion. So how has it helped us?[32]

Echoing some eminent foreign-policy thinkers, but defying the overwhelming bipartisan consensus in Washington, Trump has also called for an end to America's feud with Russia. This stance may be motivated partly by Trump's personal admiration for Vladimir Putin, but it also reflects a combination of a deep unwillingness to take on new geopolitical burdens (in this case, financial and military support for Ukraine and increased military commitment to NATO) with a desire to cooperate against more dangerous enemies such as al-Qaeda and the Islamic State.

It could also be noted that Putin, like Trump, is largely the product of a specific national reaction against the negative effects of globalisation. In this and so many other ways, Trump is also close to the nativist and populist parties in Europe, such the French National Front, which are reacting against the combination of economic change, the decline of the old working classes and mass migration.

*   *   *

David Brooks has written that the conflict between 'open' and 'closed' versions of US identity and policy will, over the next decade, destroy the existing configuration of party politics, and define politics for a long time to come. 'Where Trump fails', he says, 'someone else will succeed.'[33] It should be added, however, that this is not only because of the effects of globalisation on different sections of the US population. It is also because these two positions represent old, and even fundamental, traditions of US nationalism. As a result of the reaction to the almost unprecedented shock of 9/11, George Bush was able to mobilise both chauvinist and civic nationalism behind a programme of expanding US global power in the name of spreading freedom and democracy. The disastrous results, however, have helped turn the American antithesis back towards defensive chauvinism. Together with the negative effects of economic globalisation, growing inequality and mass migration on the US white working classes, it seems inevitable that the sentiments reflected by Trump will remain powerful. But so too will the forces perpetuating Hillary Clinton's version of American nationalism. And if the threats of Trump's policies to the United States and the world are self-evident, Clinton's nationalist faith in American power and righteousness also poses great dangers, given the diminishment of that power and the rise of rival states which categorically reject US dominance.

Notes

1   See Anatol Lieven, *America Right or Wrong: An Anatomy of American Nationalism* (New York: Oxford University Press, second edition 2011).

2   Walter Russell Mead, *Special Providence: American Foreign Policy and How it Changed the World* (New York: Routledge, 2002).

3   David Brooks, 'The Coming Political Realignment', *New York Times*, 1 July 2016.

4   Gunnar Myrdal, *An American Dilemma: The Negro Problem and Modern Democracy* (New York: Harper and Bros., 1944), pp. 1–25. For the original use of the term 'American Creed', see G.K. Chesterton, *What I Saw in America* (New York: Dodd, Mead and Co., 1922), quoted in Seymour Martin Lipset, *American Exceptionalism: A Double-edged Sword* (New York: W.W. Norton, 1976), p. 31.

5   Quoted in Hans Kohn, *American Nationalism: An Interpretive Essay* (New York: Collins Books, 1961), p. 13.

6   Alexis de Tocqueville, *Democracy in America*, trans. Henry Reeve (New York: Bantam Classics, 2000), pp. 544ff. and *passim*. See also the definitions of the creed in Lipset, *American Exceptionalism*, p. 19; Michael Lind, *The Next American Nation* (New York: Simon & Schuster, 1995), pp. 90–1, 219–33; and Herbert McClosky, 'Consensus and Ideology in American Politics', *American Political Science Review*, vol. 58, no. 2, June 1964. See also 'USA: The Permanent Revolution', by the editors of *Fortune* magazine, 1951, quoted in Louis Hartz, *The Liberal Tradition in America* (New York: Harcourt Brace Jovanovich, 1955), p. 305.

7 Frances FitzGerald, *Fire in the Lake: The Vietnamese and the Americans in Vietnam* (New York: Vintage Books, 1973), p. 9.

8 Samuel Huntington, *American Politics: The Promise of Disharmony* (Boston, MA: Harvard University Press, 1981), pp. 2–3, 25.

9 De Tocqueville, *Democracy in America*.

10 Russell Nye, *This Almost Chosen People: Essays in the History of American Ideas;* quoted in William J. Cobb, Jr, *The American Foundation Myth in Vietnam: Reigning Paradigms and Raining Bombs* (New York: University Press of America, 1998), p. 4.

11 Hillary Clinton, *Hard Choices* (New York: Simon & Schuster, 2015), p. xiv. For a compilation of Clinton's statements on foreign policy, see http://www.ontheissues.org/2016/Hillary_Clinton_Foreign_Policy.htm.

12 Joseph Lelyveld, 'Hillary', *New York Review of Books*, 25 September 2014, http://www.nybooks.com/articles/2014/09/25/hillary-clinton-hard-choices/.

13 George W. Bush, graduation speech at West Point, 1 June 2002, http://www.usma.edu/classes2/sitepages/grad-speech02.aspx.

14 Clinton, *Hard Choices*, p. 390.

15 Lelyveld, 'Hillary'.

16 'Suddenly the phrase "We Take Care of Our Own" has an exclusivist, menacing and even racist tinge. That phrase and its two possible interpretations sit at the centre of election 2016. Donald Trump's supporters stand for the exclusionist meaning. America's first loyalty is to its own workers, its own culture, its own citizens.' David Brooks, 'We Take Care of Our Own', *New York Times*, 15 July 2016.

17 Donald Trump, speech to the Center for the National Interest, 27 April 2016, https://www.donaldjtrump.com/press-releases/donald-j.-trump-foreign-policy-speech.

18 Phyllis Schlafly, 'Beware of Clinton's "Web" of Treaties', speech to the Christian Coalition, Washington DC, 18 September 1998, http://www.eagle-forum.org/topics/EO/cc_speech.html.

19 A key question concerning the electoral success of Trump and future versions of him is how far they can extend this camp into the Midwest.

20 Michael Kazin, *The Populist Persuasion: An American History* (Ithaca, NY: Cornell University Press, 1998); Anatol Lieven, 'Frontier Injustice', *Nation*, 12 October 2005, https://www.thenation.com/article/frontier-injustice/.

21 Donald Trump, speech after winning New Jersey primary, 7 June 2016, transcript available at http://time.com/4360872/donald-trump-new-jersey-victory-speech-transcript/.

22 Both Trump and Sanders would endorse the hostility to foreign interventions expressed in George Washington's farewell address, and in the following famous passage by president John Quincy Adams in 1821: 'America does not go abroad in search of monsters to destroy. She is the well-wisher to the freedom and independence of all. She is the champion only of her own. She will recommend the general cause by the countenance of her voice, and the benignant sympathy of her example. She well knows that by once enlisting under other banners than her own, were they even the banners of foreign independence, she would involve herself beyond the

powers of extrication, in all the wars of interest and intrigue, of individual avarice, envy, and ambition, which assumed the colors and usurped the standards of freedom … She might become the dictatress of the world. She would be no longer the ruler of her own spirit.' Quoted in Mead, *Special Providence*, p. 185.

23 *Ibid*, pp. 236, 245.

24 Richard Hofstadter, *The Paranoid Style in American Politics* (New York: Vintage reprint, 2008).

25 Mack Walker, *German Home Towns: Community, State and General Estate, 1648–1871* (Ithaca, NY: Cornell University Press reprint, 1998).

26 See Tony Manfred, 'Why is the Internet so Racist?', Business Insider, 24 May 2012, http://www.businessinsider.com/internet-racism-2012-5; Sean McElwee, 'The Hidden Racism of Young White Americans', PBS *Newshour*, 24 March 2015, http://www.pbs.org/newshour/updates/americas-racism-problem-far-complicated-think/; and 'Racism is Still Alive and Well in Online Comment Sections', NewsOne, http://newsone.com/777255/racism-is-still-alive-and-well-in-online-comment-sections/.

27 See, for example, https://www.facebook.com/White-Lives-Matter-1530416620562173.

28 A compilation of Trump's views on foreign and security policy can be found at http://www.ontheissues.org/2016/Donald_Trump_Foreign_Policy.htm.

29 See, for example, the letter signed by 50 Republican experts and former officials, 7 August 2016, http://i2.cdn.turner.com/cnn/2016/images/08/08/trumpletter.pdf.

30 For a well-argued rebuttal of the 'free riding' line of argument about US allies, see Alexander Lanoszka, 'Do Allies Really Free Ride?', *Survival*, vol. 57, no. 3, June–July 2015, pp. 133–52.

31 Thom Shanker, 'Defense Secretary Warns NATO of "Dim" Future', *New York Times*, 10 June 2011, http://www.nytimes.com/2011/06/11/world/europe/11gates.html.

32 'Transcript: Donald Trump on NATO, Turkey's Coup Attempt and the World', *New York Times*, 22 July 2016, http://www.nytimes.com/2016/07/22/us/politics/donald-trump-foreign-policy-interview.html.

33 Brooks, 'The Coming Political Realignment'.

Information Warfare and the US Presidential Election

Nigel Inkster

On Friday 22 July 2016, some 20,000 emails stolen from the servers of the Democratic National Committee (DNC) were published on the WikiLeaks website. The emails, a selection of which had already been passed to American media organisations, were to varying degrees embarrassing to the DNC, in particular by demonstrating that the party organisation was biased in favour of Hillary Clinton at the expense of Bernie Sanders, her rival for the Democratic presidential nomination. The immediate consequence of the leaks was the resignation of DNC chairperson Debbie Wasserman Schultz. But the ripples of this incident, which revealed no evidence of significant wrongdoing within the Democratic Party, spread far and wide, raising serious questions about the extent to which the United States presidential election had become weaponised in the context of a wider geopolitical confrontation.

The DNC had suspected since March 2016 that its network had been penetrated, and had in June sought the assistance of CrowdStrike, a cyber-security company with a strong track record of investigating cyber intrusions that turn out to have a state connection. CrowdStrike claimed to have uncovered two separate intrusions. The first was attributed to a group known as APT 29 (APT standing for Advanced Persistent Threat), which had been inside the DNC network for the preceding year. The second was attributed to APT 28, which had gained entry to the network in April 2016

Nigel Inkster is Director of Future Conflict and Cyber Security at the IISS. He previously served for 31 years in the British Secret Intelligence Service (SIS).

Survival | vol. 58 no. 5 | October–November 2016 | pp. 23–32   DOI 10.1080/00396338.2016.1231527

and appeared to be operating independently of APT 29. An investigation was subsequently launched by the FBI.[1]

Two days after the emails were leaked, Clinton's campaign manager, Robby Mook, alleged that the emails had been 'leaked by the Russians for the purpose of helping Donald Trump'.[2] The Trump campaign promptly denied any connection between the Republican presidential candidate and the Russian government. Russia denied responsibility and complained of the '"poisonous anti-Russian rhetoric" coming out of Washington'.[3] Donald Trump added fuel to the flames, however, by publicly inviting the Russian intelligence services to find and publish the 30,000 emails that had been deleted from the private server used by Clinton while serving as secretary of state.[4] The US media made much of the fact that Trump had adopted an ambivalent attitude towards Russia and had expressed doubts about his willingness to defend NATO allies – by implication against Russian aggression. Reference was also made to the previous involvement of Trump campaign chairman Paul Manafort in providing consultancy services to former Ukrainian president Victor Yanukovych. Michael Morell, the former deputy director of the Central Intelligence Agency (CIA), was even more direct in accusing Trump of having succumbed to Russian President Vladimir Putin's flattery, thereby making himself an 'unwitting agent of the Russian Federation'.[5]

Problems of attribution

The two sets of intruders identified by CrowdStrike are apparently well known to US intelligence. APT 29 is widely assumed to be operated by the Russian Federal Security Service (FSB), which is at once Russia's internal-security agency and its signals-intelligence agency. APT 29 is believed to be responsible for intrusions earlier in 2016 into the unclassified networks of the White House and the US State Department. APT 28 is generally assumed to be operated by the Main Intelligence Directorate (GRU), the Russian military-intelligence service.[6] Quite how the emails were passed to WikiLeaks is unclear, and the picture was further muddied by the emergence of an individual calling himself Guccifer 2.0, who first launched a blog in which he claimed responsibility for the hacking of the DNC network and then made himself available to journalists. His credibility was called into question, however, when, after claiming to be a Romanian national, he proved unable to conduct a conversation in what was supposedly his native language.[7] Guccifer also took the initiative in asserting that the Russian state had not attacked the DNC network, though it was far from obvious how he could have known that.

From a technical perspective, the case for Russian state responsibility is hard to prove beyond reasonable doubt. Forensic examination has identified malware and an IP address used by one of the groups involved in earlier exploits thought to be the work of the Russian state; some of the attack files used had been opened by computers set to the Russian language; and the timings of the intrusions appeared to coincide with the Russian working day, including an absence of activity during Russian national holidays.[8] None of these points are in and of themselves conclusive, however. In the cyber domain, it is relatively easy to engage in 'spoofing' (assuming a false identity); the kind of malware used in the DNC attacks is widely available on the black market; and language settings on a computer are simple to change.[9] Similar points were made about the 2014 attack on the Sony network, which the US government publicly attributed to North Korea – though in that case it became apparent from the revelations of rogue National Security Agency (NSA) contractor Edward Snowden that US agents had penetrated the North Korean networks to the point where they could be entirely confident of attribution.[10] It is unclear whether the US intelligence community has achieved anything like the same level of confidence in relation to Russia, an altogether more sophisticated adversary. If it has, it is unlikely to want to advertise that fact. But it is a safe assumption that the US intelligence community will have spent abundant time and resources studying the techniques and behaviours behind cyber intrusions conducted by, or on behalf of, the Russian state, and will be familiar with the 'signatures' or idiosyncratic characteristics of all the relevant actors.

Furthermore, the most egregious lapses appear to emanate from the GRU, which traditionally has operated to lower standards than its civilian counterpart. In this context, it is noteworthy that the two attack groups appear not to have sought to deconflict each other's presence on the DNC network, and may not even have realised that the other was there.[11] This raises questions about the extent to which the release of the emails was officially sanctioned, and, if so, at what level. In private, US officials have indicated that the intrusions were probably linked to the Russian state, though they have avoided saying so publicly. Shortly after the release of the DNC emails, the Russian FSB reported the discovery of a virus in the networks of some 20 Russian state organisations, scientific and defence corporations, and elements of critical infrastructure.[12] From the scant details provided, it seems unlikely that this represented US retaliation, and may have been an attempt to further muddy the already murky waters.

If we do assume that, on a balance of probabilities, the Russian state was behind the attack on the DNC network and the resultant leaking of its contents, what purpose was this meant to serve? It should hardly be surprising that the intelligence services of a foreign power in a con-frontational relationship with the United States should take an interest in the latter's presidential election and seek to gather intelligence on the process and candidates, including through computer-network exploita-tion. This is particularly true of an election in which, for the first time in living memory, the two presidential candidates appear to have very dif-ferent attitudes towards relations with Russia. While Clinton has adopted a generally hawkish approach, Trump has expressed a desire to 'get along with Russia', and has compared Putin favourably with President Barack Obama.[13] To the extent that Trump has said anything about his approach to foreign policy more generally, he appears to incline towards greater isolationism and reluctance to act as the world's policeman.

Gathering intelligence, however, is one thing. Using it to influence the outcome of an election is altogether different. It is not unimaginable that Russia's intelligence services might have been tempted to try to tilt the US electoral scales in favour of 'their' candidate. But that would be a high-risk strategy for all sorts of reasons, not least because Trump is an unknown and unpredictable quantity whose positions on almost every issue he has addressed during his campaign have been wildly and unashamedly inconsistent.

Russia's new model of conflict

To understand what is probably at issue here, it is necessary to take a few steps back and examine the way in which Russian strategic thinking has evolved since the end of the Cold War, with particular reference to the role of information operations. As Russia has adopted a more assertive nationalist stance – and one that is increasingly at odds with Western interests and values – it has been increasingly seized by the conviction that the West is out to undermine it through the use of soft-power tools such as the internet and social media, and the use of NGOs to promote Western values. This sentiment was first articulated by Russia in 1998, when the country's foreign minister, Igor Ivanov, wrote a letter to the UN secretary-general highlighting Russia's concerns about 'the creation of information weapons and the threat of information wars, which we understand as actions taken by one country to damage the information resources and systems of one country while at the same time protecting its own infrastructure'.[14] This letter was written just as Russia was starting to come to terms with an internet seen by the FSB as almost entirely negative in terms of its implications for Russia's strategic stability.

Over the ensuing decade, a succession of developments reinforced in the minds of senior Russian policymakers the perception that Western countries were attempting to subvert and contain Russia through methods such as the eastward expansion of NATO and the European Union. The sequence of 'colour revolutions' that affected the Arab world and Central Asia starting with Iran in 2009 was seen as further evidence of malign Western intent. In February 2013, Valery Gerasimov, Russia's chief of General Staff, summed up in an obscure Russian journal what he thought was happening and what he believed Russia should do about it:

> In the 21st century we have seen a tendency towards blurring the lines between the states of war and peace. Wars are no longer declared and, having begun, proceed according to an unfamiliar template. The experience of military conflicts – including those connected with the so-called colour revolutions in north Africa and the Middle East – confirm that a perfectly thriving society can in a matter of months and even days be transformed into

an arena of fierce armed conflict, become a victim of foreign intervention and sink into a web of chaos, humanitarian catastrophe and civil war … The very rules of war have changed … The focus of applied methods of conflict has altered in the direction of the broad use of political, economic, informational, humanitarian and other non-military measures – applied in coordination with the protest potential of the population.[15]

The answer, as Gerasimov saw it, was to turn the West's playbook against it via an approach characterised as non-linear war. In this conception, information warfare is seen not as ancillary to other activities, but as something which in many cases replaces conventional conflict. To conduct such warfare first requires taking control of one's own 'information space', thereby ensuring that one's own population cannot access competing narratives that challenge the state's legitimacy. It is a form of conflict that takes place at all times, collapsing traditional distinctions between war and peace and between the military and civilian domains.

In one sense, information warfare can be seen as a lineal descendant of the 'active measures' (*aktivnyye meropriyatiya*) conducted during the Soviet era, a significant portion of which involved putting into the public arena news stories that sought to portray the West in a negative light. The best-known example of this was the planting in an Indian newspaper in 1984 of a story that the AIDS virus, then sweeping through sub-Saharan Africa, was the outcome of a US genetic-engineering experiment.[16] But such efforts, undertaken by Service A of the KGB's First Chief Directorate, were of limited impact before the advent of the information age. In today's post-Cold War world, Russia has many more options to engage in information warfare with the West, including through the use of Russian media outlets such as RT (formerly Russia Today) and Sputnik, which are actually located in the West, and of social media in a variety of languages. A new feature of Russian information warfare has been the 'troll factory', in which Russian state employees masquerading as ordinary members of the public maintain a barrage of social-media posts supporting the Russian government, attacking foreign politicians and commentators, and spreading disinformation. Efforts have also been made to automate some of these activities using bots.[17]

The truth?

The kind of stories disseminated by Russian media outlets are often not much more sophisticated or convincing than those put out during the Cold War by Service A. Many are patent fabrications, even if built around a kernel of truth. But in Russian information warfare truth is the first casualty. The purpose of the country's barrage of mendacity is not to convince but to create doubt and uncertainty to the point where it becomes hard to discern where the truth lies, a case in point being the torrent of mutually contradictory and implausible accounts surrounding the downing of Malaysia Airlines Flight 17 over eastern Ukraine in 2014. The head of RT, which has sought to portray itself as an American organisation, has explicitly stated that 'there is no such thing as objective reporting'.[18] Information operations of this kind rely on the fact that Western governments simply lack the resources that would be required systematically to refute or debunk the huge number of stories put out, and on the Western media's professional obligation to report both sides of a story, thereby giving a veneer of legitimacy to Russian fabrications. Moscow's goal is not to rebut, but to obfuscate. Nor does Russia perceive any need to show itself as morally superior to its adversaries. Faced with extensive Western reporting that Putin stole the 2011 presidential election, the response has been not to demonstrate that the election was in fact free and fair, but rather to suggest that elections in other countries are no better. In this context, it may well be sufficient, for Russia's purposes, to cast doubt on the integrity of the US electoral process and to call into question the legitimacy of the eventual victor. Russia may be assisted in this task by the Trump campaign: acting on the suggestion of his advisers, Trump raised the possibility of electoral fraud at a campaign event in Columbus, Ohio, stating, 'I'm afraid the election is going to be rigged, I have to be honest.'[19]

If Russia did have the ambition to interfere directly with the presidential voting process, it might well be able to do so given the weaknesses of the US electoral system. Secretary of Homeland Security Jeh Johnson's suggestion that elections may need to be regarded as part of the country's critical infrastructure reflects an awareness of how vulnerable to malign interference that system is.[20] Following the 2000 US presidential election, the outcome of which was famously decided by a few hanging chads in the state of Florida, many US states invested in Direct Record Electronic (DRE) voting systems using federal funding provided under the 2002 Help America Vote Act. The outcome of this has been a confusing patchwork of processes, with some states reliant solely on DRE technologies of various vintages. Some of these use Windows XP or Windows 2000 software which is no longer supported by Microsoft, while others do not produce Voter Verifiable Paper Audit Trails, making it difficult, if not impossible, to double-check vote counts. And even though some 75% of votes in the 2016 presidential election will be cast using paper ballots, these results may well be stored, transmitted or tabulated electronically (without benefit of encryption) in ways that might be subject to covert interference. In short, the potential for electoral fraud seems all but limitless, and even if fraud cannot be conclusively demonstrated, the potential to cast doubt on the legitimacy of the process is enormous. As CrowdStrike CEO Dmitri Alperovitch has pointed out, if a hacker claimed after the election that he had attacked a state's electoral system and swung the vote one way or another, it might not be possible to prove or disprove that claim given the current state of the technology.[21]

*   *   *

It is unclear when the full story behind the attack on the DNC network will become clear, if indeed it ever does. Meanwhile, further information from the cache of stolen emails could still be leaked, timed to coincide with upcoming debates or major campaign announcements. The FBI's investigation is ongoing, but the incident has been highly politicised, and it is hard to imagine a response from the White House being interpreted as anything other than partisan. Nevertheless, the presidential policy directive released by Obama on 26 July, which categorises cyber incidents according to their severity, suggests that an incident that is 'likely to result in demonstrable harm to the national security interests, foreign relations, or economy of the United States or to the public confidence, civil liberties, or public health and safety of the American people' should trigger a coordinated response.[22]

This episode is perhaps emblematic of a world in which a plethora of instantly available information perversely makes certainty harder to achieve; in which liberal democracies appear increasingly to be suffering from a crisis of confidence that lends itself to exploitation by authoritarian adversaries espousing very different values; and in which these adversaries are willing and able to exploit a new generation of information weapons. If the US presidential election results in a Trump victory, heralding a shift toward greater isolationism and a realist approach to international relations, that would on the face of it seem a setback for liberal values. The same might be said of a presidential election that becomes mired in incessant challenges to its legitimacy. But it may also be the case that, if the Russian state was indeed behind the attacks and the leaking of the emails, it has overplayed its hand. Perhaps this incident has raised awareness of Western society's vulnerability to information warfare to the point where a more focused and structured fightback can begin.

Acknowledgements

The author wishes to thank Harriet Ellis for assisting with the research for this article.

Notes

1   Max Fisher, 'Why Security Experts Think Russia Was Behind the D.N.C. Breach', *New York Times*, 26 July 2016, http://www.nytimes.com/2016/07/27/world/europe/russia-dnc-hack-emails.html.

2   David E. Sanger and Nicole Perlroth, 'As Democrats Gather, a Russian Subplot Raises Intrigue', *New York Times*, 24 July 2016, http://nyti.ms/2a8P5hy.

3   'Russia Cyber Attack: Large Hack "Hits Government"', BBC News, 30 July 2016, http://www.bbc.co.uk/news/world-europe-36933239.

4   Ashley Parker and David E. Sanger, 'Donald Trump Calls on Russia to Find Hillary Clinton's Missing Emails', *New York Times*, 28 July 2016, http://www.nytimes.com/2016/07/28/us/politics/donald-trump-russia-clinton-emails.html.

5   Rhys Blakely, 'Trump an Unwitting Agent of Russia Says ex-CIA Boss', *The Times*, 6 August 2016, http://www.thetimes.co.uk/article/trump-an-unwitting-agent-of-russia-says-ex-cia-boss-pzkdfvwvp.

6   David E. Sanger and Eric Schmitt, 'Spy Agency Consensus Grows That Russia Hacked D.N.C.', *New York Times*, 26 July 2016, http://nyti.ms/2asxxjG.

7   Fisher, 'Why Security Experts Think Russia Was Behind the D.N.C. Breach'.

8   *Ibid*.

9   Sandro Gaycken, 'Blaming Russia for the DNC Hack Is Almost Too Easy', Net Politics, Council on

Foreign Relations, 1 August 2016, http://blogs.cfr.org/cyber/2016/08/01/ blaming-russia-for-the-dnc-hack-is-almost-too-easy/.

10 Tim Walker, 'Sony Pictures Hack: US Had Hacked North Korea First, Leaked Documents Show', *Independent*, 19 January 2015, http://www.independent.co.uk/news/world/americas/sony-pictures-hack-us-had-hacked-north-korea-first-leaked-documents-show-9988969.html.

11 Sanger and Schmitt, 'Spy Agency Consensus Grows That Russia Hacked D.N.C.'.

12 'Russia Cyber Attack: Large Hack "Hits Government"'.

13 Damien Sharkov, 'Where Do Hillary Clinton and Donald Trump Stand on Russia?', *Newsweek*, 5 August 2016, http://europe.newsweek.com/where-do-clinton-and-trump-stand-russia-487777.

14 Igor Ivanov, 'Letter Dated 23 September 1998 from the Permanent Representative of the Russian Federation to the United Nations Addressed to the Secretary-General', A/C.1/59/3, 30 September 1998.

15 Mark Galeotti, 'The "Gerasimov Doctrine" and Russian Non-Linear War', 6 July 2014, https://inmoscowsshadows.wordpress.com/2014/07/06/the-gerasimov-doctrine-and-russian-non-linear-war/.

16 Christopher Andrew and Vasili Mitrokhin, *The Mitrokhin Archive: The KGB and the World* (London: Lane Allen, 2005), pp. 339–40.

17 Keir Giles, 'Russia's New Tools for Confronting the West', Chatham House, 21 March 2016, pp. 44–6, https://www.chathamhouse.org/publication/russias-new-tools-confronting-west.

18 Peter Pomerantsev, 'Inside the Kremlin's Hall of Mirrors', *Guardian*, 9 April 2015, https://www.theguardian.com/news/2015/apr/09/kremlin-hall-of-mirrors-military-information-psychology.

19 Reid J. Epstein, 'Donald Trump: I'm Afraid the Election Is Going to Be Rigged', *Wall Street Journal*, 1 August 2016, http://blogs.wsj.com/washwire/2016/08/01/donald-trump-im-afraid-the-election-is-going-to-be-rigged/.

20 Kate O'Keefe and Byron Tau, 'U.S. Considers Classifying Election System as "Critical Infrastructure"', *Wall Street Journal*, 3 August 2016, http://www.wsj.com/articles/u-s-considers-classifying-election-system-as-critical-infrastructure-1470264895.

21 Josh Meyer, Ken Dilanian, Stephanie Gosk and Brenda Breslauer, 'Could Russian Hackers Spoil Election Day?', NBC News, 28 July 2016, http://www.nbcnews.com/news/us-news/could-russian-hackers-spoil-election-day-n619321.

22 'Presidential Policy Directive – United States Cyber Incident Coordination', PPD-41, 26 July 2016, https://www.whitehouse.gov/the-press-office/2016/07/26/presidential-policy-directive-united-states-cyber-incident.

Republican Foreign Policy After Trump

Kori Schake

From abroad, it must look as though America has lost its collective mind. For those who rely on the United States' protection, it must unsettle to be reminded how wide open the American political system truly is. For those who care about effective governance, it might mystify that 13 million Republicans cast their ballots in favour of an erratic novice instead of a dozen or so experienced governors and congressmen. For those doubtful of America's decency, Republican nominee Donald Trump's behaviour and the belligerence of many of his supporters must be an affirmation. Republicans are seemingly in thrall to a candidate who repudiates both their principles and their policies.

The American humorist Will Rogers is said to have joked about not being a member of an organised political party, because he was a Democrat.[1] This election has turned the tables on that joke, and much else. Democrats had an orderly nominating process in which the party elders' preferred candidate enjoyed a comfortable 15% cushion of 'superdelegates', while Republicans experienced a second consecutive election cycle with an unwieldy scrum of candidates. The Democratic candidate has cosy ties with Wall Street and a wealthy charity, while Republicans run against the establishment. Democrats have become the party of free trade; Republican voters want to repeal the North American Free Trade Agreement (NAFTA), and oppose the Trans-Pacific Partnership (TPP). Democrats have even become the

Kori Schake is a research fellow at Stanford University's Hoover Institution, and the editor, with Jim Mattis, of *Warriors and Civilians: American Views of Our Military* (Hoover Institution Press, 2016). She is a signatory of several letters deeming her party's presidential candidate unfit for office.

Survival | vol. 58 no. 5 | October–November 2016 | pp. 33–52   DOI 10.1080/00396338.2016.1231528

party of optimism, while Republican voters sound like they have lost faith in the American Dream. As Peter Beinart has argued, Democrats are the new conservatives.[2]

Trump questions whether the United States should honour its treaty obligations to America's allies, while admiring authoritarians. He denies Russia invaded Ukraine, advocates allying with Russia in the Middle East and seems to endorse Russian President Vladimir Putin's sphere of influence.[3] He thinks the American military is a 'disaster', is unashamed to castigate a family grieving the loss of a son in combat, and considers himself to have better military training than those in service because 50 years ago he attended a military high school.[4] He favours 'extreme vetting' of Muslim immigrants, and advocates torturing prisoners and killing their families.[5] He would withdraw from free-trade treaties, advocates a 45% tariff on Chinese imports, and believes the US is falling further and further behind global competitors.[6] 'We don't win anymore', in either war or commerce, is his message; we need to 'make America great again'.[7] Under Donald Trump, American foreign policy could become indistinguishable from the zero-sum, coercive mercantilism of Russia and China.

Republican national-security leaders have denounced their party's candidate as unfit for office.[8] More prominent Republicans have crossed party lines to endorse the Democratic candidate than in any election in memory. Even John Yoo, author of the George W. Bush administration Justice Department's famous memo on the use of torture, counsels that Supreme Court appointments are not a good enough reason to support the Republican presidential nominee.[9]

If Donald Trump wins the election, we will see a historically important test of the institutional checks and balances built into American democracy. In all likelihood, America would be consumed for the duration of a Trump presidency with domestic policy, as he attempted to enact legislation and take executive action against congressional and judicial challenges. That could mean an America disengaged from the world, with all the costs and benefits that would entail for its friends and enemies. But Trump has shown no great perseverance in unpleasant but important tasks; it seems just as likely that he would leave the quotidian negotiations of domestic affairs to Mike Pence, his choice for vice president, and expend his energies on foreign policy, where a US president has greater autonomy. In that case, for foreign policy, Trump would rewrite what it means to be a Republican.

As it happens, Donald Trump could yet defeat Hillary Clinton. It was her very weaknesses as a candidate that drew so many Republicans to contest the nomination. In late August, she was comfortably ahead in national polls, and in polls of crucial swing states such as Florida and Pennsylvania. But margins of error are high, polls have been volatile, and given the unusual nature of this year's election cycle, as well as the transition away from landline telephones (making sample voters harder to reach), the accuracy of polling could be off significantly. While there is currently no evidence Trump supporters are unwilling to admit their voting preferences, that, too, could tilt outcomes.[10] As recently as late July, the FiveThirtyEight polls-only forecast (published by Nate Silver, who predicted the 2008 and 2012 elections more accurately than any other pollster) gave Trump a greater than 50% chance of winning.[11]

Trump would rewrite what it means to be a Republican

Should Clinton win, American foreign policy is likely to be a fairly reassuring prospect: she will continue much of the Obama administration's policies, albeit in ways more congenial to America's friends and with less aversion to the use of military force. We can expect her to find some rhetorical contortion to allow her to support TPP, probably via unilaterally achievable adjustment assistance (welfare payments to people whose jobs are determined to have been lost due to the trade deal). If she wins, the margin of victory will have a significant effect on Republican policies after Trump.

An emphatic victory for Clinton would demonstrate the limited appeal of Trumpism, but probably would not reconcile his supporters to establishment policies. A narrow victory would validate Trumpism as a movement rather than just a moment, sharpening conflict within the party and making even more illusory the Republican National Committee's ambitions of broadening the base of party support.

Whatever the outcome, Republicans have a lot of hard work to do to reclaim the loyalty of Trump's supporters. This election cycle has shown that Republican leaders at the national level have failed at the essential task of providing policy responses to voters' most pressing concerns. Those who argue Trump's supporters can be ignored, or that they will submit to leaders' superior wisdom once repudiated on election day, or that Republicans just need to fine tune their message, are consigning the Republican Party to a generation of electoral losses at the national level, and wholesale destruction of the party of Lincoln via internecine warfare. US policy elites face an anti-establishment moment because our choices have caused a significant slice of the electorate to lose confidence – in expertise, in the fundamental fairness of the system, and in the ability of government to make things better rather than costly, intrusive and worse.

Republicans are still debating the legacies of George W. Bush: big-government conservatism and Wilsonian internationalism. Neither sit comfortably with conservatives. Members of the policy elite who complain that Trump supporters are demolishing the system without anything to replace it are effectively countered, even beyond Trump's base, with the charge that the system is only working for people like them, while the people most in need of opportunities are excluded.[12] Elites will have to respect these views in order to regain voters' trust. And that trust is needed to earn their votes for a foreign policy that keeps the United States prosperous and confronts international challenges in sustainable ways.

What is needed is a careful analysis of who Trump's supporters are, empathy for and engagement with their problems, an understanding of the issues that are motivating their rejection of establishment answers, and the building of a track record of conservative solutions. This is more difficult in domestic than in foreign policy, but Republicans, including 30 governors and hundreds of legislators, are already looking past Trump's candidacy on policy across the board.[13] Even before Trump thundered onto the presidential hustings, House Speaker Paul Ryan was attempting to coalesce conservatives around his Better Way agenda of reform; Yuval Levin's *The Fractured Republic* is an example of thinking about building a foundation of conservative principles that are socially cohesive.[14]

In foreign policy, the key lies in returning to first-order questions. Trump supporters – Republican voters – are genuinely questioning America's role in the world, the relationship between immigration and security, the value of trade and alliances, and whether the United States bears too much of the cost and responsibility of preserving the international order. Republicans owe them persuasive answers on their own terms.

The Trump voter

While it is tempting to see in Donald Trump a clever opportunist uniquely capable of capturing the populist zeitgeist, it would be a mistake to singularise his appeal. This is not the first time the United States has flirted with reckless populism. Americans are a people made great by distrust of their own government, and the populist strain surfaces periodically when change feels especially turbulent, government too slow or disinterested, or avenues of opportunity foreclosed.

The populist strain surfaces periodically

This election resembles the presidential contest of 1824, in which a highly experienced and well-connected candidate was challenged by a celebrity political upstart who cast himself as 'the scourge of a corrupt and abandoned aristocracy' in the midst of a crowded electoral field. Personalities trumped policies in a bitter campaign that narrowed to John Quincy Adams and Andrew Jackson. The speaker of the house cast aspersions on Jackson's record in the War of 1812, declaring him unsuited to the presidency. When the House of Representatives declared Adams president, Jackson denounced the outcome as a 'corrupt bargain', an election stolen from the people's candidate by the political establishment. Jackson spent the next four years building a formidable political machine, and was elected in 1828. In war, Jackson had abandoned his Native American allies and decided, without the permission of his government, to invade Spanish territory. As president he governed equally intemperately, disestablishing the bank serving as a federal reserve, dispossessing Native Americans and refusing to uphold Supreme Court judgments (when told the court had ruled in favour of Native American land claims, Jackson said 'let them enforce it'.)

Only recently have public attitudes shifted enough to remove Jackson from his honoured place on the $20 bill.[15]

Sarah Palin was the leading edge of the current revolt that brought Donald Trump to electoral prominence. Both have billed themselves as outsiders intent on roiling the establishment, compelled media attention and seemed to care little for the practice of governance or norms of political expression. Both have captured support from voters exasperated at costly and intrusive government, and an establishment that seemed to control access to opportunity for its own advantage. Trump has taken Palin's soap opera full-scale operatic.

And, of course, Donald Trump is not the only anomaly in this election. Fifty-three percent of Republican voters are voting *against* Clinton rather than *for* Trump. To give a sense of proportion, that is an increase of 18 points over Republicans who were voting against Barack Obama in 2008.[16] Donald Trump's success is a function of distaste for Clinton's style of politics; to his supporters, she looks like someone who played the system to maximum advantage, whose family connections produce wealth and opportunity unavailable to average Americans, and who suffers no consequence for acts that would land others in prison.

Trump supporters are frequently described as uneducated and racist, their economic prospects dimmed by globalisation. The candidate's own behaviour, as well as that of some of his adherents at rallies and on social media, provides some evidence for this proposition. It does an injustice to Trump's supporters to lump them all into this description, however. Moreover, it is politically unwise, since many of them have previously been mainstream Republican voters: much of the increased turnout of primary voters on the Republican side was provided not by new voters, but by reliably Republican general-election voters who hadn't bothered to vote in primaries before.[17] These are winnable, mainstream voters.

Gallup's Jonathan Rothwell surveyed Trump supporters and found that they

> are less educated and more likely to work in blue collar occupations, but
> they earn relative [sic] high household incomes, and living in areas more

exposed to trade or immigration does not increase Trump support. There is
stronger evidence that racial isolation and less strictly economic measures
of social status, namely health and intergenerational mobility, are robustly
predictive of more favorable views toward Trump, and these factors predict
support for him but not other Republican presidential candidates.[18]

Status and race-based anxiety may matter more to Trump voters than
money, worries about the direction of their country more than their immediate circumstances.

The statement most quoted in focus groups about Trump is that 'he tells
it like it is'.[19] But, of course, Trump doesn't tell it like it is – he tells it like
people with no responsibility for outcomes fantasise about it being. Voters
clearly preferred this to the careful limning of policy on offer from other candidates. Do voters have the stomach for tough but necessary reforms? That
is an untested proposition this election cycle. Still, the strength of Trump
voters' concern about politicians' hedging is an indicator of their belief that
politics does not take their interests into account.

Eighty-one percent of Trump supporters believe life is worse for people
like them in America compared to 50 years ago.[20] Sixty-eight percent of
Trump supporters think free trade is a bad thing; only 17% of them support
TPP.[21] That represents a significant shift, attributable to Trump's candidacy,
since the majority of Republicans supported free trade in May 2015, before
he entered the presidential race.[22] Support for Trump is found less among
those negatively affected by social and economic change than among those
who have not yet been affected, but rightly understand that its continued
advance will leave them behind. They are agitating to rescind change they
anticipate being disruptive to a way of life unsustainable amidst wider
social and economic competition, both domestically and internationally.

As American columnist Sarah Kendzior has emphasised, Trump has
succeeded in positioning himself as a tribune for 'forgotten Americans'.[23]
These are people who worry about the size and cost of government, and
an establishment that funds itself in ways unsustainable for a household.
Many were Tea Party supporters, are exasperated that a wave of opposition
to government resulted in so little change and have grown more tolerant of

symbolic gestures, such as Senator Ted Cruz's efforts to shut down the government, as their confidence in government reform has withered.

Despite the ugly racial politics of Donald Trump and some of his most vocal supporters, the broad social norms of American society have traction. Trump voters, like other Americans, believe in the country's ability to fix its problems. And while they are more suspicious of diversity than other Americans, only 16% of Trump supporters say diversity has actively made the US a worse place.[24] Republican policymaking elites can still find common ground with Trump supporters. But in order to do so, we need to address their legitimate concerns about America's role in the world.

Understanding America

Part of the reason Republican leaders have lost ground with their own voters is that they hold these truths to be self-evident: the United States has an outsize role to play in the world, and that role should not be dictated by its immediate economic circumstances. Voters simply do not understand why a wealthy Europe relies on the US for so much of its security. To be fair, Dwight Eisenhower would not understand it, either. As incoming NATO commander in 1951, he viewed the deployment of American troops to Europe as a temporary measure until Europe regained its strength. What looks to economic- and foreign-policy elites as self-evidently in the American interest is not evident to Trump voters.

It will not be good enough to argue that the United States has a special mandate to create and sustain a peaceful and prosperous international order. That is the argument that has brought us to this point. Americans have lived so long without the prospect of conquest that voters consider all wars to be wars of choice. Internationalists need to make their case in terms that connect to people's interests, which means beginning by talking about the economy. Foreign policy tends to be a field bifurcated between political science and economics. Few of us are truly proficient in both, but we must learn to be in order to persuasively make the case for an America engaged in the world. Otherwise, we will lose the argument.

Americans are in the midst of a profound economic revolution. The combined effects of globalisation and technological innovation are sweeping through the US economy like a wildfire. These forces disproportionately benefit the well-educated and creative while making obsolete not just jobs but entire professions of those least capable of moving to emerging sectors. The history of innovation suggests that as economies adjust, more and better jobs will burgeon around new technologies, so this is a transient rather than permanent fixture of the knowledge economy. But politics is a lagging indicator of economic change; the United States' current discourse, and its proposed solutions, are more apt for 2005 than 2016.[25]

Trump voters, like Bernie Sanders voters, believe there has never really been a reckoning for the economic catastrophe of 2008; bankers who caused it continue to prosper, while those with the shakiest prospects in the knowledge economy suffer. Conservatives will be unable to regain the trust of Trump voters on the economy until they have a credible story to tell about why 2008 happened and what has been done to ensure it will not happen again. Only then can the role of trade in Americans' collective prosperity be justified.

Trade is a particular sticking point with Trump supporters, but it is a recently acquired attitude, so may be malleable if Republicans can craft an explanation that does not sound insensitive to the displacement that blue-collar Americans, in particular, have experienced since the mid-1990s, when the current round of globalisation and technological innovation really picked up speed. Foreign trade saves the average American household $10,000 per year.[26] Yet conservative voters remain unpersuaded: 68% of Trump supporters believe that trade has hurt their family's finances.[27]

Trade is not the job-killing villain so many voters imagine. The Peterson Institute for International Economics calculates that even if all of the $60 billion in merchandise imports to the US displaced American workers, the total would amount to less than one-fifth of job losses in the US.[28] Voters know from their own experience that churn in the American economy destroys lots of jobs; in the 12 months ending in June 2016, the US economy suffered 59.8m job losses and generated 62.3m hires.[29] Voters are less concerned about preserving specific jobs than the disorientation of professions disappearing. That these changes have coincided with major trade agreements such as NAFTA makes for easy scapegoating, but the deeper trend is technological. Mexican drivers are not the long-term threat to long-haul truckers – driverless vehicles are. Yet driverless vehicles will also spur the invention of new jobs. Every age of technological disruption breeds concern about the end of labour — think of Britain's nineteenth-century Luddites — but new and better jobs emerge as the ecosystem forms. Managing the transition is the political challenge.

The most satisfying solution to the United States' current malaise would be faster economic growth that distributed broadly.[30] This would restore conservatives' self-confidence and would make debates about trade less heated. Such growth, however, will be extraordinarily difficult to deliver. US growth relies on global demand, which is currently slack and heading into even choppier waters. Regulatory burdens, so often decried, are devilishly hard to unravel – and in any case contribute to popular environmental and safety outcomes. Labour mobility, education and training can all be nudged by policy, but will also need to be made consistent with fiscal discipline to garner widespread conservative support.

Absent faster growth, restoring support for trade among conservatives will require shifting perceptions of what gets imported, and what creates jobs. Voters mistakenly believe that an avalanche of cheap foreign goods coming into the US is crowding out domestic manufacturing. They get that idea from politicians' emphasis on the trade imbalance, and because practically the only argument conservatives make to counter voter anguish about job losses is to say: 'but everything you buy is cheaper because of trade!' Yet 60% of US imports are intermediate goods that go into manufacturing US products. Trade deals reduce foreign tariffs on US exports and protect that most valuable of American products, intellectual property. Intellectual property is what creates manufacturing jobs for Americans, not just fortunes for Silicon Valley millennials. Conservatives need to tell a story of job creation resulting from the great American tradition of incremental improvement.

There are other good arguments to make, as former US trade representative Robert Zoellick has demonstrated: 'US manufacturing workers whose jobs depend on exports earn on average 18% more than other workers … More than 11 million U.S. workers and one million farmers gain from this global competitive edge.'[31] But getting Trump supporters to listen will require acknowledging a fundamental truth that Republicans have been denying: that trade produces winners and losers. We have too often promoted the 'net benefits' of trade without admitting how much disruption is encapsulated in that antiseptic term.[32]

Former Minnesota governor Tim Pawlenty is the Republican leader best attuned to communicating this problem. His description of the transition that occurred during his father's working life is compelling and recognisable to Trump supporters: as a truck driver, his father could support a family with a homemaker wife and six children, but such jobs are vanishing. Trade and technology have made them obsolete. Many Republicans speak as though adjustment to change is less than the wrenching sense of loss that most people experience. Until Republicans find an answer to the anxiety of people like Pawlenty's father – both a language to connect to their concerns and policy prescriptions that will facilitate transition – they will not recapture support for free trade.

It will not be enough to publish encomia to the benefits of trade in the *Wall Street Journal* or to debunk myths of steel manufacturing in the *Washington Post*,[33] valuable as those approaches are to the policy community. It will not be enough to warn that tariffs were high during the Great Depression, something experienced by few living Americans. We must make converts. Republicans need to actually address the practical problems voters are confronted with: healthcare tied to employment; the hardship of uprooting a family and migrating to where jobs are; wage stagnation that has resulted from international competition and technological substitution. Add to that economy-shaping welfare policies, such as proposals for the solvency of entitlement programmes on which working Americans rely, and one has a pretty solid economic policy.[34] Ryan's Better Way contains these elements.

Understanding the world

Listening to Trump on the campaign trail, one marvels at the reckless abandon with which he would cast away 70 years of painstaking work to construct an international order so beneficial to America's interests. Listening to Trump, one scarcely recognises a world in which the United States is the preferred partner, an establisher of rules that serve its own interests and, because they also benefit others, are not excessively costly to enforce.[35] Crucially, there is no alternative path to prosperity than to opt in to the US-led order; it is American success that ultimately keeps the cost of maintaining order acceptably low. Donald Trump is right that the United States needs to succeed in order for the system to work, which is yet another reason to ground foreign-policy discussions on economic foundations. If the American experiment is seen to falter, the cost of enforcing global order will grow too high for the American public to support.

Where Trump is mistaken is in concluding that the United States is not succeeding. This is a failure of messaging, not policy. The cost of maintaining a beneficial order has never been lower. Defence spending is under 4% of GDP, the lowest it has been since the Second World War, yet no enemy can reasonably believe it could defeat the American military in direct combat. The only winning strategy against the United States is attrition of its willingness to fight. The US has the luxury of stable, law-abiding and cooperative neighbours. The strongest countries in the world are US treaty allies. The only two aspiring great powers, China and Russia, have significant economic and political constraints both in maintaining domestic stability and in attracting international support – and neither has a political model emulated other than by despots. Barriers to US commerce in foreign markets have been reduced, and trade deals, corporate governance and publicity are slowly raising labour and other standards to American levels among US trading partners. The American economy is the engine of global innovation. What country wouldn't trade its problems for ours?

This message has failed to gain traction for two reasons: the messengers, and the moment. Because we are in a time of rapid change, public anxiety is high. Politicians of both parties have failed to provide context, adjust the provision of government services and encourage people to face change bravely. President Obama tried to do this with healthcare, and although both the policy and the way it was passed made it unacceptable to the right, conservatives failed the fundamental test of providing better alternatives. Rebuilding public faith in governance is now a challenge for both parties.

President Obama bears a fair amount of blame in foreign policy because of his strangely passive view of his own administration – listening to him, one would scarcely know he has actually been in charge these last seven years.[36] He also genuinely does not seem to believe that military force can achieve anything other than the most limited of political ends.[37]

Nevertheless, conservatives have veered too far in the other direction with the shrillness of our insistence on American exceptionalism, and adamancy that the president take the advice of military leaders – an attitude both George Washington and Dwight Eisenhower would have found dangerous. Conservatives in the United States are over-invested in military solutions, unpractised in the art of combining political, economic and military elements of strategy, and near-blind to the need for strengthening government capacity beyond the military and intelligence communities. Our mistakes in Iraq – both in the inception of the war and its management up until 2006 – will cast a long shadow over public support for the use of military force. Republicans need to own those mistakes before Trump voters, and other Americans, will trust our judgement. That reckoning is overdue and must be faced squarely.

Getting foreign policy right is difficult

To Trump supporters, we must also say, humbly but firmly, that getting foreign policy right is objectively difficult, even for experienced and well-intentioned people. There are many difficult balances to strike, many elements one can't control or sometimes even influence, and many actors involved. One must often choose from among bad options, deciding which bad outcomes are least objectionable. All of this is much more difficult without experienced people at the helm. This is a tough case to make in this populist moment, but it happens to be true.

Donald Trump is also right that Americans bear too much of the cost and responsibility of preserving the international order. Since NATO's founding, American defense secretaries have been pleading with Europeans to do more, and every NATO summit duly features a policy initiative to more equitably distribute the burden of expenditure. President Obama's exasperation shows through not only in his recent interview with the *Atlantic*'s Jeffrey Goldberg, but also in his limited support for operations by allies in Libya, Mali and elsewhere. Foreign-policy elites on both sides of the aisle have for too long made excuses for allies not doing more.

Trump's policy proposals – declining to honour US defence commitments if allies do not spend enough, repudiating the US–Japan defence agreement, encouraging nuclear proliferation by allies – would further aggravate the problem, however. They would alienate the largest contributors to America's successes, punish the countries most exposed to security threats and encourage international predators, all of which would make the international order more dangerous and reduce the United States' ability to shape outcomes. The relationship between risk and alliance contribution needs more thought. Nice as it would be to rearrange the map such that the most deserving allies have the safest positions, in reality the reverse is usually true. Free riding is a systemic problem in alliance relationships.[38] But privately acknowledging that the US will do more for allies that do more for themselves begins to incentivise different choices over time. Many of America's allies *are* making brave and important changes, especially Japan, and deserve both credit and more assistance.

There are additional ways to incentivise desired behaviour: encouraging initiative, quietly providing gap-filling support and celebrating allied achievements.[39] The Clinton administration's support to Australia in East Timor is an example of this strategy done well. The problem cropped up just after the United States' debacle in Somalia, after which there was no possibility that Congress would allow American military forces to participate in stabilising the breakaway province and keeping peace between a resentful populace and the Indonesian military. John Howard's government in Australia had a strong interest in the success of East Timor's independence, building cooperation with the Indonesian government and supporting an active UN role. The Clinton administration encouraged Australia to lead the operation, while promising any support the Australian military asked for. Australia's success encouraged the Howard government to see itself as a regional leader, emboldening its military in complex operations from which the US has benefited ever since.

As the Council on Foreign Relations' Jennifer Harris and Robert Blackwill point out, other countries more assertively use geo-economics than does the United States.[40] The US uses mostly carrots, rather than sticks. But that restraint garners significant reputational benefits: soft power is largely the power of attraction, not coercion.

Beyond commercial incentives, another proven means of getting allies to do more, neglected of late, is simply to compromise. This is the arrogance of post-Cold War American dominance: US foreign policy demands compliance on the part of allies, instead of the give and take normal in negotiating a mutually beneficial outcome. The Bush administration insisted that countries were either 'with us or against us' on terrorism; the Obama administration will not modify its Syria policy to build a common approach with Turkey, Egypt or Saudi Arabia. If we expect allies to do more, we ought to make the outcomes more worth their while. The same logic applies to Europe, where we fail to reinforce European policies, for example in Ukraine, but complain loudly that they fail to support ours.

Foreign-policy elements are connected to one another: trade creates well-paying jobs; security fosters trade; alliances sustain security cheaply. The US makes the rules by its active involvement with the rest of the world, and prevents the emergence of undesirable rules made by China, Russia or other ambitious states.

Immigration from Mexico is net negative

Immigration has played an outsized role in Trump's campaign as both foreign policy, in the form of the infamous wall on the Mexican border, and security, in his proposed ban on Muslims entering the United States. Trump's broadcasting of anti-immigrant nativism to the world as American policy is a foreign-policy problem. It also threatens prosperity: technology businesses agitate for H-1B visas, while the agrobusiness and construction industries rely on migrant labour. Trump supporters are principally concerned about the relationship between immigration and security – but here, again, politics is out of touch with reality.

Trump supporters wrongly conflate immigration and border control. Immigration is not only America's lifeblood, but is also extremely well regulated. Screening processes are rigorous and adequate to prevent known threats from entering the country. Dealing with unknown threats is a harder problem, but intelligence and law enforcement are more reliable tools than immigration bans.

Meanwhile, immigration from Mexico is negative in net terms.[41] When a surge of Central American immigrants caused public concern, the government of Mexico was the United States' best policy partner, strictly controlling immigrants crossing its own southern border. The main source of illegal immigration to the United States is legal immigrants overstaying their visas; the main violators are Canadians.[42]

Trump supporters are right to believe, however, that the southern border is too porous. Weirdly indicative of this problem is the fact that drug cartels are a major force against terrorist threats along the US–Mexico border. Organised criminals understand that it is in their interest not to induce better border enforcement, so they profit from monitoring terrorist risks. They have become a civil-society contributor, of sorts, to American foreign policy. The United States needs to approach border control with the seriousness of purpose and resources with which it treats military challenges. To this end, House homeland-security committee chair Congressman Michael McCaul proposes a combination of physical barriers, use of data, human-intelligence networks and other means to improve border control and begin rebuilding public trust.[43]

*   *   *

Without answers to the problems motivating Trump supporters, Republicans will not be competitive in national elections. We do not have the luxury of writing off those who have taken the reins of the nominating process. Even if we could, we shouldn't. Trump supporters are not the modern equivalent of the John Birch Society. They are frustrated at their inability to change government policy, and offended by elite condescension. They are worried about their country's future. They want a foreign policy that makes sense to them and connects to their economic concerns. They deserve the respect of Republican leaders, and changes to our policies. If we give them those entirely reasonable things, together we can advance the cause of conservatism and our country's well-being.

Notes

1   P.J. O'Brien, *Will Rogers: Ambassador of Good Will, Prince of Wit and Wisdom* (Philadelphia, PA: John C. Winston, 1935), p. 162.

2   Peter Beinart, 'How Democrats Became the Conservative Party', *Atlantic*, 19 August 2016, http://www.theatlantic.com/politics/archive/2016/08/democrats-conservative-party/496670/.

3   Eric Bradner and David Wright, 'Trump Says Putin Is "Not Going to Go into Ukraine", Despite Crimea', CNN, 1 August 2016, http://www.cnn.com/2016/07/31/politics/donald-trump-russia-ukraine-crimea-putin/.

4   See Glenn Kessler, 'Here's a Guide to Clinton's Claims About Donald Trump', *Washington Post*, 2 June 2016, https://www.washingtonpost.com/news/fact-checker/wp/2016/06/02/heres-a-guide-to-clintons-claims-about-donald-trump/; David Wright, 'VFW Slams Trump, Gold Star Families Demand Apology', CNN, 1 August 2016, http://www.cnn.com/2016/08/01/politics/gold-star-families-trump-apology/; and Michael Barbaro, 'Donald Trump Likens His Schooling to Military Service in Book', *New York Times*, 8 September 2015, http://www.nytimes.com/2015/09/09/us/politics/donald-trump-likens-his-schooling-to-military-service-in-book.html.

5   See 'Donald Trump Calls for "Extreme Vetting" of Immigrants to US', BBC, 16 August 2016, http://www.bbc.com/news/election-us-2016-37086578; and 'Trump: I Would Intentionally Kill Families to Defeat ISIS', ThinkProgress, 15 December 2015, https://thinkprogress.org/trump-i-would-intentionally-kill-families-to-defeat-isis-b5484a36a7a2#.s6psqtuog.

6   Nick Corasaniti, Alexander Burns and Binyamin Appelbaum, 'Donald Trump Vows to Rip Up Trade Deals and Confront China', *New York Times*, 28 June 2016, http://www.nytimes.com/2016/06/29/us/politics/donald-trump-trade-speech.html.

7   'Trump: "We Don't Win Anymore"', Reuters, 18 April 2015, http://www.reuters.com/video/2015/04/18/trump-we-dont-win-anymore?videoId=363906433.

8   David E. Sanger and Maggie Haberman, '50 G.O.P. Officials Warn Donald Trump Would Put Nation's Security "At Risk"', *New York Times*, 8 August 2016, http://www.nytimes.com/2016/08/09/us/politics/national-security-gop-donald-trump.html.

9   John Yoo and Jeremy Rabkin, 'Filling Supreme Court Vacancies Isn't a Good Enough Reason to Vote for Trump', *Los Angeles Times*, 16 August 2016, http://www.latimes.com/opinion/op-ed/la-oe-yoo-rabkin-trump-supreme-court-20160815-snap-story.html.

10 David Rothschild, 'There's No Evidence of the "Bradley Effect" in Trump Polls', *Huffington Post*, 17 August 2016, http://www.huffingtonpost.com/entry/no-evidence-of-bradley-effect_us_57b48764e4b03dd53808f5b9.

11 See http://projects.fivethirtyeight.com/2016-election-forecast. The

polls-plus measure still had Clinton comfortably ahead.

12 Ross Douthat and Reihan Salam, 'A Cure for Trumpism', *New York Times*, 15 July 2016, http://www.nytimes.com/2016/07/17/opinion/sunday/a-cure-for-trumpism.html.

13 Jackie Calmes, 'They Want Trump to Make the G.O.P. a Workers' Party', *New York Times*, 5 August 2016, http://www.nytimes.com/2016/08/06/us/politics/as-trump-rises-reformcons-see-chance-to-update-gops-economic-views.html.

14 Yuval Levin, *The Fractured Republic: Renewing America's Social Contract in the Age of Individualism* (New York: Basic Books, 2016). See also Nicholas Lemann, 'Why Conservative Intellectuals Hate Trump', *New York Times*, 21 June 2016, http://www.nytimes.com/2016/06/26/books/review/the-fractured-republic-by-yuval-levin.html.

15 This section is summarised from my book *Safe Passage: The Transition from British to American Hegemony*, forthcoming in 2017 from Harvard University Press.

16 'Election 2016: Clinton, Trump Supporters Have Starkly Different Views of a Changing Nation', part 1, Pew Research Center, 18 August 2016, http://www.people-press.org/2016/08/18/1-voters-general-election-preferences.

17 Shane Goldmacher, 'Donald Trump Is Not Expanding the GOP', *Politico*, 17 May 2016, http://www.politico.com/magazine/story/2016/05/donald-trump-2016-polling-turnout-early-voting-data-213897.

18 Jonathan T. Rothwell, 'Explaining Nationalist Political Views: The Case of Donald Trump', draft working paper, Gallup, 1 August 2016, http://papers.ssrn.com/sol3/papers.cfm?abstract_id=2822059.

19 '"He Says It Like It Is": Why These New Hampshire Voters Love Donald Trump', Bloomberg Politics, 31 July 2015, http://www.bloomberg.com/politics/videos/2015-07-30/-he-says-it-like-it-is-why-these-nh-voters-love-trump.

20 'Election 2016: Clinton, Trump Supporters Have Starkly Different Views of a Changing Nation', part 2, http://www.people-press.org/2016/08/18/3-views-of-the-country-and-feelings-about-growing-diversity/.

21 'Election 2016: Clinton, Trump Supporters Have Starkly Different Views of a Changing Nation', part 5, http://www.people-press.org/2016/08/18/5-issues-and-the-2016-campaign/.

22 *Ibid.*

23 Sarah Kendzior, 'Donald Trump and His Followers Could Destroy America Even If He Loses', Quartz, 5 August 2016, http://qz.com/751320/donald-trump-and-his-followers-could-destroy-america-even-if-he-loses/.

24 'Election 2016: Clinton, Trump Supporters Have Starkly Different Views of a Changing Nation', part 3, http://www.people-press.org/2016/08/18/3-views-of-the-country-and-feelings-about-growing-diversity/#how-has-increasing-diversity-impacted-the-country.

25 I am grateful to Philip Zelikow for sharing his views on this issue.

26 Robert B. Zoellick, 'Trump Gets

It Wrong: Trade Is a Winner for Americans', *Wall Street Journal*, 7 August 2016, http://www.wsj.com/articles/trump-gets-it-wrong-trade-is-a-winner-for-americans-1470606915.

27 'Election 2016: Clinton, Trump Supporters Have Starkly Different Views of a Changing Nation', part 5.

28 Pedro Nicolaci da Costa, 'Dump Globalization: The Word, Not the Idea', World Economic Forum, 18 August 2016, https://www.weforum.org/agenda/2016/08/dump-globalization-the-word-not-the-idea/.

29 Bureau of Labor Statistics, 'Job Openings and Labor Turnover – June 2016', news release, 10 August 2016, http://www.bls.gov/news.release/pdf/jolts.pdf.

30 Michael J. Boskin, 'The Domestic Landscape', in George P. Shultz (ed.), *Blueprint for America* (Stanford, CA: Hoover Institution Press, 2016), pp. 1–13.

31 Zoellick, 'Trump Gets It Wrong: Trade Is a Winner for Americans'.

32 Robert Verbruggen, 'The GOP Platform and the Working Class', *American Conservative*, 18 July 2016, http://www.theamericanconservative.com/articles/the-gop-platform-and-the-working-class/.

33 See, for example, Robert Samuelson, 'The (Largely False) Globalization Narrative', *Washington Post*, 7 August 2016, https://www.washingtonpost.com/opinions/the-largely-false-globalization-narrative/2016/08/07/7a095582-5b25-11e6-9aee-8075993d73a2_story.html?utm_term=.a2654fb8689b; and Zoellick, 'Trump Gets It Wrong: Trade Is a Winner for Americans'.

34 Michael Gerson, 'Trump's Applause-Line Economic Plan Was a Disaster', *Washington Post*, 11 August 2016, https://www.washingtonpost.com/opinions/reagan-revolution-leftovers/2016/08/11/eb36ce24-5ff8-11e6-9d2f-b1a3564181a1_story.html.

35 John Ikenberry, *Liberal Leviathan: The Origins, Crisis, and Transformation of the American System* (Princeton, NJ: Princeton University Press, 2011).

36 David Frum, 'The Dangers of Obama's Passive Foreign Policy', CNN, 9 April 2014, http://edition.cnn.com/2014/04/09/opinion/frum-obama-passive-foreign-policy/.

37 Jeffrey Goldberg, 'The Obama Doctrine', *Atlantic*, April 2016, http://www.theatlantic.com/magazine/archive/2016/04/the-obama-doctrine/471525/.

38 Mancur Olsen, *The Logic of Collective Action: Public Goods and the Theory of Groups* (Cambridge, MA: Harvard University Press, 1965). For a more sceptical take on the idea of free riding, see Alexander Lanoszka, 'Do Allies Really Free Ride?', *Survival*, vol. 57, no. 3, June–July 2015, pp. 133–52.

39 Peter Dombrowski and Simon Reich, 'The Strategy of Sponsorship', *Survival*, vol. 57, no. 5, October–November 2015, pp. 121–48.

40 Jennifer Harris and Robert Blackwill, *War by Other Means: Geoeconomics and Statecraft* (Cambridge, MA: Harvard University Press, 2016).

41 Jie Zong and Jeanne Batalova, 'Mexican Immigrants in the United States', Migration Policy Institute, 17 March 2016, http://www.migrationpolicy.org/article/mexican-immigrants-united-states.

42 Cedar Attanasio, 'Canadian Immigrants Lead World in Illegal U.S. Visa Overstays, According to First-Ever DHS Estimates', *Latin Times*, 4 February 2016, http://www. latintimes.com/canadian-immigrants-lead-world-illegal-us-visa-overstays-according-first-ever-dhs-367906.

43 See https://mccaul.house.gov/issues/border-security.

Removing Nuclear Weapons from Turkey

Mark Fitzpatrick

A few short years ago, in most of the NATO countries that still hosted American tactical nuclear weapons, public attitudes towards those weapons were becoming increasingly negative. In 2009, Germany began seeking their withdrawal; the following year, Belgium and the Netherlands, along with some other non-weapons-hosting NATO allies, followed suit in calling for a debate on the future of the weapons and on disarmament goals. Italian disarmament advocates campaigned against the weapons hosted in their country. There was also some debate in Turkey,[1] although the weapons there were mostly seen as providing an assurance of assistance from the United States in the event of a security threat, and tethering Turkey to the European mainland.[2]

Russia's seizure of Crimea, intervention in eastern Ukraine and nuclear sabre-rattling largely put an end to the European debate. Europeans found renewed appreciation for America's extended deterrence, and even though the 200 or so B61 gravity bombs in Europe make little practical contribution to enhancing security, their symbolic value was widely recognised. In the face of Russian aggression, unilateral withdrawal made no sense. Now, however, circumstances relating to the 15 July failed coup in Turkey have opened a debate about the wisdom of keeping US nuclear weapons there. Whereas I used to think that the US weapons in Turkey would be the last to be removed from NATO territory, I now expect they will be the first to go, and rightly so.

Mark Fitzpatrick is Executive Director of IISS–Americas.

Survival | vol. 58 no. 5 | October–November 2016 | pp. 53–58   DOI 10.1080/00396338.2016.1231529

Alliance symbol

There have been sound reasons for keeping what are estimated to be about 50 nuclear weapons at Incirlik air-force base in southern Turkey, where their presence is an open secret.[3] Forward-deployed in NATO's southeastern-most partner, the weapons have contributed disproportionately to the Alliance's deterrence posture vis-à-vis potential adversaries on two fronts; both Russia and Iran have paid close attention to them. The physical presence of the bombs has also helped reassure America's most doubtful ally. Turkey's faith in NATO guarantees has been tested repeatedly, most recently in 2003, when the Alliance rebuffed Ankara's request for Article IV consultations prior to the US-led invasion of Iraq. Weighing against Turkish angst over these occasions, the presence of tactical nuclear weapons has reinforced the credibility of the NATO nuclear umbrella.

Just as importantly, the nuclear weapons have also contributed to keeping Turkey loyal to its non-proliferation commitments. It is impossible to quantify this contribution, but it is often cited as a reason the state would have no need for indigenous nuclear weapons, even if Iran's nuclear capability had not been restricted.[4] Turkey has the means to develop nuclear weapons, based on its civilian nuclear industry, but not the motivation, since it has a far easier alternative.

The fact that Turkey no longer trains pilots to deliver the weapons, and does not permit the US to permanently station nuclear-capable aircraft in the country, weakens the ostensible purpose for positioning them there.[5] During times of crisis, air wings from US air bases in Europe would temporarily deploy to Incirlik, as they do now at sporadic intervals.[6] Yet the animosity toward America exacerbated by Washington's perceived indifference to the July coup raises questions as to whether Turkey would allow such a temporary deployment.

New threats

The coup also focused attention on the security of the weapons at Incirlik. The Turkish base commander used assets there to fuel the F-16s that bombed the parliament.[7] In response, the government closed the airspace over Incirlik, cut off its electricity and arrested the commander and nine subordinates.[8]

Labour minister Süleyman Soylu accused the US of complicity, a charge 70% of Turkish citizens believe despite the fantastical nature of the supposed evidence.[9] During previous Turkish coups and coup attempts, there was little reason to worry about the safety of the weapons. Turkey's reaction to the latest crisis, however, exposed widespread anti-American sentiment. Washington's rightful refusal to extradite Pennsylvania-based Fethullah Gülen without legitimate evidence to back up the Turkish government's claim that he instigated the coup is fanning ill will. In making the extradition request a test of the bilateral relationship, as President Recep Tayyip Erdogan, Foreign Minister Mevlüt Cavusoglu and Justice Minister Bekir Bozdag have suggested it is,[10] the Ankara government has signalled a disregard for the mutual security interests that have underpinned relations throughout the post-Second World War period.

If the July coup had succeeded, relations with the West would have been no less imperilled, because of the condemnations that would have issued from many Western capitals and the probable cut-off in US military assistance as required by law (a provision that was avoided in the case of General Abdel Fattah Al-Sisi's coup in Egypt by not calling a spade a spade). Worse for the security of the nuclear weapons, a military overthrow of the democratically elected government could well have sparked domestic strife, bordering on civil war.

The presence of Islamic State (also known as ISIS or ISIL) forces less than 200 kilometres away in Syria, and the increasing number of terrorist attacks in Turkey, has already raised concerns about the threat posed by non-state actors to the nuclear weapons at Incirlik, even though the weapons are stored in underground vaults inside protective aircraft shelters with an upgraded security perimeter. Now the United States has to worry about state actors, too. It is not hard to imagine circumstances resulting in a Turkish takeover of the US part of the base and the commandeering of the nuclear weapons. Expressing the hitherto unthinkable, Ibrahim Karagül, provocative editor-in-chief of the pro-government *Yeni Şafak* (*New Dawn*) newspaper, on 17 August tweeted: 'The nukes in Incirlik must be handed over to Turkey. Or else, Turkey should take control of them.'[11]

The bombs are not invulnerable to siege by a host nation.[12] The Permissive Action Links that protect against unauthorised use may be bypassed, given sufficient time and training.[13] The absence of nuclear-capable aircraft and trained pilots would not prevent hostile forces in Turkey from using the weapons, either in anger or as bargaining chips. As nuclear-weapons expert Hans Kristensen warned, 'You only get so many warnings before something goes terribly wrong. It's time to withdraw the weapons.'[14] Playing out the potential scenarios for further trouble, US defence planners would be negligent if they did not consider withdrawing the nuclear weapons, just as B61s were taken out of Greece in 2001 over safety concerns.[15] Nuclear weapons have been consolidated for security reasons under less worrisome conditions elsewhere. Following a review of security deficiencies, they were withdrawn in 2008 from Royal Air Force Lakenheath in the United Kingdom, and in 2004 from Ramstein Air Base in Germany.[16]

*   *   *

Over the past several years, world leaders have made securing nuclear material a high priority. Among other steps to protect against nuclear terrorism, the four nuclear-security summits held between 2012 and 2016 prompted consolidation and elimination of vulnerable nuclear materials. The entire focus of this summit process has been on civilian-use nuclear material. Consolidation should also extend to the vast bulk of such material that is in military sectors. The most important step is to remove nuclear weapons themselves from situations of vulnerability.

Moving the weapons from Turkey would have its downsides, of course. Signalling lack of confidence in an ally would reinforce Turkey's own perception of US untrustworthiness. Feeling increasingly isolated, Turkey might seek an ally in Russia, or see reason to consider nuclear options of its own. The best outcome might be if Turkey itself asked for the nuclear weapons to be withdrawn on disarmament grounds. Making Turkey nuclear-weapons-free would enhance nuclear security. It would also contribute to the goal espoused – with varying degrees of sincerity – by all members of the United Nations for a Middle East nuclear-weapons-free zone, something in which Erdogan might see some advantage.

Notes

1 Mustafa Kibaroglu, 'Isn't it Time to Say Farewell to Nukes in Turkey?', *European Security*, vol. 14, no. 4, December 2005, pp. 443–57.

2 Mark Fitzpatrick, 'How Europeans View Tactical Nuclear Weapons on Their Continent', *Bulletin of the Atomic Scientists*, vol. 67, no. 2, March 2011, pp. 57–65.

3 Amy F. Woolf, 'U.S. Nuclear Weapons in Turkey', Congressional Research Service, 2 August 2016, available at http://www.fas.org/sgp/crs/nuke/IN10542.pdf.

4 See, for example, Kori Schake, 'Should the U.S. Pull Its Nuclear Weapons from Turkey? They Are Safe and Increase the World's Safety', *New York Times*, 20 July 2016, http://www.nytimes.com/roomfordebate/2016/07/20/should-the-us-pull-its-nuclear-weapons-from-turkey.

5 Woolf, 'U.S. Nuclear Weapons in Turkey'.

6 Aaron Stein, 'Nuclear Weapons in Turkey Are Destabilizing, but Not for the Reason You Think', War on the Rocks, 22 July 2016, http://warontherocks.com/2016/07/nuclear-weapons-in-turkey-are-destabilizing-but-not-for-the-reason-you-think/.

7 Humeyra Pamuk and Orhan Coskun, 'At Height of Turkish Coup Bid, Rebel Jets Had Erdogan's Plane in Their Sights', Reuters, 18 July 2016, http://www.reuters.com/article/us-turkey-security-plot-insight-idUSKCN0ZX0Q9.

8 Eric Schlosser, 'The H-Bombs in Turkey', *New Yorker*, 17 July 2016, http://www.newyorker.com/news/news-desk/the-h-bombs-in-turkey.

9 See Gardiner Harris, 'John Kerry Rejects Suggestions of U.S. Involvement in Turkey Coup', *New York Times*, 17 July 2016, http://www.nytimes.com/2016/07/18/world/europe/john-kerry-rejects-suggestions-of-us-involvement-in-turkey-coup.html; and 'Duplicity Coup', *The Economist*, 17 August 2016.

10 See Mevlut Cavusoglu, 'Turkey: The Night of the Ordinary Heroes', Al-Jazeera, 25 July 2016, http://www.aljazeera.com/indepth/opinion/2016/07/turkey-night-ordinary-hero-160725175106299.html; 'Ankara Calls on US Not to Sacrifice Bilateral Relations Over Gulen', Deutsche Welle, 8 August 2016, http://www.dw.com/en/ankara-calls-on-us-not-to-sacrifice-bilateral-relations-over-gulen/a-19460202; and Euan McKirdy and Hande Atay Alam, 'Turkey's Erdogan to US: Hand Over Exiled Cleric Gulen', CNN, 11 August 2016, http://www.cnn.com/2016/08/11/politics/turkey-us-fethullah-gulen-ultimatum/.

11 See https://twitter.com/aksnmrt/status/765857907971911680.

12 Jeffrey Lewis, 'America's Nukes Aren't Safe in Turkey Anymore', *Foreign Policy*, 18 July 2016, http://foreignpolicy.com/2016/07/18/americas-nukes-arent-safe-in-turkey-anymore/.

13 Schlosser, 'The H-Bombs in Turkey'.

14 Julian Borger, 'Turkey Coup Attempt Raises Fears Over Safety of US Nuclear Stockpile', *Guardian*, 17 July 2016, https://www.theguardian.

com/us-news/2016/jul/17/
turkey-coup-attempt-raises-fears-over-
safety-of-us-nuclear-stockpile.

15 Lewis, 'America's Nukes Aren't Safe
in Turkey Anymore'.

16 Hans M. Kristensen, 'U.S. Nuclear
Weapons Withdrawn from the
United Kingdom', Federation of
American Scientists, 26 June 2008,
https://fas.org/blogs/security/2008/06/
us-nuclear-weapons-withdrawn-from-
the-united-kingdom/.

Brexit: What Have We Learned So Far?

Sophia Besch and James Black

On 23 June 2016, the British electorate defied the expectations of political leaders, financial markets and foreign allies by voting to withdraw from the European Union. Political shock and market upheaval followed. Theresa May replaced David Cameron as prime minister, the opposition Labour party began a leadership contest and the future status of those areas of the United Kingdom (Scotland, Northern Ireland, London and even Gibraltar) that voted to 'Remain' was thrown into doubt. The 'Leave' campaign hailed its 51.9% share of the vote as the declaration of Britain's 'Independence Day'.[1]

Other commentators drew a different revolutionary parallel. For the *Irish Times* and *National Review*, Brexit was 'the world turned upside down' – the tune (perhaps apocryphally) played by disbelieving British troops as they marched out of Yorktown in 1781 after surrendering to George Washington.[2] This cast Brexit as a historic and inglorious retreat, leaving Britain's role and influence on a continent uncertain, perhaps permanently diminished.

Several major questions about the consequences of Brexit cannot yet be answered: What is the future of the UK economy? How will any deal with the EU navigate Parliament? Will there be a second referendum, or a general election? Will other countries follow the Brexit example? Nonetheless, events since June have shed some light on the issues that will shape the answers to these questions in the years to come.

Sophia Besch is a research fellow at the Centre for European Reform, where her work focuses on NATO, EU defence issues and UK–EU relations. **James Black** is a defence and security analyst at RAND Europe, part of the global RAND Corporation, where his work focuses on international security, defence policy and technology and acquisition issues.

Survival | vol. 58 no. 5 | October–November 2016 | pp. 59–67   DOI 10.1080/00396338.2016.1231530

Failure to plan

In the week prior to the referendum, Number 10 Downing Street had grown increasingly bullish about the prospects of victory. Polls showed a consistent swing towards Remain, and financial markets in the UK and Europe priced in the expectation of a vote to stay.[3]

This failure of prediction was matched by a failure of planning. If the latter stages of its campaign increasingly came to resemble the manifesto of a government-in-waiting, the Leave camp had nevertheless refused to set out any detailed explanation of what Brexit would actually mean. The lack of clarity was exacerbated by a ban on contingency planning within the UK government – aside from limited efforts by HM Treasury and the Bank of England – in the light of fears that any such plans could be leaked in order to influence the vote.[4]

During general-election campaigns, of course, there are mechanisms in place to ensure a smooth transition between governments, no matter the outcome, with civil servants producing different sets of briefing notes in order for the opposition to implement its programme if necessary. The referendum did not follow that practice. Subsequent leadership contests in the Conservative, Labour and UK Independence parties, and dramatic oscillations in the political fortunes of key Brexit-supporting figures such as Boris Johnson (now foreign secretary), have done little to provide direction to those who now begin the difficult task of drawing plans together.

Negotiating Britain's withdrawal from the EU, overhauling the domestic legislation affected by withdrawal, and building new institutional, diplomatic and trade relations with Europe and the rest of the world presents Whitehall's most daunting, resource-intensive bureaucratic challenge since the Second World War.[5] Up to 12,295 EU regulations will require careful review in order to be copied or replaced.[6] The scale, complexity and urgency of the task will strain British institutions, and might be too much for their finite human, intellectual and organisational resources.

Particularly problematic is the shortage of British trade negotiators – the UK has some 12–20 in service, by government estimates, compared to around 600 working for the EU, which has managed trade talks for Britain since 1973. To address this deficit, the government has advertised for 300 new positions and begun reaching out to law firms, industry and non-EU allies.[7] Efforts are also under way to persuade British experts working for the EU in Brussels to return home, though some may be reluctant to unpick the same ties of European integration that they have spent their careers building. Initial attempts by the new Department for Exiting the European Union, and its counterpart for international trade, to draw staff from the Foreign Office and other departments have reportedly met with resistance from ministers and lukewarm enthusiasm from civil servants.[8]

Art of the deal

London urgently needs people who know what they are doing. Difficult political choices and years of detailed technical wrangling lie ahead. Those who were hoping the referendum would put an end to Britain's tortuous European debate will be disappointed. If 'Brexit means Brexit', as Theresa May insists, it is less clear which kind of Brexit voters had in mind.[9] The act of leaving does not remove the tension at the heart of Britain's long-standing quarrel with the EU: the economic benefits of the single market are conditional on the free movement of labour and the pooling of sovereignty. The mandate to leave could be upheld through a wide variety of possible arrangements, all of which require compromise.

At one end of the spectrum, economists and business leaders have pushed for Britain to follow the example of Norway and join the European Economic Area (EEA), either permanently or as a stop-gap measure to allow time for further negotiation.[10] In this model, full membership of the single market – including 'passporting' rights, which allow UK banks to do business across the EU while being regulated in Britain – is offset by an obligation to pay into the EU budget and accept freedom of movement.

Alternatively, Boris Johnson has previously backed a free-trade agreement with the EU, perhaps similar to the deal currently in the works between the EU and Canada.[11] That agreement, once ratified, will grant Canadians limited access to the single market, removing most tariffs on goods, but excluding most of the services at which the UK excels. In return, Canada will have no obligation to allow free movement of workers from the EU.

A third model is the bilateral treaty between the EU and Switzerland. Switzerland is closely integrated into the EU's goods market, signing up to EU rules and standards to ensure tariff-free trade. In exchange, its access to EU financial markets is limited, and the Swiss have had to accept the free movement of labour (which has recently been the cause of much political difficulty).

In the weeks since the referendum, any scenario in which free movement of labour can be fully preserved has become increasingly unlikely. It has quickly become the conventional wisdom that a large proportion of Leave voters were strongly motivated by hostility to immigration.[12] As a result, many MPs across party lines, even if themselves in favour of EU immigration, feel bound by their constituents to support tighter controls.

Some hope that Britain will get a better deal than any of the existing agreements and adopt a bespoke arrangement.[13] They count on European leaders' and business lobbies' interest in ensuring that the EU maintains a close economic relationship with its biggest export market, the UK, and are thus aiming for an 'EEA-minus' with substantial curbs on immigration, or a 'Switzerland-plus' allowing passporting rights.[14] A bespoke Brexit sounds like a luxury, but it may be a necessity, as none of the extant models meet all the UK's needs.[15]

Such hopes depend, however, on the goodwill of Britain's negotiating partners. There will not be one set of negotiations, but many: between Britain and the EU; between the various EU institutions and the 27 member states; and between governments and their electorates. Britain's negotiators have the short-term advantage in deciding when to invoke Article 50, which initiates the process for withdrawal. Once triggered, however, the EU immediately gains the upper hand. If no agreement is reached within two years (or an extension approved by unanimous decision), the UK faces the prospect of an unceremonious exit without any new arrangement. To make things worse, new trade deals, and talks with the World Trade Organisation and others, may not be able to proceed until the UK–EU relationship is resolved.[16]

Given these deadlines, one or more member states could hold negotiations hostage. EU members might also seek to punish Britain to deter further departures. Brexit has alarmed many European leaders, who have seen the referendum result welcomed by their own populist parties. It could be that the political and economic fallout of the UK's vote proves deterrent enough – but in any case, elections in France and Germany in 2017, as well as the next round of EU budget talks and European elections in 2019, could all make negotiations more difficult.[17]

Still, Britain is not the only EU country in which a large portion of the population is calling for reform of free movement. Across Europe, there are increasing doubts whether the principle is politically sustainable in the long term, especially given the ongoing refugee crisis.[18] Britain might benefit, or rethink its own position, if this core EU tenet appears to have become negotiable.

Britain's global role

Though the economy and immigration dominated the referendum campaign, Brexit supporters also warned that an independent EU defence policy – more tendentiously, an 'EU army' – risked undermining NATO. Others warned that Brexit was the true threat to the Alliance, as without the UK's strong veto on EU defence matters, less Atlanticist forces would prevail in Brussels.[19] The Kremlin has already expressed hopes for 'more positive relations' with Britain, and Russian state media has hailed Brexit as a sign of weakening Western solidarity.[20] Allies fret that Brexit could signal a more isolationist outlook from the UK. Indeed, Labour leader Jeremy Corbyn – whose lukewarm support for the EU is said by his critics to have contributed to the referendum result – is one notable NATO sceptic.[21]

Western leaders have been quick to emphasise that the business of European defence will continue. Shortly after the referendum, the French and German foreign ministers issued a joint declaration 'recommitting' to Europe as a 'security union' able to effectively plan and conduct military operations.[22] At the Warsaw summit in July, NATO leaders reaffirmed the Alliance's intention to deepen cooperative ties with the EU. And even though its publication was overshadowed by the Brexit vote, the new EU Global Strategy (EUGS) in June set out the EU's strategic ambitions for the first time since 2003.

Nonetheless, the EU has lost one of its most capable military powers, a nuclear-armed permanent member of the United Nations Security Council and a leading intelligence actor. The EUGS quickly risks obsolescence if Brussels does not follow up with an EU defence 'White Book' that takes account of this new reality.[23] Given Britain's continuing interest in and relevance to European security, there is a real desire among many EU members to keep the UK and its capabilities as closely associated as possible.

The UK government also has a continuing interest in investing time and resources into Europe's defence, via NATO, bilateral arrangements or ad hoc support for EU operations. It does so not only to protect its own national interests, but also to buy goodwill abroad as Brexit negotiations unfold, and to demonstrate to other allies (not least the United States) Britain's enduring ambition to be a global player. The Warsaw summit duly saw the announcement that 650 British troops would be deployed to Estonia and Poland as part of a new deterrent force on NATO's eastern flank.[24]

Maintaining Britain's global clout will not be without its difficulties, however. If uncertainty over Europe slows the UK economy, and the fall in sterling continues to harm Britain's purchasing power, the British military may find additional pressure on its already ambitious procurement plans – including the F-35 Joint Strike Fighter, new frigates, armoured vehicles and a *Successor* programme to its *Vanguard*-class nuclear-armed submarines.[25] In terms of bureaucratic capacity, the UK is starting the process of leaving the EU with a civil service 18% smaller than it was in 2010. The Foreign Office has cut a quarter of its budget and lost hundreds of staff, as well as closing embassies and several consulates overseas. Some Brexit advocates insist the need is for quality, not quantity: MP Bernard Jenkin speaks of 'the Northcote–Trevelyan bit of the civil service', referring to the highly trained analytic cadre that Britain has attempted to develop since the nineteenth century.[26] But as a non-EU member, without representation at the European External Action Service or the monthly meetings of European foreign ministers, the UK will need numerous well-connected people in Brussels to network and lobby for British interests outside the negotiating room.

* * *

For the UK, it is already becoming clear that Brexit is the lens through which all policy decisions must now be re-examined, a task made more difficult by the lack of prior planning. How might new contributions to NATO affect the EU negotiations, for instance? How might postponing construction of a nuclear power plant at Hinkley Point affect the negotiating stance of France, or prospects of a trade deal with China? Understanding links between different Brexit negotiations and wider policy could consume much of the government's political and intellectual capital over many years to come.

Negotiations over which model UK–EU relations should now adopt are in some ways a proxy for a wider debate among the remaining EU members about the type of union they wish to build. As such, the talks will test the limits of supra- and inter-governmental decision-making, and the ability of European leaders to pursue collective policy goals while managing political challenges at home. Will European and British leaders find common ground? Will European leaders be able to use Brexit as a catalyst for reform?

At this early stage, it is enough to conclude that the referendum found many basic political and strategic assumptions wanting. At a time when policy elites are increasingly disconnected from their electorates, it was a mistake not to plan seriously for the possibility that those assumptions could be wrong. As a result, for Europe and for the United Kingdom, this is only the beginning of a long and messy process.

Notes

1   Ryan Browne, 'Pro-Brexit Britons Claim Their Own Independence Day', CNN, 4 July 2016, http://www.cnn.com/2016/07/04/politics/brexit-independence-day/.

2   See Denis Staunton and Suzanne Lynch, 'Brexit: Political World Turned Upside Down in Britain', *Irish Times*, 25 June 2016, http://www.irishtimes.com/news/world/uk/brexit-political-world-turned-upside-down-in-britain-1.2699077; and Arthur Herman, 'The World Turned Upside Down', *National Review*, 24 June 2016, http://www.nationalreview.com/article/437085/brexit-britain-votes-independence.

3   Overnight, markets in the UK saw a 10% swing in the value of sterling and some £120 billion wiped off the value of the FTSE 100. Eurozone markets dipped even further: 6.8% in Germany, and 12.5% in Italy and Spain. See Ben Chu, 'Brexit: "Black Friday" for Financial Markets Sparked by EU Referendum Vote',

Independent, 24 June 2016, http://
www.independent.co.uk/news/
business/news/brexit-black-friday-
financial-markets-eu-referendum-
vote-recession-a7101896.html; and
Matt O'Brien, 'The World's Losers
Are Revolting, and Brexit Is Only the
Beginning', *Washington Times*, 27 June
2016, https://www.washingtonpost.
com/news/wonk/wp/2016/06/27/
the-losers-have-revolted-and-brexit-
is-only-the-beginning/.

4   Larry Elliot, 'Mark Carney
Says Brexit Contingency Plans
Under Way', *Guardian*, 24 June
2016, https://www.theguardian.
com/business/2016/jun/24/
bank-of-england-mark-carney-says-
brexit-contingency-plans-under-way.

5   See Lawrence Freedman, 'Brexit
and the Law of Unintended
Consequences', *Survival*, vol. 58, no. 3,
June–July 2016, p. 10.

6   'Building the Brexit Team', *The
Economist*, 16 July 2016, http://
www.economist.com/news/
britain/21702229-bureaucratic-
marathon-lies-ahead-does-britain-
have-enough-pen-pushers-building-
brexit.

7   Peter Spence, 'Government Faces
Worldwide Hunt for Trade
Negotiators, Experts Warn',
Telegraph, 3 July 2016, http://www.
telegraph.co.uk/business/2016/07/03/
government-faces-worldwide-hunt-
for-trade-negotiators-experts-wa/.

8   John Ashmore, 'Theresa May
"Unimpressed" by Brexit Turf War
Between FCO and Trade Department',
Civil Service World, 15 August 2016,
https://www.civilserviceworld.
com/articles/news/theresa-may-

unimpressed-brexit-turf-war-between-
fco-and-trade-department.

9   See Mark Mardell, 'What Does "Brexit
Means Brexit" Mean?', BBC News, 14
July 2016, http://www.bbc.co.uk/news/
uk-politics-36782922.

10 See Wolfgang Münchau, 'The Norway
Option Is the Best Available for the
UK', *Financial Times*, 28 June 2016;
and, for more on the timing of negotiations, Charles Grant, 'Theresa May
and Her Six-Pack of Difficult Deals',
CER Insight, 28 July 2016, http://www.
cer.org.uk/insights/theresa-may-and-
her-six-pack-difficult-deals.

11 Rowena Mason, 'Boris Johnson on
Brexit: "We Can Be Like Canada"',
Guardian, 11 March 2016, http://www.
theguardian.com/politics/2016/mar/11/
boris-johnson-on-brexit-we-can-be-
like-canada.

12 See Michael Ashcroft, 'How the
United Kingdom Voted on Thursday
… and Why', Lord Ashcroft Polls, 24
June 2016, http://lordashcroftpolls.
com/2016/06/how-the-united-king-
dom-voted-and-why/; and Sunder
Katwala et al., 'Disbanding the Tribes:
What the Referendum Told Us About
Britain (and What It Didn't)', *British
Future*, July 2016, pp. 6–10, http://
www.britishfuture.org/articles/news/
disbanding-the-tribes/.

13 Daniel Hannan, 'What Brexit Would
Look Like for Britain', *Spectator*, 23
January 2016, http://www.spectator.
co.uk/2016/01/what-brexit-would-
look-like-for-britain/.

14 Ashley Armstrong, 'The City Pushes
for Swiss-style Brexit', *Telegraph*,
18 August 2016, http://www.
telegraph.co.uk/business/2016/08/18/
the-city-pushes-for-swiss-style-brexit/.

15 For an analysis of the difficulties with all existing deals, see John Springford, 'Britain's Limited Options', *CER Bulletin*, no. 109, July 2016, http://www.cer.org.uk/publications/archive/bulletin-article/2016/britains-limited-options.

16 Shawn Donnan, 'WTO Warns of Tortuous Brexit Trade Talks', *Financial Times*, 25 May 2016, https://www.ft.com/content/745d0ea2-222d-11e6-9d4d-c11776a5124d.

17 Polls suggest a surge in public support for the EU in Denmark, France, Finland and Germany. See Peter Levring, 'EU Support Surges in Denmark as Brexit Scare Spreads in Nordics', Bloomberg, 4 July 2016, http://www.bloomberg.com/news/articles/2016-07-04/eu-support-surges-in-denmark-as-brexit-scare-spreads-in-nordics; Hortense Goulard, 'German Support for EU, Angela Merkel Surges After Brexit: Poll', *Politico*, 8 July 2016, http://www.politico.eu/article/support-for-angela-merkel-rises-after-brexit-poll-eu-referendum-germany/; and Michel Rose, 'EU Support Surges in Big European Countries After Brexit Vote', Reuters, 20 July 2016, http://uk.reuters.com/article/uk-britain-eu-poll-idUKKCN1002A0.

18 'Migrant Crisis: EU at Grave Risk, Warns France PM Valls', BBC News, 22 January 2016, http://www.bbc.co.uk/news/world-europe-35375303.

19 Paul Taylor, 'Brexit Would Leave the EU Less Liberal, Less Atlanticist', Reuters, 6 June 2016, http://www.reuters.com/article/us-britain-eu-future-analysis-idUSKCN0YR0BH.

20 See Ivan Nechepurenko and Neil MacFarquhar, 'Despite Russia's Somber Facade, Glimpses of Joy Over E.U. Referendum', *New York Times*, 24 June 2016; and Christopher Chivvis, 'The Future of Transatlantic Security', *US News & World Report*, 24 June 2016.

21 George Eaton, 'Jeremy Corbyn's NATO Stance Is a First for a Labour Leader', *New Statesman*, 19 August 2016, http://www.newstatesman.com/politics/uk/2016/08/jeremy-corbyns-nato-stance-first-labour-leader.

22 Jean-Marc Ayrault and Frank-Walter Steinmeier, 'A Strong Europe in a World of Uncertainties', Federal Foreign Office, 27 June 2016, https://www.auswaertiges-amt.de/EN/Europa/Aktuell/160624-BM-AM-FRA_ST.html.

23 Or, if not a White Book, an equivalent document that sets out the EU's level of military ambition.

24 NATO, 'Warsaw Summit Communiqué', 9 July 2016, http://www.nato.int/cps/en/natohq/official_texts_133169.htm.

25 Andrew Chuter, 'After Brexit, What's Next for Defense?', Defense News, 24 June 2016, http://www.defensenews.com/story/defense/2016/06/24/after-brexit-whats-next-defense/86333926/.

26 Jess Bowie and Matt Foster, 'Former Civil Service Head Lord Kerslake: Brexit Challenge Should Prompt Rethink on Job Cuts', Civil Service World, 27 June 2016, http://www.civilserviceworld.com/articles/news/former-civil-service-head-lord-kerslake-brexit-challenge-should-prompt-rethink-job.

Noteworthy

Dramatic exit

'Nothing is really impossible if you put your mind to it.'

> David Cameron addresses Parliament for the last time as prime minister on 13 July 2016, having resigned after the United Kingdom's 23 June vote to leave the European Union.[1]

'We expect the UK to experience a marked economic slowdown in the second half of this year and throughout 2017. There is an even chance of a technical recession in the next 18 months while there is an elevated risk of further deterioration in the near term.'

> Simon Kirby, principal research fellow at the National Institute of Economic and Social Research (NIESR).[2]

'Upside: Boris Johnson as UK Foreign Secretary is an absolute godsend for social media satire. Downside: Most other things.'

> US political scientist (and Survival contributing editor) Ian Bremmer responds, via Twitter, to Johnson's appointment.[3]

35,022

Number of people detained, according to Turkey's justice minister, for their alleged role in the 15 July coup attempt

17,740

Number of people arrested on specific charges, including 5,226 military personnel

81,494

Number of people fired or suspended from various institutions and state departments, including more than 42,767 from the Ministry of Education

2,000

Number of institutions shut down that the government says are linked to suspected coup leader Fethullah Gülen[4]

Life after Nice

'We would like to tell the French people that we will never give in. We will not give in to the terrorist threat. The times have changed, and France should learn to live with terrorism.'

> French Prime Minister Manuel Valls makes a statement following the terror attack in Nice on 14 July that killed 86 people.[5]

'A lot of this stuff is at the fringes of what we would historically think of as terrorism. The Islamic State and jihadism has become a kind of refuge for some unstable people who are at the end of their rope and decide they can redeem their screwed-up lives.'

> Daniel Benjamin, a former State Department coordinator for counterterrorism and a professor at Dartmouth College.[6]

Numbers game

'Turn to Page 459, No. 35; Page 913, No. 55; Page 135, No. 86 …'

Pyongyang Radio broadcasts what the announcer described as 'a mathematics review assignment for investigative agent No. 27', a coded message, on 15 July 2016.[7]

Gold Star response

'Donald Trump … Let me ask you: Have you even read the United States constitution? I will gladly lend you my copy.'

Khizr Khan, father of late US military Captain Humayun Khan, speaks at the Democratic National Convention on 28 July 2016.[8]

Britain's difficult war

'We have concluded that the UK chose to join the invasion of Iraq before the peaceful options for disarmament had been exhausted. Military action at that time was not a last resort.'

The Chilcot inquiry delivers its assessment of the decision by British prime minister Tony Blair to join the US-led invasion of Iraq in 2003, in a report released on 6 July 2016.[9]

'Whether people agree or disagree with my decision to take military action against Saddam Hussein, I took it in good faith and in what I believed to be the best interests of the country.'

Blair responds, in a public statement issued on the day of the report's release.[10]

Chinese hopes dashed

'The Tribunal concluded that there was no legal basis for China to claim historic rights to resources within the sea areas falling within the "nine-dash line".'

The Permanent Court of Arbitration in The Hague delivers its ruling on a case brought by the Philippines against Chinese actions and claims in the South China Sea.[11]

'China will take all necessary measures to protect its territorial sovereignty and maritime rights and interests. China in the past was weak … but now has multiple means at its disposal. Provocateurs are doomed to fail.'

The ruling Communist Party's official People's Daily *responds in a front-page commentary.[12]*

Peace at last

'May this be the last day of the war.'

Timoleón 'Timochenko' Jiménez, head of the Colombian guerrilla group FARC, signs a ceasefire agreement with the Colombian government on 23 June 2016.[13]

'Now that we have agreed peace, as head of state and as a Colombian, I will argue, with equal determination their right to express and to continue their political struggle by legal means, even if we never agree. That is the essence of democracy to which we welcome them.'

Colombian President Juan Manuel Santos.[14]

Sources

1 Peter Walker, 'David Cameron Delivers Parting Shots at Jeremy Corbyn in Final PMQs', *Guardian*, 13 July 2016, http://www.theguardian.com/politics/2016/jul/13/david-cameron-parting-shots-at-labour-final-pmqs.

2 Sean Farrell, 'UK "Has 50% Chance of Slipping into Recession Within 18 Months"', *Guardian*, 3 August 2016, https://www.theguardian.com/business/2016/aug/03/bank-of-england-urged-to-use-sledgehammer-to-combat-brexit-slump.

3 Ian Bremmer, Twitter, 14 July 2016, https://twitter.com/ianbremmer/status/753348314653876225.

4 Lauren Said-Moorhouse, 'This Is How Many People Turkey Has Arrested Since the Failed Coup', CNN, 13 August 2016, http://edition.cnn.com/2016/07/29/europe/turkey-post-coup-arrest-numbers.

5 Alissa J. Rubin et al., 'Scores Die in Nice, France, as Truck Plows into Bastille Day Crowd', *New York Times*, 14 July 2016, http://www.nytimes.com/2016/07/15/world/europe/nice-france-truck-bastille-day.html.

6 Mark Mazzetti and Eric Schmitt, 'In the Age of ISIS, Who's a Terrorist, and Who's Simply Deranged?', *New York Times*, 17 July 2016, http://www.nytimes.com/2016/07/18/world/europe/in-the-age-of-isis-whos-a-terrorist-and-whos-simply-deranged.html.

7 Choe Sang-Hun, 'North Korea Revives Coded Spy Broadcasts After 16-Year Silence', *New York Times*, 21 July 2016, http://www.nytimes.com/2016/07/22/world/asia/north-korea-spy-radio-broadcasts.html.

8 Paul Owen, 'Fallen Muslim American Soldier's Father Scolds Trump: "Have You Even Read the Constitution?"', *Guardian*, https://www.theguardian.com/us-news/2016/jul/29/khizr-khan-democratic-convention-constitution-trump.

9 'Statement by Sir John Chilcot: 6 July 2016', Iraq Inquiry, 6 July 2016, http://www.iraqinquiry.org.uk/media/247010/2016-09-06-sir-john-chilcots-public-statement.pdf.

10 'Chilcot Report: Read Tony Blair's Full Statement in Response to the Iraq War Inquiry', *Independent*, 6 July 2016, http://www.independent.co.uk/news/uk/politics/chilcot-report-tony-blair-read-response-statement-in-full-iraq-war-inquiry-a7123251.html.

11 'Press Release: The South China Sea Arbitration', Permanent Court of Arbitration, The Hague, 12 July 2016, https://assets.documentcloud.org/documents/2990864/Press-Release-on-South-China-Sea-Decision.pdf.

12 Ben Blanchard and Martin Petty, 'China Vows to Protect South China Sea Sovereignty, Manila Upbeat', Reuters, http://www.reuters.com/article/us-southchinasea-ruling-stakes-idUSKCN0ZS02U.

13 Sibylla Brodzinsky and Jonathan Watts, 'Colombia and Farc Rebels Sign Historic Ceasefire Deal to End 50-Year Conflict', *Guardian*, 23 June 2016, https://www.theguardian.com/world/2016/jun/23/colombia-farc-rebel-ceasefire-agreement-havana.

14 *Ibid.*

The New Oil Regime

Pierre Noël

The oil-price collapse that started in June 2014 was not just a correction typical of commodity markets. It will be seen retrospectively as the inauguration of a new era.

The oil industry has gone through a constant process of change since the oil-price shocks of the 1970s, but one key, structural feature has endured. The sovereign owners of the cheapest resources on earth – notably Saudi Arabia and other Gulf producers – have exploited them much less intensively than would have been the case under a competitive market structure. Because of the relative unresponsiveness of both supply and demand for oil to changes in price, the Saudi-led oil cartel of low-cost Gulf producers has been able to withhold cheap oil from the market, shifting marginal supply to more expensive oil fields. Hence, for decades, oil has been sold for more than it would have cost in a competitive industry. This strategy has generated huge economic rents for the industry's key players, including Gulf sovereigns and publicly traded oil companies. Today, however, this structure is being eroded, and may even be collapsing before our eyes.

The emergence of the North American shale-oil industry as a large and price-responsive source of supply is a key component of this change. However, it is the strategic response of Saudi Arabia, and by extension other low-cost resource owners, to the shale-oil revolution that has triggered the emergence of a new regime. Countries such as Saudi Arabia and the United Arab Emirates (UAE) are investing to produce more oil in an attempt to

Pierre Noël is the Sultan Hassanal Bolkiah Senior Fellow in Economic and Energy Security at the IISS.

Survival | vol. 58 no. 5 | October–November 2016 | pp. 71–82   DOI 10.1080/00396338.2016.1231532

displace higher-cost sources of supply – including US shale. This strategy is supported by growing fears among Gulf producers that long-term demand – and therefore the value of their reserves – may be under threat from environmental regulations and technological advances.

Reflecting the latter risk, Saudi Arabia is embarking on a radical economic overhaul. Moving away from being a rentier society will involve painful change, and will only succeed if Saudis can be convinced that oil prices cannot durably move back up. Lower prices were initially imposed on Saudi Arabia by the shale revolution; today, the Kingdom's leaders need sustainably low prices to succeed in weaning the country off its oil-export dependence.

Shale oil appears to be bringing profound, lasting change to the oil industry. What it will not do, however, is reduce the importance of the Middle East. Under the new regime, the oil market's reliance on the Gulf will increase, diversity of supply will shrink, US oil imports will rise once again and Middle Eastern geopolitics will present a serious risk to global oil security.

The shale revolution

The US shale revolution has transformed the global oil market. Qualitatively, shale oil changed the economics of the industry, causing supply to become more price-responsive and therefore making it inherently more difficult to form cartels. Quantitatively, the US shale industry has been a key contributor to the gradual emergence of the oil surplus that eventually led to the fall in global prices from mid-2014 onwards. Between March 2010 and March 2015 – when US shale-oil output peaked – the average daily US production of liquid fuels grew by 6 million barrels (from 9m barrels per day to 15m bpd), accounting for three-quarters of global net growth (see Figure 1).[1] Shale added 4m bpd (or 200m tonnes per year) to the world's crude oil supply, the largest such addition, over a period of five years, since the ramp-up of Middle Eastern production in the early 1960s. The remaining 2m bpd were contributed mainly by the shale-gas industry, in the form of liquid fuels pumped alongside natural gas, with a minor contribution from biofuels.

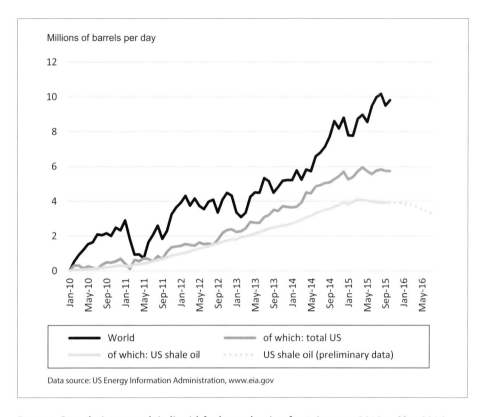

Millions of barrels per day

Legend:
— World
— of which: total US
of which: US shale oil
US shale oil (preliminary data)

Data source: US Energy Information Administration, www.eia.gov

Figure 1: **Cumulative growth in liquid-fuels production from January 2010 to May 2016**

Figure 2 reveals that, if US oil production had actually remained unchanged during this period, and this growth had instead corresponded to the emergence of a new oil producer outside of the United States, in 2014 this new producer would have ranked fourth in the world, behind Saudi Arabia, the Russian Federation and the US at its 2010 production level.

The emergence and rapid growth in US shale-oil production was the product of a sustained period of high prices, from the early 2000s onwards, itself largely the consequence of Saudi Arabia's conservative oil-supply policy in the face of emerging economies' surging demand and declining renewal rates for conventional reserves. While the International Energy Agency (IEA) and the US Energy Information Administration (EIA) predicted that low-cost producers from the Gulf would dramatically increase production in order to meet the growing needs of China and other developing countries, some economists pointed out that this would be an irrational

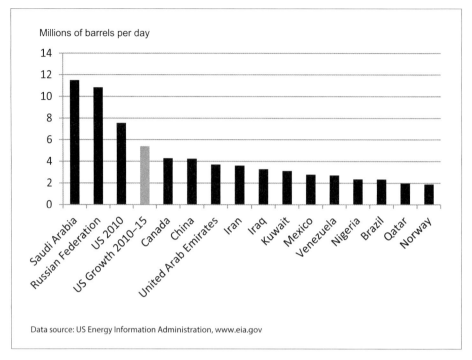

Figure 2: **Ranking of oil producers in 2014**

move.[2] Given the limited price-responsiveness of both supply and demand for oil, low-cost producers had an interest in limiting expansion and instead enjoying far higher prices than the world had become accustomed to since the mid-1980s.

These economists proved to be correct. Limiting supply delivered much higher export revenues to Gulf producers than they would have enjoyed had they expanded production capacity and export volumes as the EIA and IEA projected they would. However, this strategy by Saudi Arabia and other Gulf producers pushed prices to levels way above what was in their long-term interest.[3] Once prices of $80–$100 per barrel started to be perceived as the new normal, consumption behaviour changed in key markets such as the US; investment in efficiency and alternative transport technologies, such as electric cars, sharply increased; fuel-economy regulations became cheaper to implement; and supply-side technological innovation was significantly incentivised. The latter delivered the shale oil and gas revolution.

Understanding Saudi strategic choices

To understand the Saudi response to the 2014–16 price drop, one needs not just to look at the pace of shale-output growth, but consider its economics as well. In essence, the price-responsiveness of the shale industry left Saudi Arabia and other low-cost producers with no option but to let the price go down. Cutting production would have been self-defeating, as shale output would have simply substituted for oil from the Gulf, with no durable impact on prices.

Hydrocarbons from shale formations are quite different, economically speaking, from conventional oil and gas. Instead of a large upfront investment that buys a steady flow for a long period of time – provided appropriate field maintenance is carried out – maintaining the production of shale hydrocarbons in a given area typically entails drilling large numbers of wells that have a high decline rate. When prices drop, operators may continue to produce from conventional fields, as long as operational expenditures are covered. Shale-oil producers, on the other hand, will almost immediately drill fewer wells. Shale production is therefore much more responsive to price than conventional production: it declines quickly – though not instantaneously – when prices drop, and recovers swiftly when prices rise.

When the oil price collapsed in mid-2014, Saudi Arabia's response was informed by the economic characteristics of shale oil. Cutting back production – as it did when demand abruptly collapsed with the financial crisis of 2008–09 – would only have sustained shale-oil drilling and led to the creeping displacement of Saudi oil by US shale oil, with no or limited impact on prices. Thus, the only option was for the low-cost producers of the Gulf to allow the price to fall. Only time would tell by how much, how fast and at what price level US shale-oil output would stop growing and begin to shrink.

The information that this price decline revealed about the shale industry's costs would be very important to Saudi Arabia's strategic thinking. If most shale oil were to prove relatively costly, the market might rebalance fairly quickly. In such a scenario, shale would be mainly a good thing for Saudi Arabia, as it would tend to cap prices, thus preserving long-term demand, without destroying Saudi Arabia's ability to defend a relatively high floor

– thereby safeguarding the Kingdom's revenues. In this sense, Gulf producers must have been encouraged by mounting doubts, even before the price collapse, about the profitability of the shale-oil industry.[4]

If, however, a large fraction of the shale industry were to survive the price collapse, either because its costs were low or because it was able to cut them quickly and deeply enough, then Saudi Arabia and any other economic actors that benefited from high oil prices would face a much bigger problem. The emergence of a new, large, low-cost, price-elastic competitor that would never cooperate with Saudi Arabia would leave the country with two broad strategic options: expand the boundaries of its existing cartel by bringing in Russia so as to significantly increase the ability of cartel members to defend prices; or flood the market with some of the cheapest oil in the world, and accept a permanently lower mid-cycle oil price.

Explaining Saudi behaviour

The impact of falling prices on US shale-oil drilling was almost immediate (see Figure 3). Production rates took more time to respond, but output eventually did plateau, and then start to decline. In some producing regions, such as Bakken, Eagle Ford and Niobrara, the decline has been precipitous (by 15%, 30% and 21% respectively between the shale-oil production peak in March 2015 and June 2016). Overall, US shale-oil output declined by 654,000 bpd (12%) between March 2015 and June 2016 (see Figure 4).

This slowdown and eventual decline in US shale-oil production was, however, more than compensated for by a surge in production elsewhere in the world, especially in Saudi Arabia and Iraq (see Figure 5). Not only did Saudi Arabia refuse to cut production in the face of falling prices, it seems also to be implementing a programme of investment to increase its production capacity. Even as the Kingdom was supposed to be negotiating a 'freeze' in output with Russia and others – it blamed the failure of that negotiation on Iran[5] – more drilling rigs were active in the Arabian Peninsula than ever before.[6] The announcement in June 2016 of the partial flotation of Saudi Aramco may be a sign that the era of conservative resource management is over, as national oil companies tend to increase production rates after partial privatisation.[7]

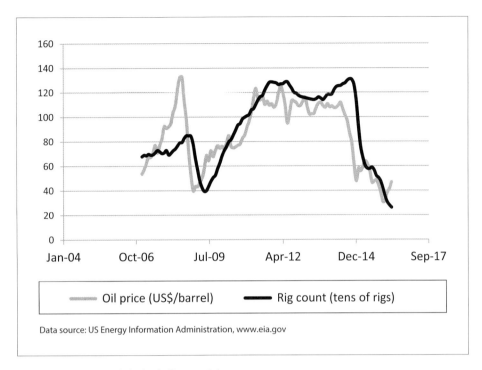

Figure 3: **Oil price and shale drilling activity**

Thus, the long-term Saudi response to US shale, as it emerges, seems to be to flood the market with, or at least to produce significantly more, cheap oil, and to accept a structurally lower price. This strategy seems to have been decided early on, perhaps even before the onset of the price collapse in mid-2014, in anticipation of what was to come. Saudi Arabia may have predicted a dynamic cost reduction in the US shale-oil industry, as well as a possible spread of shale-oil production to other regions of the world.

In April 2016, the OPEC countries and Russia met at Doha with the purported aim of expanding a conditional Saudi–Russian agreement to freeze production. The talks failed to achieve this outcome, however. This failure was not because of Iranian obstructiveness, as Riyadh claimed, but because Saudi Arabia did not want to revive the oil cartel. While Iran had only a limited ability to increase its production capacity in any case, Riyadh was deeply distrustful of Iraq. Not only is Iraq a de facto oil con-federation, with very limited – if any – central control over investment and production decisions by the Kurdish Regional Government, but Saudi

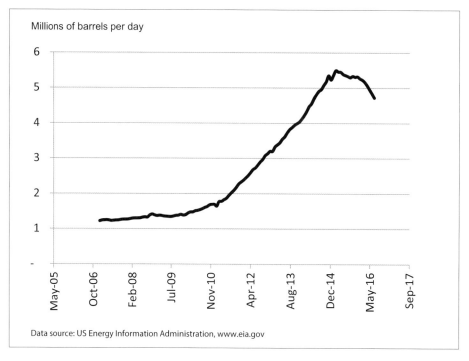

Figure 4: **US shale-oil production**

trust in the Shia-dominated government in Baghdad is very low. Iraq is blessed with abundant, low-cost oil reserves and is desperate for revenues. There is no way that it could seriously and durably cooperate in oil-market management.

A few days after the Doha meeting, Saudi Arabia announced its plan, long in the making, to transform the nation's economy and move it beyond oil dependence.[8] It appeared that Riyadh had begun to take seriously the threat to long-term demand for petroleum products. For a country like Saudi Arabia, with large oil reserves and, until recently, a high degree of market power, there is always a trade-off between extracting more monopoly rents in the short term and preserving long-term demand. Oil prices between 2010 and 2014 were much higher than the long-term optimum for low-cost producers with abundant reserves. They spurred an acceleration in efficiency gains, regulatory interventions in the US and China, inter-fuel substitution and technological advances in transport fuels and technologies that put long-term demand for oil at risk. In addition, the problem of

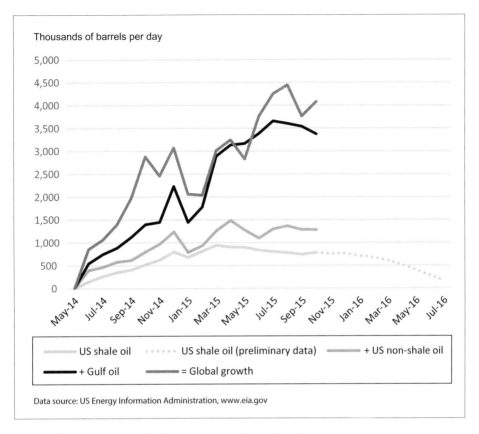

Figure 5: **Cumulative growth of oil production from May 2014**

climate change is being taken more seriously by an ever-increasing number of countries and will, over time, support more aggressive policies to curb emissions from the transport sector.

In short, it seems that Saudi Arabia has concluded that it will no longer be possible to defend high prices. Additionally, leaders in Riyadh clearly have become convinced that high prices, however comfortable in the short term, have created a false sense of security by deepening the country's dependence on oil rents. In the face of credible threats to long-term oil demand, this poses a very serious risk to the country's economic security. The Saudi plan, called 'Vision 2030', makes sense in broad terms: if the Kingdom is losing control of the oil market, investing in a process to reduce the country's dependence on oil-export revenues may be the only way forward. However, in order for the plan to succeed, Saudi citizens need to be disabused of their belief that the good days can come back, and instead convinced that the rentier model has run its course. For that, the oil price has to stay low. The Vision 2030 plan establishes a reference price for oil of $30 per barrel. It is a new era.

Economic and political implications

The emergence of the shale-oil industry, the threats to long-term demand and the strategic response from Saudi Arabia will produce a more competitive oil market than has existed since the 1970s. More cheap oil will be available, displacing supplies from more expensive territories and resulting in a lower mid-cycle price.

This shift will have far-reaching economic implications. The shale-oil industry may never again be as large as it was at its peak, with only the cheapest part of the industry surviving. US oil imports will start growing again. Most importantly, the overall level of rent in the oil system will shrink. The barrels that 'clear' the market and therefore set the price will be cheaper than before, meaning that, for any producer, the difference between price and average cost of production will be lower. For many producers, it will be much lower. For producing countries and oil companies alike, the business will be much less lucrative. The market valuation and size of oil companies will come under pressure, while rentier states will be forced into painful fiscal choices and difficult processes to reduce their dependence on oil-export revenues. The Saudi plan will be emulated elsewhere.

Another key feature of the new oil era will be the increased exposure of the global economy to Middle Eastern political risk. As oil from Saudi Arabia, Iraq, the UAE and Iran displaces more expensive production elsewhere, the global oil market will become more reliant on the Persian Gulf. Moreover, Saudi Arabia's new strategy means that it will maintain less spare production capacity than it used to, weakening an important tool in managing oil-supply emergencies.

It is doubtful, therefore, that the shale-oil revolution is making the Middle East less relevant to the United States' economic security, as President Barack Obama is said to have suggested.[9] The long-term risk to global oil security – the risk of scarcity – is indeed receding, but the short-term security risk – the risk of oil-supply disruption – is actually increasing, unless Middle Eastern politics can take a decisive turn for the better.

This does not mean, however, that regulating shale oil out of the market, as the two leading Democratic presidential candidates pledged to do during the primaries, would have no consequences. US shale-oil production may be much smaller under the new Saudi strategy than it would have been otherwise, but it will still act as a disciplinary mechanism: absent the shale-oil industry's ability to surge back quickly if prices were to durably increase, it would prove irresistible for Saudi Arabia to re-engineer high prices. Thus, an important aspect of the emerging oil regime is a new, implicit oil-policy compact between the United States and Saudi Arabia.

Under the new Saudi strategy and oil-market structure, the shale-oil industry may be significantly and durably smaller than it had become at $100/barrel, reducing the political pressure to regulate it on environmental grounds. In turn, by not regulating away the price-responsiveness of shale oil, the United States will maintain the industry's disciplinary effect and therefore lock in the economic benefits associated with lower oil prices. Shale may shrink, but the threat of its resurgence is still credible enough that Saudi Arabia will not go back to its old policy – at least not in the absence of effective and sustainable cooperation with Russia and Iraq.

For Saudi leaders, the discipline of market forces will act as a quasi-constitution – something that binds their hands, helping them stay the painful course of economic transformation. They will be able to claim that a lower oil price – and the difficult adaptation it demands – is not only vital to the success of the country's new economic strategy, but something that has been imposed on Saudi Arabia by forces beyond its control.

None of this is to suggest that the new oil-market situation will help Saudi Arabia and the United States bridge their disagreements and restore the trust that has been eroding for 15 years. There is no explicit, government-to-government agreement. It is likely that American and Saudi leaders do not even talk about the oil market when they meet. Rather, what is suggested here is an overlap of interests: a self-enforcing, implicit agreement whereby each player helps the other to reach its goals by pursuing its own. This should prove to be a stable political–economic equilibrium.

Acknowledgements

The author is grateful to Guillaume de Bergues and Geoffroy Gueyffier for research assistance.

Notes

[1] 'Liquid fuels' include crude oil, liquids associated with natural-gas production and biofuels.

[2] See Dermot Gately, 'How Plausible Is the Consensus Projection of Oil Below $25 and Persian Gulf Oil Capacity and Output Doubling by 2020?', *Energy Journal*, vol. 22, no. 4, Fall 2001, pp. 1–27.

[3] See David Greene, 'Future Prices and Availability of Transport Fuels', Discussion Paper No. 2007-15, International Transport Forum, Joint Transportation Research Center, OECD, Paris, 2007.

[4] See David Einhorn, presentation to the Sohn Investment Conference, 4 May 2015, Greenlight Capital, https://www.greenlightcapital.com/926698.pdf.

[5] See Rania El Gamal and Reem Shamseddine, 'Saudi–Iran Tensions Scupper Deal to Freeze Oil Output', Reuters, 18 April 2016, http://www.reuters.com/article/us-oil-meeting-draft-idUSKCN0XE02Y.

[6] See John Kemp, 'Arabia Sees Record Oil and Gas Drilling as Rest of World Slumps', Reuters, 13 April 2016, http://www.reuters.com/article/us-arabia-oil-kemp-idUSKCN0XA1LA.

[7] See David Keohane, quoting from a report by Bernstein Research, 'Saudi Aramco: A Race to the Bottom?', FTAlphaville, 6 June 2016, http://ftalphaville.ft.com/2016/06/06/2164840/saudi-aramco-a-race-to-the-bottom/; and Christian Wolf, 'Does Ownership Matter? The Performance and Efficiency of State Oil vs. Private Oil (1987–2006)', *Energy Policy*, vol. 37, no. 7, July 2009, pp. 2,642–52.

[8] See Myra Saefong, 'Four Things Saudi Arabia's Economic Reform Plan Says About Oil', Market Watch, 26 April 2016, http://on.mktw.net/1TtlCQq.

[9] See Jeffrey Goldberg, 'The Obama Doctrine', *Atlantic*, April 2016, http://theatln.tc/1UUZ50W. In seeking to present President Obama's thinking, Jeffrey Goldberg writes: 'the Middle East is a region to be avoided – one that, thanks to America's energy revolution, will soon be of negligible relevance to the U.S. economy.' Note that this sentence is not presented by Goldberg as a direct quotation from Obama.

EU–Iran Relations After Brexit

Seyed Hossein Mousavian

The decision by British voters to leave the European Union coincides with improving relations between Europe and Iran. Since the 1979 Islamic Revolution, Iran's relationship with Europe's major powers has been characterised by periods of economic cooperation followed by near-complete disengagement. The nuclear deal struck between Iran and world powers in July 2015 – which the EU played a major role in negotiating – removed the economic sanctions that since 2006 have stood in the way of deeper ties. A new chapter in Iranian–European relations has already begun. But the impending exit of the United Kingdom from the EU further paves the way for a new paradigm in Europe's relationship with Iran: strategic EU–Iran engagement that is separate from, but parallel to, high-level UK–Iran talks.

Separating the UK

London and Tehran have not had sustainably good relations since before the revolution. Over the course of the past century, Iranians of all walks of life have come to view Britain differently, and with far more suspicion, than they view other European states. At the root of this mistrust is Britain's colonial-era history in Iran. Nearly every Iranian bitterly recalls incidents such as the Anglo-Russian Convention of 1907, which split Iran into Russian and British spheres of influence; the engineering by the British of Reza Khan's (later Reza Shah Pahlavi) ascension to the throne in 1925; Britain's opposition to

Seyed Hossein Mousavian is a Professional Specialist at Princeton University and a former head of the Foreign Relations Committee of Iran's National Security Council. He is the author of *Iran and the United States: An Insider's View on the Failed Past and the Road to Peace* (Bloomsbury, 2014).

Survival | vol. 58 no. 5 | October–November 2016 | pp. 83–94   DOI 10.1080/00396338.2016.1231533

the nationalisation of Iranian oil; and its infamous 1953 plot with the CIA to oust prime minister Mohammad Mossadegh. This history has been so seared into the consciousness of Iranians that many believe Britain is to this day still trying to manipulate events inside Iran to its benefit.

These feelings have been reinforced since the revolution by Britain's support for forceful US policies against Iran, and its continuing refusal to acknowledge its historical offences. This was most evident during the early years of the nuclear crisis, when Iran negotiated with the E3 powers (Germany, France and the United Kingdom) over its nuclear programme. During this period, I served as the spokesman for Iran's negotiating team. In spring 2005, I privately presented a similar proposal to my counterparts

Relations with the UK hit rock bottom

in Germany, France and the United Kingdom. While it was met with support in Berlin, my meeting with French nuclear negotiator Stanislas Lefebvre de Laboulaye led me to conclude that France would accept the proposal only if the UK did. However, London's nuclear negotiator, John Sawers, would ultimately turn down the offer in my talks with him,

telling me that Washington would not tolerate even one centrifuge spinning in Iran.[1] This episode served as a striking example of America's hold, through Britain, on the foreign-policy decision-making of other EU states. Jack Straw, then UK foreign minister, would later say: 'Had it not been for major problems within the US administration under President Bush, we could have actually settled the whole Iran nuclear dossier back in 2005.'[2]

The period of negotiations between Iran and the E3 from 2003–05 was nevertheless significant, as it marked an effort by the EU to play a strategic role in the Middle East. The subsequent eight years, however, would see Iran's relations with the EU, and the UK in particular, hit rock bottom. The format of the negotiations changed in 2006 to include other major world powers, adding the United States along with China and Russia to what became the E3+3, also known as the P5+1. As negotiations stalled during the second term of George W. Bush and President Barack Obama's first term, the US and its allies imposed an increasingly draconian sanctions regime while Iran increased the size and capacity of its nuclear programme.

In late 2011, the crisis reached its peak. Iran's 'breakout time' – the amount of time it needed to amass the quantity of fissile material needed for a single weapon if it made the decision to do so – reached just a few months, according to some estimates. In November 2011, the United States and its allies also imposed what would be their hardest-hitting sanctions on Iran, effectively cutting the country out of most international trade and banking.[3]

Immediately following this move, Iran's parliament passed a bill to expel the British ambassador to Tehran and reduce diplomatic contact. This was not a spontaneous decision, but rather the result of years of increasingly louder calls in Iran to downgrade relations with Britain. The origin of the feud went back to the protests that rocked Iran following Mahmoud Ahmadinejad's re-election in 2009, during which Iranian authorities arrested nine local British embassy staff, including chief political analyst Hossein Rassam, for allegedly playing a 'significant role' in the post-election protests of that year. At the time, then-foreign minister Manouchehr Mottaki warned that Iran would downgrade ties, and intelligence minister Gholam-Hossein Mohseni-Eje'i even alleged that some of the violent protesters had been caught with British passports.[4] Iranian authorities subsequently tried Rassam for espionage.[5] The British government vigorously denied the charges.

A day after the bill was passed in 2011, a group of angry young protesters surrounded the British embassy in Tehran, chanting slogans and pushing up to the embassy walls. They eventually overcame police guards and stormed the embassy, setting fire to the first floor and causing extensive damage to the rest of the compound. The action spurred outrage across the world. The foreign ministry called it 'unacceptable'.[6] Supreme Leader Ayatollah Ali Khamenei later said of the protesters, 'The feelings of the youth were correct, but their behavior was not correct.'[7] The British government argued, however, that the protests could not have taken place without a degree of institutional consent.[8]

The 2011 attack on the British embassy exemplified the vehement animosity against Britain that continues to exist in segments of Iranian society. It also contributed to escalating EU–Iran tensions and tipped the EU into firmly supporting additional US sanctions against Iran. As a result, the EU's total trade with Iran dropped to €6 billion by 2013, down from a high of roughly €27bn in 2011.[9]

With the election of President Hassan Rouhani in June 2013, and a decision by second-term President Obama to pivot from a position of no enrichment in Iran to no nuclear weapons, the path to reconciliation between Iran and the UK, and by extension the EU, was cleared. The British embassy in Tehran reopened one month after the Joint Comprehensive Plan of Action (JCPOA) was reached, nearly four years after it was attacked. For many in Iran, it had become clear that the EU's position was heavily influenced by the UK and that Iran could not have a meaningful economic relationship with the EU if it continued to have poor relations with Britain.

One implication of an EU without the United Kingdom is that British, and by extension American, influence on EU–Iran relations will be diminished. This was one reason why Hamid Aboutalebi, Rouhani's deputy chief of staff for political affairs, tweeted after the vote that 'Brexit is a "historic opportunity" for Iran'.[10] Continental Europe has always been friendlier towards Iran and far more willing to do business with it. This has been evident since the JCPOA was reached, with EU–Iran trade picking up dramatically (serious banking issues notwithstanding)[11] and political delegations travelling back and forth.

Iranian leaders should bear in mind, however, that despite Britain's exit from the EU, Iran's relations with the UK will still affect the kind of relationship Iran can have with the West. If tensions between Iran and the US and UK were to increase to the levels seen during the nuclear crisis, EU–Iran relations would almost certainly deteriorate again as well. As such, in light of Brexit, there is a vital need for direct high-level talks between London and Tehran aimed at defining a new relationship. These talks should focus on eliminating mistrust, and give Britain the opportunity to address Iranian grievances and acknowledge past wrongdoings. Given the unique history between Iran and the UK, the talks need to be held within their own framework and separately from efforts aimed at EU–Iran engagement. And for the UK–Iran relationship to be reconstructed, it is also imperative that regional policies be discussed, as many Iranian officials firmly believe that London has always pursued a strategy of dividing Iran from its Arab neighbours.

Britain today has strong ties with many of Iran's Arab neighbours, particularly the Gulf Cooperation Council (GCC) countries. By engaging Iran at a deeper level, it stands to play an instrumental role in fostering detente between Iran and the GCC states and facilitating the creation of a regional cooperation system. This would have a stabilising effect in the region and benefit Britain by diminishing the threat of terrorism, stemming refugee flows and securing the Persian Gulf as an economically prosperous area where investments can be made and safe passage for energy resources is guaranteed.

A new relationship with Europe

Iran and the rest of the EU have a different history, and the opportunity exists for deeper, strategic engagement between them. Since 1979, tensions between EU member states and Iran have centred on four major issues: terrorism, human rights, weapons of mass destruction and the Israeli–Palestinian conflict. When I became Iran's ambassador to Germany in 1990, I tried to establish a joint working group to address these differences. These efforts led to a 'critical dialogue' between Iran and the EU from 1992–97 followed by a 'comprehensive dialogue'. While then-German chancellor Helmut Kohl was receptive to these initiatives, he was met with opposition from the United States. Nevertheless, the EU and Iran developed amicable ties over time, and Europe even became Iran's largest trading partner, until the nuclear crisis emerged.[12]

While EU–Iran relations suffered greatly during the nuclear-crisis era, especially from 2011 to 2013, the EU played an instrumental role in the diplomacy that eventually led to the JCPOA. EU foreign-policy chief Catherine Ashton and her successor, Federica Mogherini, spearheaded the negotiations between the E3+3 and Iran, and the EU's High Representative now holds the decisive role of Coordinator of the Joint Commission that will oversee the JCPOA's implementation.[13]

Following the conclusion of the JCPOA, Europe has the opportunity to shift towards a more constructive approach towards Iran. The increasingly shared interests and threats between the two sides have created room not just for tactical cooperation and increased trade, but for broader strategic dialogue on a host of decisive issues.

Western Asia today is a significantly different place than it was a decade or even five years ago. Large swathes of Iraq and Syria have become battle-fields or been occupied by violent terrorist groups, the most notorious of which is the Islamic State (also known as ISIS or ISIL). Other Arab states, such as Libya, Egypt and Bahrain, are either in complete disarray or on shaky foundations. Refugees in their millions are entering Europe, testing the continent's social cohesion and public services in unprecedented ways. A two-state solution to the Israeli–Palestinian conflict is also a more distant prospect than ever. Europe simply cannot turn its back on the turmoil in the Middle East, and urgently needs to help foster a stabilising regional order for its own well-being.

In the face of all this disorder, Iran is a strong state with functioning insti-tutions and significant influence throughout the region. It has a pluralistic political system, by regional standards, and regularly holds elections. It is at the forefront of the fight against ISIS and other terrorist groups, and is engaged in Iraq, Syria, Yemen and Afghanistan. Simply stated, Iran stands to be an effective partner in helping the EU alleviate the trifecta of serious challenges it faces today: terrorism, migration and a stumbling economy. The differences that once existed between Iran and the EU are either no longer pertinent or can be mitigated through deeper engagement.

On the issue of terrorism, Iran is among the few countries in the Middle East fighting terrorist groups that have been responsible for the deaths of many Americans and Europeans, including ISIS, al-Qaeda and al-Qaeda's Syrian affiliate, Jabhat al-Nusra (now Jabhat Fatah al-Sham). By contrast, US Vice President Joe Biden has accused US regional allies of support-ing extremists in Syria in their eagerness to oust Syrian President Bashar al-Assad.[14] Former secretary of state Hillary Clinton also stated at the Brookings Institution last year: 'Much of the extremism in the world today is the direct result of policies and funding undertaken by the Saudi govern-ment and individuals. We would be foolish not to recognize that.'[15]

The nuclear deal also resolved, at least for the moment, the long-standing issue of Iranian nuclear proliferation. Through diplomacy, the EU, Iran and other world powers not only managed to reach the most comprehensive agreement on nuclear non-proliferation in history, but also established a model that can be used to address proliferation concerns in other countries, particularly in the Middle East. The initiative of a Middle East Nuclear Weapons Free Zone (MENWFZ) was first proposed by Iran and Egypt in 1974. If the principles of the JCPOA are implemented regionally, it would finally be realised.

On the issue of human rights, differences will undeniably continue to exist. However, there is also room for dialogue on human rights that focuses on identifying ways to minimise differences and cooperate on common interests. One possible area for cooperation is the refugee crisis, which has had unique consequences for both the EU and Iran. Europe has found itself taking in more than one million refugees and migrants in 2015 alone, posing unprecedented security, political, demographic and economic challenges. Iran, on the other hand, is surrounded by several of the failed states from which many of the refugees are fleeing, greatly threatening its national security. Iran and the EU both stand to benefit from changing this status quo, and could work together to foster stable orders in Iraq, Syria and Afghanistan in order to allow refugees to return.

On other human-rights issues, it is important for the EU to hold Iran to the same standards it does other regional countries, of which Iran is often far ahead on human rights. For example, whereas Iranian women are active in nearly all walks of professional life, vote and seek elected office, women in Saudi Arabia are not even allowed to drive.

An agenda for cooperation

Strategic EU–Iran engagement would entail deep and long-lasting cooperation in economics, security and regional stability. Iran is strategically located at the crossroads of the Middle East, Central Asia and Europe, and in between the energy-rich Caspian Sea and Persian Gulf. Its geographic position also makes it an ideal alternative to conventional shipping routes to Asia, Eastern Europe and the Commonwealth of Independent States (CIS). In short, Iran is a significant regional player that the EU can no longer afford to ignore.

Iran is resource-rich, with the fourth-largest oil reserves and the largest natural-gas reserves in the world. It could be an integral part of Europe's efforts at energy diversification.[16] In order to foster broader energy cooperation, a working committee of European and Iranian energy executives could be set up to explore opportunities for EU companies to become commercial partners in investing in and developing Iran's energy sector.

On the security front, there is a vital need for the EU and Iran to cooperate in the fight against terrorism. Since ISIS and other terrorist groups established a foothold in Syria, there has been a dramatic rise in both the number and scope of terrorist attacks around the world. Whether in ISIS-inspired attacks like the Orlando shooting that left 49 dead, or the ISIS-directed attack at Istanbul's Atatürk Airport, which killed 44, it is clear that the group's reach is not limited to any specific territory. Terrorism from ISIS and like-minded groups is now the number-one security threat not just to the Middle East, but also to Europe. Iran is leading the fight on the ground against terrorist groups in Syria and Iraq. While cooperation in Syria is highly unlikely until a settlement is reached between the Syrian government and members of the opposition, the EU can work more closely with Iran in Iraq to combat ISIS and strengthen the Iraqi government. Formal intelligence sharing is one possible and immediate step the EU and Iran could pursue.

Strategic engagement between the EU and Iran also promises to be a great boost to regional security. Iran and the E3+3 could agree to a model for crisis management based on the template of the nuclear negotiations, which succeeded in large part because the end state was agreed to at the beginning of the negotiating process. The conflicts raging in Syria, Yemen and Bahrain all share a common root cause: the social and political marginalisation of a major group within society. In Syria, this group was the majority Sunni Arab population; in Bahrain, the majority Shia population; and in Yemen, the Zaydi Muslims who constitute a large minority. EU–Iran cooperation on solving the discord in these countries should centre on bringing about a solution that emphasises majority rule, minority rights, power sharing and free elections.

EU leaders should be aware of the fact that the free flow of hydrocarbons out of the Persian Gulf is dependent on regional stability. While the EU imports most of its oil and gas from Russia, Central Asia and North Africa, stability in the Persian Gulf would ensure a lower price for energy and provide the EU with a viable alternative energy source, thereby lowering the leverage of its current suppliers.[17] To ensure the continued secure flow of energy resources out of the region and boost regional stability at the same time, the EU could work with Iran and the GCC countries to develop plans for regional energy interconnectivity. Iran's natural-gas endowment, in particular, could serve as a source of energy for GCC countries whose own energy exports are being cut by their growing domestic energy demands. This would give countries on all sides of the Gulf a real stake in each other's well-being, promoting regional cooperation.

The EU can also help bring order to the region by supporting the establishment of a system that allows Iran and the GCC to have substantive dialogue on security issues. Establishing a regional security structure was once the initiative of former German foreign minister Hans-Dietrich Genscher, who pushed for a system of cooperation that would include Iran and the GCC states. Such a system would, importantly, allow Saudi Arabia and Iran to mend their differences, take into account each other's interests and cooperate to stabilise the region. It would help to end the proxy wars that have for so long tormented the region, and usher in a durable peace.

Another fruitful area for dialogue and increased cooperation between the EU and Iran is the environment, and averting man-made disasters more broadly. Iran is wrestling with severe environmental challenges, ranging from drought to heavy pollution. Its quest for nuclear energy has also seen it construct a nuclear power plant in the coastal city of Bushehr, which sits on seismic fault lines. European businesses and specialists can help in both of these cases: by developing water-efficiency programmes, and sharing methods for enhancing nuclear safety.

*   *   *

The most immediate potential obstacle to strategic Iran–EU cooperation would be a failure to live up to JCPOA commitments. US sanctions legislation still in place has inhibited EU financial institutions from facilitating trade with Iran, preventing Iran from receiving the sanctions relief it expected under the nuclear deal. If this impasse can be overcome, the EU will find a strong partner in Iran. If not, Iran will turn further towards non-Western countries and the EU will be left with its hands tied in the Middle East.

The Middle East is on the verge of total collapse, and there is no sure-fire way to bring it back from the brink. There is no doubt, however, that strategic EU–Iran engagement would be a step towards order and away from further chaos. For decades, the Middle East has been a battleground for outside powers vying for control. In the past, the turmoil created in the region largely stayed there. Today, this is no longer the case. This new world calls for abandoning counterproductive policies of exclusion, and pursuing new partnerships that offer a real opportunity to make the region, and the world, a safer and more prosperous place.

Notes

1 Seyed Hossein Mousavian, *Iran and the United States : An Insider's View on the Failed Past and the Road to Peace* (London: Bloomsbury, 2014), pp. 204–5.

2 David Morrison and Peter Oborne, 'Why the West Will Strike a Nuclear Deal with Iran', *Telegraph*, 21 November 2014, http://www.telegraph.co.uk/news/world-news/middleeast/iran/11245730/Why-the-West-will-strike-a-nuclear-deal-with-Iran.html.

3 Mark Landler, 'United States and Its Allies Expand Sanctions on Iran', *New York Times*, 21 November 2011, http://www.nytimes.com/2011/11/22/world/middleeast/iran-stays-away-from-nuclear-talks.html?_r=1.

4 Ian Black, 'Iran Arrests UK Embassy Staff', *Guardian*, 28 June 2009, https://www.theguardian.com/world/2009/jun/28/uk-embassy-tehran-arrests.

5 Colin Freeman, 'British Embassy Official, Hossein Rassam, Appears in Spy "Show Trial" in Iran', *Telegraph*, 8 August 2009, http://www.telegraph.co.uk/news/worldnews/middleeast/iran/5994520/British-embassy-official-Hossein-Rassam-appeas-in-spy-show-trial-in-iran.html.

6 Saeed Kamali Dehghan, 'Hague Says Iran Will Face "Serious Consequences" Over Embassy Attack', *Guardian*, 29 November 2011, https://www.theguardian.com/world/2011/nov/29/iranian-students-storm-british-embassy.

7 Arash Karami, 'What Does Khamenei Think of Saudi Embassy Attacks?', Al-Monitor, 4 January 2016, http://www.al-monitor.com/pulse/originals/2016/01/iran-condemn-saudi-attack-embassy-nimr.html.

8 William Hague, statement to the House of Commons, 30 November 2011, https://www.gov.uk/government/news/foreign-secretary-statement-to-the-house-of-commons-on-british-embassy-tehran.

9   European Commission, 'European
     Union, Trade in Goods with Iran', 21
     June 2016, p. 3, http://trade.ec.europa.
     eu/doclib/docs/2006/september/
     tradoc_113392.pdf.

10   Esfandyar Batmanghelidj, 'The Brexit
     Risk to the Iran Deal', LobeLog,
     24 June 2016, http://lobelog.com/
     the-brexit-risk-to-the-iran-deal/.

11   Seyed Hossein Mousavian and Reza
     Nasri, 'Obama Needs to Protect
     the Iran Deal', *New York Times*, 20
     June 2016, http://www.nytimes.
     com/2016/06/21/opinion/obama-needs-
     to-protect-the-iran-deal.html.

12   European Commission, 'Trade: Iran',
     http://ec.europa.eu/trade/policy/
     countries-and-regions/countries/iran/.

13   Joint Comprehensive Plan of
     Action, Annex 4, available at
     https://eeas.europa.eu/statements-
     eeas/docs/iran_agreement/
     annex_4_joint_commission_en.pdf.

14   'Biden "Clarifies" Comments
     Implying UAE Support for
     Extremists', AP, 5 October 2014,
     https://www.theguardian.com/
     us-news/2014/oct/05/uae-clarification-
     joe-biden-remarks-extremists.

15   'Hillary Clinton Addresses the
     Iran Deal', transcript, Brookings
     Institution, 9 September
     2015, p. 18, https://www.
     brookings.edu/wp-content/
     uploads/2015/09/20150909_clinton_
     iran_transcript.pdf.

16   BP, 'Statistical Review of
     World Energy', June 2015, pp.
     6 and 20, https://www.bp.com/
     content/dam/bp/pdf/energy-
     economics/statistical-review-2015/
     bp-statistical-review-of-world-energy-
     2015-full-report.pdf.

17   European Commission, 'Energy:
     Supplier Countries', https://
     ec.europa.eu/energy/en/topics/
     imports-and-secure-supplies/
     supplier-countries.

Cryptography and Sovereignty

Ben Buchanan

Cryptography has gone mainstream. Now more than ever, encryption is used by ordinary citizens, often without their knowledge, and is a subject of national debate.[1] Intelligence and law-enforcement officials warn of the dangers of messages they cannot read.[2] Presidents and prime ministers weigh in on the way cryptography shapes the balance between liberty and security.[3] The Edward Snowden revelations drive encryption-related coverage in major newspapers, even as the technology is rolled out by increasing numbers of companies over government objections.[4] All told, it may be the most international attention a mathematical concept has received since the space race.

These ongoing debates exist at the intersection of at least three fields: law, applied mathematics and international relations.[5] The legal debate varies by country, and centres on what restrictions on cryptography the government may enact under each state's domestic political system. The debate in applied maths, drawing on computer science and software engineering, addresses whether or not it is technically feasible to place limitations on cryptographic implementations, such as those desired by some governments, without sacrificing security or the right to privacy. The international-relations debate, which is only nascent, questions what the widespread use of cryptography means for the future of states in the international system.[6]

Ben Buchanan is a Postdoctoral Fellow at Harvard University's Belfer Center for Science and International Affairs, where he conducts research on the intersection of cyber security and statecraft. His first book, *The Cybersecurity Dilemma* (Oxford University Press and Hurst), comes out this year.

Survival | vol. 58 no. 5 | October–November 2016 | pp. 95–122   DOI 10.1080/00396338.2016.1231534

For all the recent discussion and increasing use of cryptography, however, many of the core concepts of the modern debate are not entirely new. In legal and applied-maths circles, similar debates took place in the 1980s, as powerful new forms of encryption came to the fore. Another round of discussion took place in the 1990s, as the spread of the internet dramatically increased the number of encryption users and raised the prospect that the security and privacy offered by cryptography would spread beyond American borders. Much can be learned from these previous debates that can help to ascertain the implications of cryptography for international relations.

In several important respects, the increasing implementation of secure cryptographic systems reshapes the concept of state sovereignty. It is clear that the seemingly irreversible rise of strong encryption will place particular types of communication beyond the state's reach, while at the same time leaving policymakers with alternative means of reasserting state power. In this way, encryption is similar to other potential challenges to sovereignty, such as globalisation. In practice, the widespread use of cryptography alters how states relate to one another, and to their own citizens. It raises important questions about the legitimate use of a state's own power, and the ways in which this power is constrained by the power of other states.[7]

A primer on sovereignty

The centrality of sovereignty in geopolitics and international relations is nicely captured by the political scientist Stephen Krasner's description of it as 'the master variable of the international system'.[8] Krasner's framework for understanding sovereignty[9] can shed light on the ways in which cryptography might affect the future of the state.[10] This framework posits four interrelated types of sovereignty, each of which represents an area in which the state wields some legitimate power, but also faces limits on that power. The first type of sovereignty is what Krasner calls 'domestic sovereignty'. This is what most people have in mind when they think of sovereignty. The term refers to a state's control over its domestic affairs, and suggests that, broadly speaking, the relationship between the state and its citizens is a matter of national, not international, affairs. The implementation of the social contract, the use of force, the demands placed on citizens and the benefits rendered by the state in return are all issues of domestic sovereignty. National governments typically possess robust authority in these areas, subject to the limitations arising from their political systems and the relationship those systems define between citizens and the state.

A second kind of sovereignty is what Krasner calls 'Westphalian sovereignty', after the 1648 Peace of Westphalia that heralded – in theory, if not always in practice – the beginning of the modern international system. That peace, achieved between neighbouring Catholic and Protestant princes, dictated that each locality would follow the religion of its ruler, and that rulers would not interfere with the practice of religion outside their own domains. Thus, Westphalian sovereignty holds that states have a negative right to non-interference. Likewise, they may not interfere with the exercise of other states' domestic sovereignty, nor may they, absent some extenuating circumstances discussed below, upend another state's political system or meddle in its domestic affairs.

The third type of sovereignty, known as 'international legal sovereignty', extends the Westphalian idea. It comes into play when states provide explicit recognition of one another's rights. Frequently, this recognition centres on issues such as territory and borders, as when states acknowledge one another's frontiers, marking the end of their own sovereignty and the beginning of their neighbours'. When disputes do occur, this system of recognition provides a foundation for resolving them. Indeed, the clear recognition of mutually respected limits can minimise disputes in the first place. This type of sovereignty is largely unaffected by the cryptography debate.

Krasner's final type of sovereignty is what he calls 'interdependence sovereignty'. This refers to the ways in which states seek to regulate what crosses their borders. The movement of capital, people and information across national borders presents at once a positive opportunity for states – in the form of trade, growth and immigration – and a potential challenge, as it allows citizens to be influenced by external forces in a variety of ways. As a result, the incoming and outgoing flows of capital, people and information affect domestic sovereignty, including the relationship between the state and its citizens. Interdependence sovereignty, then, refers to a state's power, or lack thereof, to manage cross-border flows through controls such as immigration rules, import and export restrictions, and financial regulations. Because interdependence sovereignty is so frequently exercised at international borders, it is naturally linked to a state's relationship with other states.

For the most part, the system of sovereignty works. No state can credibly claim unlimited power and influence. Nonetheless, Krasner identifies four areas in which the international community acknowledges limitations on sovereignty, permitting interference in another state's national affairs: the preservation of religious toleration, the protection of the rights of minorities, the upholding of human rights and the maintenance of international stability. When one of these four goals is seriously threatened – a condition that is subject to wildly differing interpretations – countries may consider interfering with the offending state's sovereignty.[11]

Cryptography is hardly the first challenge to the system of sovereignty. As noted, globalisation too has been theorised as a threat to sovereignty because of the way it tightens relationships between states and creates strong multinational organisations, such as corporations and non-governmental organisations. States have seen fit to empower supranational institutions in some key areas, recognising limits on the wisdom and feasibility of using the levers of interdependence sovereignty to slow globalisation. Generally speaking, people, information and money flow across borders more quickly and freely than they used to.

Krasner's response to the globalisation challenge is instructive for any consideration of cryptography and its impact on sovereignty. Globalisation can in some ways change the relationship between states, but Krasner contends that these changes do not in fact undermine the concept of sovereignty itself. Viewed in the context of history, states have responded to modern trends much as they have in the past, and have continued to assert comparable levels of control and influence, though in new ways. For example, in the nineteenth and early twentieth centuries, many states were buffeted by boom-and-bust flows of capital and credit; today, central banks permit states to partake in the global financial system while also providing some protection against the risks of financial contagion. Aside from the European Central Bank, which Krasner notes as an exception, these banks

9 European Commission, 'European Union, Trade in Goods with Iran', 21 June 2016, p. 3, http://trade.ec.europa.eu/doclib/docs/2006/september/tradoc_113392.pdf.

10 Esfandyar Batmanghelidj, 'The Brexit Risk to the Iran Deal', LobeLog, 24 June 2016, http://lobelog.com/the-brexit-risk-to-the-iran-deal/.

11 Seyed Hossein Mousavian and Reza Nasri, 'Obama Needs to Protect the Iran Deal', *New York Times*, 20 June 2016, http://www.nytimes.com/2016/06/21/opinion/obama-needs-to-protect-the-iran-deal.html.

12 European Commission, 'Trade: Iran', http://ec.europa.eu/trade/policy/countries-and-regions/countries/iran/.

13 Joint Comprehensive Plan of Action, Annex 4, available at https://eeas.europa.eu/statements-eeas/docs/iran_agreement/annex_4_joint_commission_en.pdf.

14 'Biden "Clarifies" Comments Implying UAE Support for Extremists', AP, 5 October 2014, https://www.theguardian.com/us-news/2014/oct/05/uae-clarification-joe-biden-remarks-extremists.

15 'Hillary Clinton Addresses the Iran Deal', transcript, Brookings Institution, 9 September 2015, p. 18, https://www.brookings.edu/wp-content/uploads/2015/09/20150909_clinton_iran_transcript.pdf.

16 BP, 'Statistical Review of World Energy', June 2015, pp. 6 and 20, https://www.bp.com/content/dam/bp/pdf/energy-economics/statistical-review-2015/bp-statistical-review-of-world-energy-2015-full-report.pdf.

17 European Commission, 'Energy: Supplier Countries', https://ec.europa.eu/energy/en/topics/imports-and-secure-supplies/supplier-countries.

remain national institutions.[12] When it comes to exercising sovereignty in the modern world, states pick and choose their battles: in some areas they may find it useful to cede a degree of influence, while in other areas their control may perhaps be greater than ever before.[13] Emerging trends may change the policy levers that states can use to exercise sovereignty, but they rarely reduce a state's sovereignty altogether. As encryption has become more common, it has given rise to a similar dynamic.

A primer on cryptography

The word cryptography takes its origin from the Greek terms for 'secret' and 'writing'. Encoded messages are nothing new, of course, and even though modern cryptography has become increasingly sophisticated and taken a number of different forms, the core concept is straightforward. Cryptographic implementations provide a mechanism for one party, traditionally labelled Alice, to deliver a message to another party, called Bob, in such a way that the message cannot be understood or altered if a third party, Eve, intercepts it in its entirety.[14] In most cases, the medium through which the message is transferred does not matter, so long as the message itself is properly encrypted; a message can be encrypted and sent through the mail, just as it can be encrypted and sent over the internet. Computers can make cryptographic implementations more sophisticated, more usable and easier to scale, but the core ideas come from applied mathematics, not computer science.[15]

There is an obvious solution to the problem of secure messaging, one so easily implemented that it is practised even in youth sports leagues. Alice and Bob, like a pitcher and catcher in baseball, can agree in advance on a set of signals, each with a meaning that only they know. When the time comes to communicate during a game, they will transmit only those prearranged signals, trusting that the recipient will be able to work out the meaning. Even if Eve – in this example, someone on the opposing team – intercepts the signals, she will not know what the real message is.

This solution is difficult to apply on a large scale for a variety of reasons, however. If Eve is able to steal enough signals over time, she increases her odds of associating the signals with their true meanings.[16] In addition, the system requires Alice and Bob to meet beforehand, in a secure setting free from Eve's eavesdropping, in order to agree on the signals. Such a meeting is required each time they wish to establish new signals, which provides additional opportunities for Eve to eavesdrop and obtain the information she needs to break the code. Problems like these ensured that effective encryption remained out of reach for centuries. A number of partial solutions were invented, but each had its own flaws.[17] It was not until the 1970s that a solution known as public-key encryption revolutionised the traditional approach to encryption by eliminating the need for Alice and Bob to prearrange signals.[18] It is this solution that powers much of contemporary cryptography – and the legal and political debates that surround it.[19]

Public-key cryptography

A public-key-encryption system gives each participant in a conversation two so-called 'keys', one labelled public and one labelled private. These keys, which are typically long strings of letters and numbers that are chosen for their mathematical properties, are linked in a special way.[20] One of these two keys is made public for all potential conversation partners, and eavesdroppers, to see. The other key is kept private. When Alice wants to send Bob a message, she uses *his* public key to scramble the message. Because his public key is visible to everyone by definition, no prearrangement of codes is required. The process of encryption transforms Alice's unencrypted text into indecipherable nonsense called ciphertext. Due to the mathematical relationship between each pair of public and private keys, only someone with the associated private key can decrypt the ciphertext to read the original message.[21] Even Alice herself cannot decrypt the message once she has encrypted it with Bob's public key, because she lacks Bob's private key. Once the message is encrypted, Alice can send it to Bob over any medium; Eve, also lacking Bob's private key, will similarly not be able to decrypt it. When Bob wants to respond to Alice, he uses *her* public key to encrypt the message so that only someone with Alice's private key – ideally, this is only Alice – can decrypt it.

Yet even this groundbreaking system has one important weakness worth discussing here.[22] The security of all messages depends on the security of the intended recipient's private key. If Eve can steal a copy of that private key, she can decrypt every message ever written to that recipient, a massive breach of privacy and security. To remedy this problem, modern implementations of various cryptographic systems include what is known as 'perfect forward secrecy'. In these systems, the pair of public and private keys is changed with each individual message. That is, for each message Alice wants to send to Bob, she gets a new public key from Bob (which again is not secret). For each public key he gives out, Bob also has a new, mathematically related private key that is needed to decrypt the message. If for some reason a private key of Bob's is stolen, only one message is compromised, not entire conversations. Perfect-forward-secrecy systems are mathematically and technically much more complex – among other components, they require an infrastructure for distributing and verifying many more keys – but they are harder to attack, and hence superior, to the alternative. As a result, these systems are increasingly prevalent.

A final concept in modern cryptography, end-to-end encryption, can also be found at the heart of the public-policy debate. In the past, cryptographic implementations were vulnerable if the keys were stored, distributed or accessed by a middleman. To put it in terms of Alice and Bob, the two were in this case reliant upon a third party, Charlie, to facilitate the distribution of both public and private keys, and to transmit messages between the two conversation partners. Yet if Charlie – typically a major company, not an individual – had access to all the participants' private keys, he could also decrypt their messages and read them. This is a security risk. To counteract it, some modern cryptographic implementations encrypt the messages end-to-end, meaning Alice and Bob do not rely on a third party to generate their public and private keys. Instead, Alice and Bob, via software on their devices, generate and store their own keys. Even if they rely on a third party to transmit their messages to each other, that third party is unable to decrypt what is sent because it does not have access to the users' private keys. Apple's iMessage system is one of the best-known examples of this type of encryption, and Tim Cook, the company's CEO, has defended it as essential to preserving 'an individual's right to privacy'.[23] Google has promised similar security in its Android operating system, and several other applications also implement end-to-end systems.[24]

In sum, then, a properly implemented modern cryptographic system can enable two individuals who have never interacted before to communicate with each other in a way that is impossible for others to read, that does not depend on a third party for secrecy, and that is not easily attacked at scale by the theft of individual keys.[25] These are technical facts, grounded in mathematics and proven in practice over the last 40 years.[26] While in the past such implementations were only available to tech-savvy individuals, these sorts of modern cryptographic systems are increasingly enabled by default, meaning users do not even need to know they are being used. There are many examples of this default implementation, including the end-to-end encryption used by the messaging services mentioned above, as well as by certain internet applications.[27]

Users receive protection by default

In these instances, even those users who take no overt steps to safeguard the privacy and security of their communications and who have no technical proficiency receive protection by default. It is no exaggeration to say that the number of people using cryptography to protect their messages to friends, to search engines and to many other entities has grown and will continue to grow by billions, all in less than a decade. Such default systems are becoming the new normal in personal cyber security.[28] For governments, this means that the wiretapping and surveillance mechanisms they have traditionally used to target unencrypted communications are of demonstrably less value against such cryptographic systems, if the cryptography is well designed. States that were previously able to collect information on their citizens or other targets via a court-approved wiretap or other legal means are now in some circumstances unable to do so. Corporations that used to be able to comply with legal demands for assistance are sometimes technically prevented, because of their encryption designs, from complying. Intelligence agencies that used to derive great value from tapping internet cables en masse have now found that some of those communications are harder to decrypt. As a result, citizens now have a new means of more private communication. Conversely, states are arguably less secure and enjoy less domestic sovereignty because of this innovation, which has caused some policymakers to look for countermeasures.

Cryptography and state control

Because of the difficulty involved in implementing cryptography, and as a result of the United States' early head start in many high-tech areas, for a number of years cryptographic implementations were primarily built and sold by American companies. During the Cold War, such technologies were mostly restricted for use by friendly governments or large corporations, making it easier for the United States to prevent their spread to the Soviet Union and its allies. The US government could enjoy the benefits of cryptography while still being able to spy with relative ease on its adversaries overseas, and on criminal suspects at home.

The advent of personal computers and the internet changed all this. The arrival of the digital age afforded tech-savvy individuals in the United States the opportunity to use cryptography. In addition, the country's booming high-tech industry created new opportunities for overseas sales by American companies. This prospect raised concern among American policymakers. It was clear that the benefits of cryptography were immense to those who used it, as the technology could secure vital information such as financial data, health records and more. But overseas governments and other enemies could also use cryptography to secure their own secrets – and, in the process, potentially thwart the efforts of US intelligence agencies, and perhaps even harm American interests. In order to give American companies the chance to sell overseas while maintaining the government's ability to decrypt overseas communications, a compromise was sought. In 1992, one was reached in the form of a two-tiered system known as export-grade cryptography.[29]

The export-grade cryptographic regime dictated that cryptography of a certain standard could only be used within the United States. This meant that strong cryptography would be legal within American borders – though, in practice, such systems were rarely implemented, for reasons of cost and complexity. Only cryptography of a substantially weaker grade could be exported abroad. Borrowing concepts from export-control regimes for military technologies, the arrangement treated cryptography as a weapon that could, in the wrong hands, harm American security. The regime gave rise to a number of technological consequences. One notable requirement was that systems that crossed national borders have mechanisms for switching between strong cryptographic implementation (for American use) and weaker forms (for users whose access to cryptography was controlled).

As internet use became more widespread, the export-control compromise grew increasingly ineffective. Computer code is much harder to stop at national borders than are physical weapons, one of the many ways in which digital technologies generally pose a challenge to interdependence sovereignty. In addition, secure cryptography has become a more global phenomenon, desired and produced by citizens and companies all over the world. E-commerce, which requires strong cryptography to guarantee trust, has likewise gained in prominence. In response to these trends, the export-control system was partially reversed by then-president Bill Clinton in a 1996 executive order, with further amendments made after that.[30] Today, citizens of most countries have numerous cryptographic systems available to them, two-thirds of which have been developed outside the United States.[31] Even if a state were to ban the production of certain kinds of cryptographic implementations, such systems can typically be acquired, via the internet, from providers in another state. In this sense, interdependence sovereignty is not nearly as strong as it used to be.

While the United States' brief attempt to impose export controls on cryptography is largely recognised as a failure, its legacy has endured long after its demise. In 2015, information-security researchers discovered an important weakness in vital software.[32] Since code is often written to be backward-compatible, meaning new software works with older standards as well as new ones, some modern tools, such as web browsers, still supported export-grade – that is to say, vastly less secure – encryption, even though it had not been required for years. What's more, a modern-day Eve could force web browsers to switch back to this old standard under certain conditions, effectively removing a large amount of the protection afforded to Alice and Bob. Functionally, this weakness gave eavesdroppers in 2015 the ability to turn back the clock to the weaker standards of the mid-1990s. In this way, a policy misstep in the 1990s threatened to harm users 20 years later.

This example highlights an important cryptographic principle: adding requirements to systems increases their complexity, making it more likely that they will contain hidden vulnerabilities that will eventually be found and exploited by attackers. Even when systems are straightforward, it is unlikely that cryptographers will be able to produce flawless mathematics and computer code. Adding additional complications runs a high risk of weakening the protections cryptography is supposed to offer. These weaknesses, once discovered, can persist for a long time.

Mandated golden keys

National governments, even in the digital age, still have a great deal of power when it comes to domestic sovereignty. Because states have more control over what happens within their borders, policymakers concerned about the impact of cryptography might try to impose restrictions on what type of cryptographic implementations are available to citizens. The US experience demonstrated that a two-tiered cryptographic system is unlikely to work, but another option is for the state to mandate that all cryptographic systems produced within its borders contain what is known in various circles as a 'back door', a 'front door' or a 'golden key'.[33] Such a key would enable the entity holding it to decrypt any message, no matter which public key was used to encrypt it. There are various ways to implement this requirement (including some that do not involve cryptographic keys per se); but, whatever form it takes, a golden key will always function mathematically as if it were the intended recipient's private key. An entity possessing such a key will have the ability to decrypt any message, regardless of its intended recipient. A state with a golden key could therefore ensure – in a manner that was, at least in theory, consistent with its legal principles and subject to judicial oversight – that no message produced within its borders was out of its reach. As long as the golden key was secure from everyone else, this system would offer cryptographic protection to users while permitting the state to retain its domestic power.

This type of system is often proposed by law-enforcement agencies. There is strong evidence, however, that such proposals are technically suspect. A version of this system was tried during the mid-1990s, without success. Known informally as the Clipper Chip, the system allowed messages to be encrypted in such a way that the intended recipient could decrypt it but malicious eavesdroppers could not. It also provided a way for the government to decrypt the message if required, using a system known as key-escrow. This compromise was soon shown to have serious technical weaknesses, however. In 1994 and 1995, these flaws were made public by the news media. By 1996, the Clipper Chip was largely defunct.[34] In 1997, a group of the world's leading cryptographers published a landmark paper that examined not just the Clipper Chip but, more generally, the idea of key-escrow cryptography, outlining the major technical limitations of the concept.[35]

Rather than reasserting state sovereignty, the Clipper Chip exposed its limits in the digital age. Concerns about government-mandated insecure encryption prompted individuals to develop cryptographic implementations that did not provide access for governments.[36] The tools of American domestic sovereignty, bound as they were by the First Amendment, were unable to prevent this circumvention. The limitations of interdependence sovereignty also came into play. Requiring that American companies use insecure encryption while their foreign competitors did not had the potential to put the United States at an economic disadvantage. Meanwhile, individual citizens retained the ability to import cryptographic systems from overseas.

After the Snowden revelations, and as the cryptography debate re-emerged with the introduction of default end-to-end encryption, law-enforcement officials again put forward the idea of a Clipper Chip-style compromise. The director of the National Security Agency, Admiral Mike Rogers, made the case in 2015 for ensuring government had access to a 'big front door, with locks' for every cryptographic system.[37] Rogers, along with FBI Director James Comey, suggested that American companies in Silicon Valley could function as partners to the intelligence and law-enforcement communities. By providing golden keys for their cryptographic systems, these companies could provide security for their customers while also permitting the state to fulfil its own security-providing role as the domestic sovereign. Government officials suggested that such a system – which, in their view, was technically feasible – would strike the right balance between user security and state sovereignty, though they did not explicitly use the term.

A major academic study conducted by several of the world's leading cryptographers, including some veterans of the 1990s debate, concluded just the opposite, however.[38] Released in 2015, the study is unambiguous about the dangers of such a compromise. Allowing for government access to cryptographic systems drastically increases their complexity, thereby making them more vulnerable. Malicious hackers could discover flaws in the system's technical implementation and use them to gain unauthorised access to the communication of others. This is not merely a theoretical risk: in 2010, a Google system intended to allow for lawful interception was penetrated and used by adversaries.[39] In their paper, the cryptographers conclude, with reference to the Clipper Chip era, that 'the damage that could be caused by law enforcement exceptional access requirements would be even greater today than it would have been 20 years ago', in part because individuals today conduct an even greater share of their communications and economic activities in the digital sphere than they did then.[40]

Targeting providers of encryption

States have a third possible option available to them that could be used instead of or in addition to export controls and golden keys. This would involve surreptitiously targeting the providers of encryption by stealing large numbers of keys in bulk, finding mathematical weaknesses in the cryptographic system or introducing hidden vulnerabilities to be exploited at a later date. By carrying out these activities in secret, a state could effectively sidestep public debates about the limits of its domestic sovereignty. It could also use the same means to target the providers of encryption in other states, either as a way of gaining access to private information, or of compromising encryption systems that its own citizens, in an attempt to avoid domestic restrictions, might seek out.

There is some precedent for this kind of state behaviour. Gemalto, a company headquartered in Amsterdam, provides two billion SIM cards per year to more than 450 mobile-phone providers around the world, including AT&T, Verizon, T-Mobile and Sprint.[41] These four major American telecommunications providers, like many others in Western countries, used reasonably advanced mechanisms of encryption on their networks, which were linked to these SIM cards. In order for calls to be decrypted, the secret key on the SIM card needed to be in sync with the key designated for that user by the cellular-service provider. This system was not a public-key system, and did not have perfect forward secrecy. In effect, it was more akin to Alice (the SIM card) and Bob (the cellular company) arranging long-lasting baseball signs, in this case facilitated by Charlie (Gemalto).

Under this system, Gemalto manufactured billions of secret encryption keys for its SIM cards, lists of which it provided to the cellular-service providers. These lists were intercepted by GCHQ – the British intelligence agency that closely partners with the United States National Security Agency – by means of its network-intrusion and signals-intelligence capabilities. Stealing the secret keys en masse allowed the agency and its partners to decrypt calls and data in real time for a wide number of users.[42]

It is worth noting, however, that the approach of targeting providers, while technically powerful, also has important limits. Firstly, it requires the state to be willing to attack or undermine, in secret, large-scale cryptographic systems through key theft. Such efforts are likely to raise thorny legal questions if conducted domestically.[43] Secondly, it raises the possible risk of diplomatic blowback if such activity is discovered to have taken place internationally.[44] Thirdly, in the same way that a hacker might steal a golden key from a state, keys obtained from encryption providers could also be stolen, allowing malicious hackers to decrypt large amounts of data. Fourthly, the method requires targeting weaknesses in encryption providers' networks. If providers improve their security, access will be lost. In short, then, targeting keys is an effective approach for covertly gathering foreign intelligence, but it is of more limited use when it bears on matters of domestic sovereignty, such as law enforcement.

State sovereignty in an age of cryptography

States do not have a good option for overcoming properly implemented encryption systems. Each of the approaches described above has been shown in practice to carry significant costs or limitations. However, even if the state cannot target the message itself, it can still assert its sovereignty over the citizen. The state need not intercept the message as it is transmitted from

Alice to Bob if it can monitor the sender (before the message is encrypted), or monitor the recipient (after the message is decrypted), instead. Indeed, domestic police forces have a long history of conducting such surveillance operations. But where previously such monitoring would often have required extensive human involvement and generated significant expense, it is now possible to gather the required information electronically, using malicious software.[45] Widespread encryption may weaken some levers of domestic sovereignty, but the associated increases in the scale and usability of computing resources has empowered the state in other ways.

Malicious software can be inserted into a suspect's computer using a variety of methods. For example, in 2007, during an investigation into a bomb threat at a Seattle high school, the FBI targeted a potential suspect by sending him a link to what appeared to be a relevant news article. In fact, the article was a fake devised by the FBI. When the suspect clicked the link, the bogus article secretly downloaded malicious software onto his computer, which then began to generate reports on his activities.[46] The FBI has used a variant of this technique in other cases dating back to 2003, including a major 2010 operation in which it gained control over a child-pornography server and distributed malicious code to more than 1,000 visitors in a bid to identify their location.[47] Similar techniques are used routinely by law-enforcement and intelligence agencies – Britain's MI5 acknowledges it uses such measures in 'the overwhelming majority of [its] high priority investigations'[48] – as well as by cyber criminals, who employ malicious software for a range of purposes.

This technique, though sometimes unsuccessful and less straightforward than traditional methods of intercepting unencrypted communications, frequently enables whoever employs it to sidestep the target's use of cryptography. It is akin to Eve secretly watching Alice as she drafts her message before encrypting it, or Bob as he reads it following its decryption. The limitations of encryption in this regard are widely acknowledged, even by its strong advocates. In the same interview in which Edward Snowden praised the security offered by properly implemented cryptography, he lamented how often poor endpoint security renders cryptography irrelevant.[49] After a network intrusion into the systems of the US Office of Personnel Management

(OPM) resulted in the loss of tens of millions of records containing sensitive data on government employees, the agency's congressional overseers demanded to know why the records hadn't been properly encrypted. It fell to officials from the Department of Homeland Security to point out that encryption, while still important, would not have helped prevent the damage done in that particular breach. By gaining access to the OPM system's user accounts or even its servers, the intruders would have been able to access the data after it had been decrypted, or to decrypt it themselves.[50]

In addition to allowing for the copying of communications before encryption or after decryption, the system-level access that results from this sort of compromise technically permits a wide range of operations. Anyone enjoying this level of access would likely be able to completely disable the targeted device, access all the files that had been stored on it, gather all the keystrokes made with it, secretly activate its camera and microphone, and potentially even impersonate its owner or utilise his or her accounts. Legal requirements could limit what can be done in certain contexts; however, discussion of this topic in legal circles is still nascent and often contradictory.

This is a major step up from the level of access typically gained in past court-approved wiretapping operations, at least in the United States. Historically, in the case of phone wiretapping, the government would put an order in to the telecommunications company for access to a suspect's calls. As the calls transited the company's networks, government investigators would be able (at most) to listen in and make recordings, or to obtain phone records after the fact. They would almost never be able to alter the communication, or prevent it from taking place. Moreover, a court-approved wiretap would not have afforded the investigators access to large amounts of information on the suspect unrelated to his or her phone conversations. Deploying targeted malicious software, while not yet as easily scaleable as ordering wiretaps over a centralised phone system, is thus potentially far more potent. The former director of GCHQ recently warned that these sorts of intrusions onto users' devices should be expected in response to increasing encryption. He also admitted that, 'in terms of intrusion into personal privacy – collateral intrusion into privacy – we are likely to end up in an ethically worse position than we were before'.[51]

Not only does this technique provide a means of reasserting domestic sovereignty, it also marks a shift in the conceptual approach to gathering electronic communications away from passive collection carried out by a third party (such as a phone provider) to the active targeting by the state of citizens and their devices. The unchecked use of malicious software undermines not just the confidentiality of targets' communications but also the integrity of their entire digital life. It empowers the collection of an enormous amount of forensic data, far more than is possible under a wiretap. None of this is necessarily a bad development; it may make law enforcement more efficient and reduce crime. But its widespread, successful use – which would likely come at significant cost and require well-trained personnel – would more than reaffirm the power and sovereignty of the state over the citizen, rendering trends in cryptography mostly beside the point.

All told, in important respects, states hold the cards when it comes to cryptography and domestic sovereignty. They can choose one of the flawed options described above and attempt to assert power over the use of cryptography, paying whatever economic or political costs that accompany that choice. Alternatively, they can choose to sidestep the question by targeting citizens and their devices directly, bypassing the protection of cryptography but at least partially redefining the citizen–state relationship in the course of reasserting domestic sovereignty. If a state chooses this last and more aggressive route, there is little other states would be able to do about it. It is purely a domestic matter.

Interdependence sovereignty

Cryptography affects interdependence sovereignty in much the same way that other digital technologies do: states find it very difficult to manage the flow of digital information across their borders. In simple terms, states have two potential options. Firstly, they can seek to monitor such traffic as it crosses their borders, carrying out surveillance and gathering intelligence in the service of their national-security aims and other interests.[52] There are many examples of this sort of activity occurring at the landing points of the undersea cables that carry the internet's data between continents.[53] Secondly, a state can choose to block all or some of the digital information that crosses its border. This could be because the information has been deemed secret, subversive or illegal. China famously attempts to carry out such censorship using its Great Firewall.

The widespread use of cryptography would affect these two types of interdependence sovereignty differently. Properly implemented cryptography, in which the state is not able to obtain the encryption key or break the system's algorithm, could foil states' efforts to intercept traffic as it crosses national borders, thereby weakening their intelligence-collection and surveillance efforts. They would then have three options: to accept the loss of sovereignty as a price of being connected to the internet; to compensate for the loss by leaning more heavily on their tools of domestic sovereignty, such as by deploying malicious software against the communicating devices as described above; or to target the providers of the encryption, weakening the system across the board. If these providers were based in other countries, this last option could be seen as compromising the sovereignty of other states, as will be discussed below.

States have three options

When it comes to blocking digital content, states' interdependence sovereignty is somewhat limited. This is true not just of content secured by cryptography, but of all digital traffic. If a state wants to be integrated into the global economy and connected to the internet – which virtually all states do – it will likely accept the need to let large amounts of traffic through. The modern internet carries too much data at too rapid a pace to be reviewed by humans in real time. Even states that have invested large amounts of money in such censorship, such as China, still have porous and inconsistent digital borders. What is more, states that try to exert their sovereignty in this way run the risk of creating a domestic backlash, as the Chinese did when they tried to block a major technical site, GitHub, in 2013.[54] When it comes to blocking digital traffic, as opposed to monitoring or copying it, interdependence sovereignty has stark limits.

Westphalian sovereignty

Because computer code, data and services can so easily move across borders, the Westphalian principle of non-interference in states' domestic affairs is often challenged. Consider, for example, the scenario in which State A has concluded that it will permit the production of secure encryption within its borders, while State B has decided that it will mandate a golden key for all the encryption systems its companies produce. Some citizens of State B, perhaps wary of the security dangers posed by systems with golden keys, will instead employ cryptography from State A. Neither State A nor State B would be able to prevent them from doing so, given that export controls on cryptography have already been shown to be unenforceable in practice. Furthermore, State B has no authority to compel State A to change its stance on encryption. Instead, all State B can do is target the systems of secure cryptographic production used in State A, in the same way the British targeted Gemalto. This would allow State B to more easily break messages encrypted by the targeted providers in State A, possibly sparing the former the need to target its own citizens' devices in order to intercept communications.

On the one hand, this sort of activity might be considered espionage, which is quasi-accepted under the current system of Westphalian sovereignty, though usually not in any formal way. On the other hand, State B might carry out such an operation strictly for reasons of domestic law enforcement, rather than foreign intelligence or national security. For example, it might do so as a means of fighting the sort of crimes, such as kidnappings, that FBI Director James Comey believes could become impossible to solve if their perpetrators had easier access to encryption.[55] Even so, State A would likely consider it an affront to its sovereignty for State B to interfere with its companies and the security of its citizens' encryption in the service of its own domestic sovereignty. Whether State B could actually carry out such interference without suffering consequences from State A would in large measure depend on the power differential between the two, the general nature of their relationship and the ability of State B to carry out such operations in secret.

The new normal

As divisive as the encryption debate seemed in 2015, a new normal has started to emerge. Professional computer scientists and cryptographers, spurred by law enforcement's requests for access, have re-examined and reaffirmed their belief that, at a technical level, golden keys create serious risks to security and privacy. Many security officials, including former directors of the US Department of Homeland Security, the National Security Agency, the National Counterterrorism Center and the United Kingdom's MI5, have come out in support of this view – a surprising consensus, given the ways in which those agencies would benefit, or have benefited, from weaknesses in encryption.[56] While some law-enforcement and signals-intelligence professionals still believe that a golden-key system is possible, leaked documents and public statements indicate that they have lost the policy battle in the United States thus far.[57]

That this consensus reflects the one reached after the Clipper Chip and export-control failures of the 1990s suggests policymakers are slow to accept sometimes unpleasant technical realities. Nevertheless, the consensus seems poised to endure. It is clear that, for the foreseeable future, properly implemented encryption systems will be able to produce messages that even powerful states will not, by targeting the cryptography itself, be able to decrypt. States will either make their peace with this, attempt to undermine cryptography at some cost to their security or interconnectedness, or side-step the cryptography by going after users' devices instead.

At present, there is only nascent discussion of government-backed hacking into citizens' devices as a means of domestic law enforcement, and the legal complexities it poses.[58] Such discussion as has occurred has been emotionally charged on both sides, as when the FBI attempted to compel Apple's assistance in hacking into the work phone of a San Bernardino shooter possibly linked to the Islamic State. The question of government hacking and its limits is an obvious and significant gap in the academic and public conversation that must be filled if such techniques are to gain legitimacy as the appropriate domestic response to encryption. Informally, good questions have been raised about the scope of government powers when remotely accessing a device, about whether the government can keep secret the means it uses to exploit targeted devices and about how forthright law enforcement has been in requesting hacking warrants.[59] These questions have yet to be fully answered. Similarly, there has been virtually no academic consideration of what intrusions such as the Gemalto case mean for order and stability in the international system. Lastly, national-security officials, having achieved consensus on export controls and golden keys, have yet to publicly debate the security implications of targeting encryption providers overseas or citizens' devices at home. The limits, reach and consequences of these kinds of operation deserve further discussion.

The ways in which cryptography affects sovereignty is largely up to the state. In the four decades since public-key encryption was discovered, this trend has only become more evident. As encryption's new normal takes hold, the ways in which states respond will contribute to reshaping the relationship between the governing and the governed, and between one nation and another.

Acknowledgements

The author would like to thank Lance Hoffman, Shashank Joshi, Thomas Rid and Michael Specter for reviewing earlier drafts of this piece.

Notes

1   Cryptography is the study and practice of secure communication; encryption is the process through which particular communications are transformed so that, even if they are intercepted, their meaning cannot be discerned.

2   Ellen Nakashima and Barton Gellman, 'As Encryption Spreads, U.S. Grapples with Clash between Privacy, Security', *Washington Post*, 10 April 2015, https://www.washingtonpost.com/world/national-security/as-encryption-spreads-us-worries-about-access-to-data-for-investigations/2015/04/10/7c1c7518-d401-11e4-a62f-ee745911a4ff_story.html.

3   Danny Yadron, 'Obama Sides with Cameron in Encryption Fight', *Wall Street Journal*, 16 January 2015, http://blogs.wsj.com/digits/2015/01/16/obama-sides-with-cameron-in-encryption-fight/.

4   Nicole Perlroth, Jeff Larson and Scott Shane, 'N.S.A. Able to Foil Basic Safeguards of Privacy on Web', *New York Times*, 5 September 2013, http://www.nytimes.com/2013/09/06/us/nsa-foils-much-internet-encryption.html; Nicole Perlroth, 'Tech Giants Urge Obama to Reject Policies That Weaken Encryption', *New York Times*, 19 May 2015, http://www.nytimes.com/2015/05/20/technology/tech-giants-urge-obama-to-reject-policies-that-weaken-encryption-technology.html.

5   For examples of debates within the legal field see Christopher Soghoian, 'Caught in the Cloud: Privacy,

Encryption, and Government Back Doors in the Web 2.0 Era', *Journal on Telecommunications and High Technology Law*, vol. 8, no. 2, 2010, p. 359; Scott Brady, 'Keeping Secrets: A Constitutional Examination of Encryption Regulation in the United States and India', *Indiana International & Comparative Law Review*, vol. 22, no. 2, 2012, p. 317; Bela Chatterjee, 'Fighting Child Pornography through UK Encryption Law: A Powerful Weapon in the Law's Armoury', *Child & Family Law Quarterly*, vol. 24, no. 4, 2012, p. 410; Matthew Parker Voors, 'Encryption Regulation in the Wake of September 11, 2001: Must We Protect National Security at the Expense of the Economy', *Federal Communications Law Journal*, vol. 55, no. 2, 2002, p. 331; and Steven Levy, *Crypto* (New York: Penguin Books, 2001). For examples of debates with the mathematics community see Hal Abelson et al., 'The Risks of Key Recovery, Key Escrow, and Trusted Third-Party Encryption', Columbia University Academic Commons, 1997; and Harold Abelson et al., 'Keys under Doormats', Massachusetts Institute of Technology Computer Science and Artificial Intelligence Lab Technical Reports, 2015.

6   See, for example, Daniel Moore and Thomas Rid, 'Cryptopolitik and the Darknet', *Survival*, vol. 58, no. 1, February–March 2016, pp. 7–38.

7   There are a wide range of perspectives on sovereignty, some of which differ from the framework used in this study. See, for example, Thomas J. Biersteker and Cynthia Weber, *State Sovereignty as Social Construct*, vol. 46

(Cambridge: Cambridge University Press, 1996); Stephen J. Kobrin, 'The Architecture of Globalization: State Sovereignty in a Networked Global Economy', in John Dunning (ed.), *Governments, Globalization, and International Business* (Oxford: Oxford University Press, 1997), pp. 146–71; Virginie Guiraudon and Gallya Lahav, 'A Reappraisal of the State Sovereignty Debate: The Case of Migration Control', *Comparative Political Studies*, vol. 33, no. 2, 2000, pp. 163–95; Janice E. Thomson, 'State Sovereignty in International Relations: Bridging the Gap between Theory and Empirical Research', *International Studies Quarterly*, vol. 39, no. 2, 1995, pp. 213–33.

8   Stephen Krasner, *Power, the State, and Sovereignty: Essays on International Relations* (London and New York: Routledge, 2009), p. xiii.

9   Stephen D. Krasner, *Sovereignty: Organized Hypocrisy* (Princeton, NJ: Princeton University Press, 1999).

10 This is not the first attempt to apply Krasner's framework to cyber security. An earlier effort considered what cyberspace more generally means for the future of the state, but did not give much attention to cryptography in particular. See David Betz and Tim Stevens, *Cyberspace and the State*, Adelphi 424 (Abingdon: Routledge for the IISS, 2011).

11 For a range of perspectives, see Gene M. Lyons and Michael Mastanduno, *Beyond Westphalia? State Sovereignty and International Intervention* (Baltimore, MD: Johns Hopkins University Press, 1995); Richard H. Cooper, *Responsibility to Protect* (New

York: Palgrave Macmillan, 2009); and Gareth Evans and Mohamed Sahnoun, 'The Responsibility to Protect', *Foreign Affairs,* vol. 81, no. 6, 2002, pp. 99–110.

12 Krasner succinctly explains why the European system is an outlier for a variety of social, cultural and historical reasons in 'Think Again: Sovereignty', *Foreign Policy,* 20 November 2009, http://foreignpolicy.com/2009/11/20/think-again-sovereignty/.

13 For Krasner's views on globalisation see *ibid*.

14 This paper will primarily concern itself with this version of the problem – that is, with communication between two parties. Nonetheless, a slightly modified version of this problem is also important. In this version, Alice wants to store, rather than send, information in such a way that only she can later retrieve it, and so that, if the information falls into the wrong hands, it cannot be read. Cryptography that solves this problem secures the information at rest as opposed to in transit. Many of the same principles discussed here still apply, though particular technical implementations will vary somewhat.

15 It is worth noting that, despite recent advances, cryptographic implementations are still enormously difficult, in mathematical terms, to design and implement on a large scale. Sophisticated eavesdroppers will be alert for weaknesses in theory or in practice. It is for this reason, among others, that signals-intelligence agencies employ large numbers of mathematicians who attempt to uncover mathematical weaknesses in cryptographic systems that would allow large quantities of messages to be decrypted at once. See David Adrian et al., 'Imperfect Forward Secrecy: How Diffie–Hellman Fails in Practice', 22nd ACM Conference on Computer and Communications Security, Denver, CO, 2015.

16 To extend the baseball analogy, this is as if a batter successfully associates an opposing team's signals with the pitches that were thrown after they were given. It's for this reason that teams regularly change their signals.

17 For a comprehensive history see Simon Singh, *The Code Book* (New York: Doubleday, 1999).

18 The concept of public-key encryption was first elaborated in secret by the British signals-intelligence agency GCHQ, and then independently developed and put into practice by academic researchers a few years later. *Ibid*., pp. 279–92.

19 Not all modern cryptographic systems rely on public-key encryption, however. Some mechanisms, such as those that secure one's own data for later use, do not require it. Nonetheless, it is fair to say that the dawn of public-key encryption greatly increased the value of cryptography for the average citizen, and is a major driver of the current debate.

20 For an explanation of the mathematics behind this concept, see Ross Anderson, *Security Engineering* (Indianapolis, IN: John Wiley & Sons, 2008), pp. 129–84.

21 In theory, even without the private key it is still possible to perform this decryption by brute force. However, with strong cryptographic methods and carefully chosen public and pri-

vate keys, this would take billions of years.

22 In practice, if the key-generation algorithm is mathematically unsound, such that it does not generate random keys, Eve may be able to guess a private key without having to steal it. But this weakness is mostly beyond the scope of this paper, and can be managed by publishing the design – but not the individual keys – of a cryptographic system for open peer review by other experts.

23 Matthew Panzarino, 'Apple's Tim Cook Delivers Blistering Speech on Encryption, Privacy', Tech Crunch, 2 June 2015, http://techcrunch.com/2015/06/02/apples-tim-cook-delivers-blistering-speech-on-encryption-privacy/.

24 Perlroth, 'Tech Giants Urge Obama to Reject Policies That Weaken Encryption'.

25 If the cryptographic system is properly implemented, it would take billions of years to discover the private key of a target. This is why stealing keys is widely preferred.

26 When asked how individuals might secure themselves from even the most powerful state signals-intelligence agencies, Edward Snowden famously said that 'properly implemented strong crypto systems are one of the few things that you can rely on'. See Edward Snowden, 'Edward Snowden: NSA Whistleblower Answers Reader Questions', *Guardian*, 17 June 2013, http://www.theguardian.com/world/2013/jun/17/edward-snowden-nsa-files-whistleblower.

27 The particulars of web encryption are beyond the scope of this text, and depend on the task the encryption is designed to carry out.

28 Not all of these systems are entirely impenetrable or fully end-to-end, but generally speaking the rising use of default cryptography vastly increases the security of communications.

29 The cryptography debate of the 1990s took a number of forms and involved many proposals. See Levy, *Crypto*. Only two of these – export controls and the Clipper Chip – are discussed here.

30 'Executive Order 13026: Administration of Export Controls on Encryption Products', *Federal Register*, vol. 61, no. 224, 19 November 1996, https://www.gpo.gov/fdsys/pkg/FR-1996-11-19/pdf/96-29692.pdf.

31 Bruce Schneier, Kathleen Seidel and Saranya Vijayakumar, 'A Worldwide Survey of Encryptions Products', Berkman Center for Internet and Society, Harvard University, Research Publication No. 2016-2, 11 February 2016, https://cyber.law.harvard.edu/publications/2016/encryption_survey.

32 Nimrod Aviram et al., 'DROWN: Breaking TLS Using SSLv2', Proceedings of the 25th USENIX Security Symposium, August 2016, https://drownattack.com/drown-attack-paper.pdf.

33 Different participants in the debate called it different things. See Herb Lin, 'The Rhetoric of the Encryption Debate', Lawfare, 12 October 2015, https://www.lawfareblog.com/rhetoric-encryption-debate. 'Golden key' is used here because it highlights the power invested in the entity possessing the key, but implies no judgement about whether this power is legitimate.

34 Levy, *Crypto*, pp. 226–69.

35 Abelson et al., 'The Risks of Key Recovery, Key Escrow, and Trusted Third-Party Encryption'.

36 Philip Zimmermann, 'Why I Wrote PGP', 1999, https://www.philzimmermann.com/EN/essays/WhyIWrotePGP.html.

37 Nakashima and Gellman, 'As Encryption Spreads, U.S. Grapples with Clash between Privacy, Security'.

38 Abelson et al., 'Keys under Doormats'.

39 Robert McMillan, 'Google Attack Part of Widespread Spying Effort', Computerworld, 13 January 2010; Abelson et al., 'Keys under Doormats', p. 5.

40 Abelson et al., 'Keys under Doormats', p. 1.

41 A SIM card is a small and usually removable component that is placed in mobile phones to enable them to use certain cellular networks and to be billed for that usage.

42 Jeremy Scahill and Josh Begley, 'The Great SIM Heist', *The Intercept*, 19 February 2015, https://theintercept.com/2015/02/19/great-sim-heist/.

43 In the United States, the oversight and constraints on intelligence activity vary based on whether that activity takes place inside or outside of the United States. Far looser restraints apply to targets based outside of the United States, even if that target is a US company. For example, in an effort to access unencrypted data, American and British signals-intelligence agencies have targeted the links between the overseas data centres of major American firms, including Google and Yahoo. Barton Gellman and Ashkan Soltani, 'NSA Infiltrates Links to Yahoo, Google Data Centers Worldwide, Snowden Documents Say', *Washington Post*, 30 October 2013, http://www.washingtonpost.com/world/national-security/nsa-infiltrates-links-to-yahoo-google-data-centers-worldwide-snowden-documents-say/2013/10/30/e51d661e-4166-11e3-8b74-d89d714ca4dd_story.html. It is not clear that the United States would be able to use its overseas authorities to weaken domestically produced cryptography.

44 Ryan Devereaux and Cora Currier, 'European Lawmakers Demand Answers on Phone Key Theft', *The Intercept*, 20 February 2015, https://theintercept.com/2015/02/20/gemalto-heist-shocks-europe/.

45 The term 'malicious software' as used here does not cast aspersions on the state's intent or legitimacy. Rather, it is the phrase employed by cyber-security professionals to denote software that, unbeknownst to the end user, attempts to gain access to the user's device.

46 Mike Carter, 'FBI Created Fake Seattle Times Web Page to Nab Bomb-Threat Suspect', *Seattle Times*, 27 October 2014, http://www.seattletimes.com/seattle-news/fbi-created-fake-seattle-times-web-page-to-nab-bomb-threat-suspect/. It has since come to light that the FBI used this technique in earlier cases as well. Kim Zetter, 'Everything We Know About How the FBI Hacks People', *Wired*, 15 May 2016, https://www.wired.com/2016/05/history-fbis-hacking/.

47 See Matt Apuzzo, 'F.B.I. Used Hacking

Software Decade Before iPhone Fight', *New York Times*, 13 April 2016, http://www.nytimes.com/2016/04/14/ technology/fbi-tried-to-defeat-encryption-10-years-ago-files-show.html; and Joseph Cox, 'The FBI's "Unprecedented" Hacking Campaign Targeted Over a Thousand Computers', Motherboard, 5 January 2016, https://motherboard.vice.com/ read/the-fbis-unprecedented-hacking-campaign-targeted-over-a-thousand-computers.

48 Government of the United Kingdom, 'Factsheet – Targeted Equipment Interference', 30 October 2015, p. 1, https://www.gov.uk/government/ uploads/system/uploads/ attachment_data/file/473740/Factsheet-Targeted_Equipment_Interference.pdf.

49 Snowden, 'Edward Snowden: NSA Whistleblower Answers Reader Questions'.

50 Jason Miller, 'OPM's Archaic IT Infrastructure Opened Door for Massive Data Breach', Federal News Radio, 17 June 2015.

51 Melanie Newman, 'Encryption Risks Leading to "Ethically Worse" Behaviour by Spies, Says Former GCHQ Chief', Bureau of Investigative Journalism, 23 January 2015, https:// www.thebureauinvestigates. com/2015/01/23/encryption-will-lead-to-ethically-worse-behaviour-by-spies-says-former-gchq-chief/.

52 Ryan Gallagher, 'Profiled', *The Intercept*, 25 September 2015, https:// theintercept.com/2015/09/25/ gchq-radio-porn-spies-track-web-users-online-identities/.

53 Ewen MacAskill et al., 'GCHQ Taps Fibre-Optic Cables for Secret Access to World's Communications', *Guardian*, 21 June 2013, http://www.theguardian. com/uk/2013/jun/21/gchq-cables-secret-world-communications-nsa.

54 Michael Kan, 'GitHub Unblocked in China after Former Google Head Slams Its Censorship', Computerworld, 23 January 2013, http://www.computerworld.com/ article/2493478/internet/github-unblocked-in-china-after-former-google-head-slams-its-censorship. html.

55 David Sanger and Matt Apuzzo, 'James Comey, F.B.I. Director, Hints at Action as Cellphone Data Is Locked', *New York Times*, 16 October 2014, http://www.nytimes.com/2014/10/17/ us/politics/fbi-director-in-policy-speech-calls-dark-devices-hindrance-to-crime-solving.html.

56 Conor Friedersdorf, 'Encryption Backdoors Are Opposed by Former Government Officials', *Atlantic*, 30 July 2015, http:// www.theatlantic.com/politics/ archive/2015/07/former-national-security-officials-see-the-peril-of-weakening-encryption/399848/?utm_ source=SFTwitter.

57 It is worth noting that there is no law reflecting this consensus, only executive-branch decisions. Thus, while there is widespread agreement that choosing a different path on encryption would impose significant costs and limitations, there is no guarantee that a future administration would not deem these consequences acceptable. See Ellen Nakashima and Andrea Peterson, 'Obama Faces Growing Momentum to Support Widespread Encryption',

Washington Post, 16 September 2015, https://www.washington-post.com/world/national-security/tech-trade-agencies-push-to-disavow-law-requiring-decryption-of-phones/2015/09/16/1fca5f72-5adf-11e5-b38e-06883aacba64_story.htm; and Dustin Volz, Mark Hosenball and Joseph Menn, 'Push for Encryption Law Falters Despite Apple Case Spotlight', Reuters, 27 May 2016, http://www.reuters.com/article/us-usa-encryption-legislation-idUSKCN0YI0EM.

58 See Steven M. Bellovin et al., 'Lawful Hacking: Using Existing Vulnerabilities for Wiretapping on the Internet', *Northwestern Journal of Technology and Intellectual Property*, vol. 12, no. 1, 2014, p. i; Jonathan Mayer, 'Constitutional Malware', 20 July 2015, https://papers.ssrn.com/sol3/papers.cfm?abstract_id=2633247; Susan Landau, 'The Real Security Issue of the iPhone Case', *Science*, vol. 352, no. 6,292, 17 June 2016, pp. 1,398–9; and Steven Bellovin, Matt Blaze and Susan Landau, 'Insecure Surveillance: Technical Issues with Remote Computer Searches', *Computing Now*, March 2016, https://computingnow.computer.org/cms/Computer.org/ComputingNow/issues/2016/06/mco2016030014.pdf.

59 See, for example, Nicholas Weaver, 'Examining an FBI Hacking Warrant', Lawfare, 16 March 2016, https://www.lawfareblog.com/examining-fbi-hacking-warrant; Nicholas Weaver, 'The FBI's Firefox Exploit', Lawfare, 7 April 2016, https://www.lawfareblog.com/fbis-firefox-exploit; Andrew Crocker, 'With Remote Hacking, the Government's Particularity Problem Isn't Going Away', *Just Security*, 2 June 2016, https://www.justsecurity.org/31365/remote-hacking-governments-particularity-problem-isnt/?print; and Susan Hennessey and Nicholas Weaver, 'A Judicial Framework for Evaluating Network Investigative Techniques', Lawfare, 28 July 2016, https://lawfareblog.com/judicial-framework-evaluating-network-investigative-techniques.

The Case for Israeli Ground Forces

Eado Hecht and Eitan Shamir

Israel's security doctrine has traditionally distinguished between routine threats (low-intensity attacks by state armies or non-state organisations) and fundamental threats (high-intensity offensives by state armies). It has paid much less attention to the middle ground: the medium-intensity threat. That threat has grown in the wake of changes to the priorities of some Arab states; reductions in the military capabilities of others; and the emergence of non-state organisations that have acquired some state capabilities and that have successfully combined guerrilla and terror tactics (irregular warfare) with more conventional practices (regular warfare).[1] Indeed, medium-intensity warfare is now the strategic focus of some of Israel's active enemies. The country's security doctrine must address this grey area, first by defining it, and then by identifying the optimal strategies and tactics that will be required to combat it.

The range of threats Israel faces suggests that the Israel Defense Forces (IDF) would be well advised to increase investment in its ground forces.[2] This is a conclusion that the IDF itself appears to have drawn: it recently published a strategy document, signed by the IDF chief of staff, that explicitly recommends that Israel maintain an effective ground-force capability.[3] The stated tasks of this force are to defend against small- or large-scale attacks into Israeli territory (mass offensives are deemed less likely for the time being given the internal Arab wars);[4] to conduct small or large focused

Eado Hecht is a Research Fellow at the Begin–Sadat Center for Strategic Studies (BESA Center). He also teaches at the IDF Staff and Command College. **Eitan Shamir** is a Research Fellow with the Begin–Sadat Center for Strategic Studies (BESA Center) and a Lecturer in the Political Studies Department, Bar-Ilan University.

Survival | vol. 58 no. 5 | October–November 2016 | pp. 123–148   DOI 10.1080/00396338.2016.1231535

raids into enemy territory in order to destroy enemy military assets or pressure hostile leadership;[5] and to temporarily conquer large tracts of hostile territory in order to clear them of enemy artillery or other military threats.[6] To accomplish these tasks, the IDF believes it needs a ground force that enjoys better firepower, mobility and protection than its potential enemies.[7] It also believes that this force must achieve a 'critical mass' in terms of size.[8] In other words, quantity is as important as quality. Furthermore, the IDF document emphasises precision firepower (especially, but not exclusively, aerial), and even states that one of the major tactical goals of ground manoeuvres is to locate targets for the IDF's precision-fire assets to destroy.[9]

In contrast with these theoretical findings, however, the IDF has in practice disbanded six armoured brigades, two artillery brigades and an undisclosed number of rear-area security battalions over the past five years. These actions were in keeping with an ongoing, drastic decrease in Israel's ground-force combat power.[10] When viewed in conjunction with statements by senior officers questioning the utility of offensive ground operations, these reductions cast doubt on the seriousness of the military's commitment to conducting them.[11] It seems that those who defend the value of ground forces currently represent a minority.[12]

The role of ground forces in Israel's national security

During the 1990s and 2000s, the confluence of a growing sensitivity to casualties and the development of new technologies caused Israel, like other Western countries, to begin to favour stand-off fire based on aerial and artillery forces whenever possible.[13] (A major exception to this trend was the reassertion of control over the Palestinian territories during the Second Intifada between 2000 and 2006.) IDF failures in the Second Lebanon War (2006) were largely attributed to the neglect of ground warfare. After that war, the IDF invested heavily in rebuilding its ground forces. However, in 2013 it launched a five-year programme to build up its forces that refocused its limited resources on cyber, intelligence, air-force and special-operations capabilities, again at the expense of conventional ground forces.

To understand the evolving role of Israel's ground forces, one needs to revisit Israel's traditional national-security doctrine. Fighting between

Israel, Arab states and non-state organisations has been constant ever since the end of Israel's War of Independence in spring 1949, varying only in intensity and in the identity of the Arab participants. From the early 1950s, Israelis have divided the Arab threat into two categories.[14] 'Fundamental threats' describe scenarios in which an Arab actor launches a major offensive (high-intensity war) with the intent of physically annihilating Israel. 'Routine threats' cover scenarios in which Arabs conduct constant small-scale raids (low-intensity war) in order to wear down the resolve of the Jewish population to remain in Israel.

Given the awareness among Israel's military leaders that neither threat can ever be completely eliminated, the core objective of all Israeli military operations has been to deter future attacks by responding aggressively to current attacks. Fundamental threats are to be countered by a massive, rapid, overwhelming offensive – preferably a pre-emptive one. Routine threats are to be countered by a series of punitive, retaliatory actions. These are usually small, though they can occasionally become larger if the routine threat escalates to an intensity that causes major disruption of civilian life in Israel or excessive Israeli military casualties.

From its founding, the Israeli military has favoured its standing air force over its other branches, for several reasons. Firstly, the air force can produce more firepower per man than Israel's ground forces. Secondly, there is an extreme fear in Israel of air attacks on civilians, fuelled by memories of the Second World War.[15] Many worry that enemy air forces would bypass Israeli ground forces to strike the civilian population. Thirdly, if early warning fails, the air force can respond faster than ground forces. Finally, it is easier to maintain the combat readiness of air-force reserves compared with ground-force reserves.

Despite this, Israel's ground forces were originally deemed the main force for defeating any fundamental threat. Few believed that the air force would be able to defeat an Arab aggressor on its own. Instead, the air force protected the home front from enemy air attacks and assisted the ground forces in their battles.

Since 1973, no Arab state has attempted to initiate a major war with Israel. In 1982, the Syrians, reluctantly drawn into the fighting in Lebanon, refrained from opening a second front on the Golan Heights. This led many to believe that the goal of achieving long-term deterrence against fundamental threats had been achieved. The main focus of Israel's military establishment became routine security and low-intensity threats.

A gradual shift towards a preference for airstrikes over ground actions to fulfil the offensive component of routine security operations began during the War of Attrition against Egypt, Syria, Jordan and the Palestine Liberation Organization (1967–70), becoming the norm in Lebanon during the 1990s. The initial response to the particularly successful Hizbullah raid in 2006, which evolved into the Second Lebanon War, was initially exclusively aerial. Only when the results of the aerial offensive proved insufficient did Israel gradually begin to involve ground troops.

After the Israeli withdrawal from the Gaza Strip in summer 2005, Israeli ground troops were relegated to a defensive role along the border, with the offensive aspect of border defence entrusted to the air force. *Operation Cast Lead* (December 2008–January 2009) was the first large-scale operation in which the air force received an autonomous major role in Gaza. A week-long series of airstrikes was followed by a very limited ground incursion. *Operation Defensive Pillar* (November 2012) responded to the escalation of rocket fire from Gaza exclusively from the air. During all previous operations in Gaza, as in Lebanon, airstrikes had reduced but not stopped continuous rocket fire. However, the short but successful 2012 operation (which resulted in minimal collateral damage, few Israeli casualties and a quiet period following the operation) led some officers to view it as a model for future operations. When attacks again began to escalate nearly two years later, the Israelis initiated *Operation Protective Edge* (July–August 2014). In a repeat of the approach employed during *Defensive Pillar*, Israel initially adopted an air-only strategy. However, it was eventually compelled to employ ground forces to temporarily enter Gaza with the aim of destroying a system of offensive tunnels that was impervious to airstrikes.

Flawed assumptions

One of the assertions that many senior IDF commanders have repeated publicly – which is also expressed in the recently published IDF strategy document[16] – is that, for the foreseeable future, there is no threat of a major ground invasion of Israel by a state-sized army. They conclude, therefore, that the composition of forces required by the IDF requires a radical change. Many believe that ground forces can be drastically diminished in size, since the remaining threats do not require such a large force. This conclusion has been implemented over the past few years by disbanding and discharging numerous ground-force reserve units and shortening the duration of conscript service.[17] Many also believe that the internal composition of the ground force can be changed. Now required, according to this premise, are mostly light-infantry units supported by precision-fire weapons.[18] This conclusion has been made manifest in reductions to armoured and artillery units. Finally, it has been suggested that the training of infantry units should focus more on commando-style and counter-guerrilla operations than on large-unit actions and manoeuvres.[19]

It is true that no Arab state or coalition has attempted to conduct a massive invasion of Israel since 1973, but it is important to understand why this is the case. One reason has been the deterrent effect of the repeated military defeats inflicted on Arab opponents in high-intensity wars, beginning with the defeat of the Arab invasion of the newly established Israel in 1948 and culminating in the Yom Kippur War in 1973. Despite having started the latter war in the best conceivable strategic position, the Arab armies involved achieved very little, and within a few days the IDF had reversed the situation.

Israel's deterrence was enhanced by Egypt's decision to shift from Soviet to US patronage and to sign a peace treaty with Israel, removing the most powerful Arab army from the hostile line-up. The current inter-Arab wars have diverted hostile attention from Israel and decimated the Syrian army. Meanwhile, the post-Saddam, American-built Iraqi army is weak and barely competent.

The widespread belief that Israel possesses nuclear weapons is probably the ultimate form of deterrence against existential threats to the country. However, as demonstrated in 1973, high-intensity wars can be initiated to achieve limited political objectives. Thus, military leaders should be concerned not just with existential, high-intensity threats, but with limited-objective, high-intensity threats. The strategy needed to address these threats may be different, but the tactics and force composition required are similar.

It is probably true that Israel does not currently face a high-intensity threat. Even after the current inter-Arab wars come to an end, it will take years for Syria and Iraq to rebuild military forces capable of conducting a war of annihilation against Israel. However, this analysis rests on a number of assumptions, which, though valid today, might quickly change.

The peace treaty with Egypt, for instance, has been upheld because it was deemed in the interest of the military oligarchy that has mostly ruled Egypt since the treaty was signed in 1979. However, the treaty is viewed negatively by the Muslim Brotherhood, which briefly ruled Egypt from summer 2012 until the following year.[20] Had the Brotherhood not been deposed by the current regime, it is probable that Israeli–Egyptian relations would have soured, and possibly reached a state of military hostility once again. Even now, the stability of the current Egyptian regime is not clear, and the Muslim Brotherhood continues to pose a potent political threat to its existence.[21]

The changes in Egypt show how difficult it is to predict the precise array of Israel's enemies beyond the very near future. How stable is the current Egyptian regime? How stable is the Jordanian regime? If either regime collapses, will these states become like Syria? Or will they maintain their current military capability while changing their policies, as Egypt did under the Muslim Brotherhood? If Egypt loses control of its border with Israel in Sinai, will it accept Israeli operations there against aggressive jihadi groups, or resist them as a matter of principle?

The rise of the medium-intensity threat

The accepted dichotomy between fundamental threats, understood to mean threats emanating from Arab states, and routine threats presented by non-state and mostly Palestinian organisations, is not defensible.[22] Arab states have conducted both high-intensity and low-intensity operations against Israel. There have also been operations that lie somewhere between the two, including not just the high-intensity, limited-objective offensive in 1973, but also various episodes between spring 1969 and summer 1970, in which the intensity of artillery, airstrikes and ground raids rose above the usual level attributed to low-intensity operations. The Palestinians and Hizbullah may not have been capable of escalating beyond low-intensity operations in the past, but the Second Lebanon War (2006) and *Operation Protective Edge* in Gaza (2014) revealed that this has changed. Both groups are now capable of conducting medium-intensity operations, combining irregular warfare with the strategy and tactics of regular warfare.[23] The IDF's tactical mistakes against Hizbullah in 2006 can be largely attributed to the former's failure to recognise this development, and to its attempt to conduct the war with tactics designed to fight an enemy conducting irregular warfare, even though Hizbullah was conducting regular warfare – albeit of limited intensity, and with some reliance on irregular measures. As an IDF battalion commander explained to one of the authors after the 2006 Lebanon War, 'I went in as if to arrest a terrorist and collided with a regular army. It took me a couple of days to understand the situation and adapt my actions accordingly.'[24]

Similar threats have emerged as a result of the Syrian civil war, in the form of groups such as Jabhat al-Nusra (recently renamed Jabhat Fatah al-Sham), which currently controls the southern Syrian Golan Heights adjacent to Israel's border. The Assad regime in Syria has also allowed Iran and Hizbullah to operate in the northern Golan. The forces of Islamic State (also known as ISIS or ISIL) in Syria are capable of medium-intensity operations, but their attempt to advance into the Syrian Golan has been pushed back, and their affiliate forces in Sinai have been compelled to return to terrorist and guerrilla operations after being defeated by Egyptian forces in the battle for Shaykh Zuweyd in July 2015. A catastrophic defeat for the Islamic State could see many of its members migrating to Jabhat Fatah al-Sham (the two groups were originally allies). The twists and turns of the complicated Syrian civil war or an unexpected change in Egypt could allow the Islamic State to recover in either country at any time.

With the exception of the Palestinians, most of these actors are currently focused on fighting each other. Yet there is no way of knowing how long that will last. They all consider Israel an enemy, if one to be dealt with only after defeating their immediate rivals. In the past, inter-Arab rivalry might have reduced the effectiveness of Arab coalitions against Israel, but it did not prevent them from forming.

Given that the scenario Israel is most likely to face in the foreseeable future is a confrontation with either Hamas, Hizbullah (with or without support from Syria or Iran) or Jabhat Fatah al-Sham, it is important to assess these groups' military capabilities. All are essentially infantry armies equipped with light and medium weapons, and with varying sizes of artillery forces. Hizbullah and Hamas each employ tens of thousands of fighters, and Hamas is working to increase its numbers.[25] Hizbullah has provided assistance to the Assad regime in Syria, and therefore has reason to expect that, even if Assad does not employ the official Syrian army directly against Israel, he will not refuse to provide reinforcements for Hizbullah from the National Defense Forces, a grouping of pro-regime militias currently assessed at 70,000 to 80,000 men.[26] Jabhat Fatah al-Sham is smaller, but could also mobilise a variety of non-jihadi allies. Together, all these organisations have a potential combined total strength equivalent to 7–10 light-infantry divisions (though without the same number of service and support personnel associated with American or European light-infantry divisions). Though some of these enemies are rivals that are unlikely to coordinate their attacks on Israel, and are currently preoccupied elsewhere, this does not preclude a simultaneous war with them.[27]

IDF ground forces must be capable not only of defeating ground attacks into Israel, but of successfully conducting ground offensives into neighbouring territories. Since the mid-1970s, Israel has initiated a number of medium-intensity ground-force offensives against Hamas and Hizbullah to defeat low- and medium-intensity threats that had grown to an unacceptable level. Some of these offensives began at a lower intensity and then escalated, despite Israel's preference that they not do so. In each of these offensives, the IDF did not have to simultaneously employ more than three or four divisions, but only because the fighting was limited to a single front.[28]

During the 2002 *Defensive Shield* offensive in the West Bank against a much weaker foe, the IDF employed two divisions with numerous reserve units. If, simultaneously with this operation, there had been an escalation of fighting in Gaza or Lebanon, the IDF would have had to mobilise a number of reserve divisions to those fronts too. The experience of *Peace for Galilee*,

Defensive Shield, the Second Lebanon War, *Cast Lead* and *Protective Edge* shows that, to conduct simultaneous ground-offensive operations on any combination of fronts, the IDF would need a ground force at least equal in size to the combined enemy forces, and preferably larger. In other words, simultaneously defending all of Israel's borders while conducting a major offensive on at least one, and possibly two, fronts would require at least ten divisions' worth of front-line ground forces and a quantity of rear-area security forces. A force size smaller than this would not achieve the 'critical mass' the IDF has claimed it needs.[29]

Strategy and tactics of Israel's main opponents

The balance of heavy, light and artillery units within Israel's ground forces will depend on the strategy and tactics of the enemy. The Islamic State and Jabhat Fatah al-Sham have not yet fought Israel, but their goals and capabilities are variations on those of Hizbullah and Hamas. While acknowledging the differences between them, it is still possible to assess how these actors might adapt their strategy and tactics to fight Israel.

Because neither the Palestinians nor Hizbullah are capable of decisively defeating the Israeli military, their offensive strategy in past confrontations has been to gradually exhaust Israel's civilian population by terrorising it and depressing its morale. The tactical tools employed to implement this strategy have been direct attacks on Israeli civilians by individual assailants or small groups, and long-range artillery bombardments of Israeli population centres. The groups have also employed sniping, bombardment and ambushes, as well as small-unit, commando-style raids, against Israeli forces in order to inflict military casualties and thus attack the morale of the civilian population indirectly. In 2006 and 2014, Hizbullah and Hamas respectively conducted defensive battles to block, or at least delay, Israeli attacks aimed at their rocket-launcher sites and offensive tunnel networks.

An analysis of the current rhetoric and force build-up of Hamas and Hizbullah, as well as the demographic and budgetary constraints on the size and composition of their forces, suggests that a major change in their offensive strategy and tactics is unlikely for the foreseeable future. Both groups continue to emphasise long-range artillery rockets, commando units, light infantry, and advanced anti-tank, anti-aircraft and anti-ship weapons.[30] The Islamic State and Jabhat Fatah al-Sham, which lack a dependable source for more advanced weaponry and are currently fighting an enemy that differs significantly from Israel, are lagging behind in all these fields, with the exception of light infantry. Conversely, although Hizbullah and Hamas have used suicide bombers, they have never used them as frequently or effectively as have the Islamic State and Jabhat Fatah al-Sham.

The strategy of these groups may be more or less unchanging, but there have been developments in the tactical field. Although familiar tactics continue to be used, more emphasis is being placed on commando-style, cross-border raids, Hamas having learned the tactical and strategic utility of such raids during the 2014 Gaza war.[31] Using tunnels or diving gear to bypass Israeli detection systems, Hamas fighters were able to inflict casualties on Israeli forces inside Israel: one-sixth of IDF fatalities during the war occurred during infantry engagements on the Israeli side of the Gaza border. A number of Hamas commando troops have undergone parachute–glider training as well.[32] The novelty lies not in the methods, which have all been used in the past, but rather in the emphasis on planned efforts to conduct several such raids in concert, simultaneously or sequentially, rather than conducting small, isolated actions.

Hamas is contemplating deeper raids

Furthermore, though the raids from Gaza in 2014 were fairly shallow (that is, close to the border), Hamas is apparently contemplating deeper raids, with attack objectives further inside Israel.[33] Hizbullah leaders have mentioned 'liberating' the Galilee region, an operation that is currently beyond their military capability, but which could presage attempts to raid deeper objectives within Israel.[34] The concept of deep, large-force raids is a staple of Islamic State and Jabhat Fatah al-Sham tactics.

These raids could be conducted by forces ranging in size from a squad (as was seen during the summer 2014 war with Gaza) to a battalion (something that Hizbullah is capable of, and that has been seen in operations by the Islamic State).[35] Hamas is lagging behind in the size of its trained raiding forces, but could develop this capability if it wished to.

Forces are sized according to the missions they undertake: the bigger the force, the bigger the objective, and the more persistent the force will be in achieving that objective. In fact, there is a point at which, though conceived as a raid, an operation might become an attempt to capture and hold territory. This leads us to the most dramatic change seen in the tactical competence of Israel's enemies. Over the past few years, Hizbullah, Jabhat Fatah al-Sham and the Islamic State have acquired a great deal of experience employing thousands of fighters organised in ad hoc or (almost) regular combat teams to capture or hold territory, especially built-up areas. Islamic State has conducted wide-ranging offensive operations, requiring the coordination of actions separated by dozens to hundreds of kilometres towards a common operational goal. At the battle for Kobane in autumn 2014, the Islamic State employed the numerical equivalent of an infantry division – some 9,000 infantry and 30–50 tanks, supported by artillery and surveillance drones.[36]

Still, the group has much to learn. Written and video reports on the fighting in Syria and Iraq between 2012 and 2016 show that, even when larger forces were fighting around a single objective, the biggest forces seen to be operating together tactically, rather than just side by side, were equivalent to battalions. Platoon- and company-sized actions were much more common. Also observed were combined-arms teams at the platoon and company levels, using mortars, tanks, anti-tank missiles and light artillery to support mostly infantry forces.

Hizbullah is probably more advanced than the others because of Iranian mentoring and training,[37] experience working closely with Syrian army formations at the brigade and division levels, and participation with them in combined-arms battles. Thus, at the battle of al-Qusayr in spring 2013, Hizbullah employed 1,700 men with a combined-arms force of 5,000–6,000 men from the Syrian army's 1st Armoured Division, with some reports even claiming that command of the entire battle was delegated to the Hizbullah commander at the scene.[38] Hamas has only defensive experience and, as of summer 2014, did not show much capability in coordinating units larger than platoons.

All this suggests that there could very well be attempts to conduct larger operations to capture, at least temporarily, not just military posts, but Israeli villages or towns adjacent to the border, or important civilian or military installations further in, for the purpose of conducting massacres or taking hostages.[39] Given the overall disparity in military strength between Israel and these enemies, such attacks would be aimed more at exploiting their psychological value than at actually capturing and retaining territory. Nevertheless, the taking of an Israeli village or part of a town, even if the population had been evacuated prior to the attack and the occupation was temporary, would have a dramatic psychological effect on Israel.[40]

Though all the organisations fighting in Syria have employed heavy weapons such as tanks, infantry fighting vehicles and armoured personnel carriers, the numbers have been relatively small – a few dozen on occasion, but usually only a handful at a time. The groups' attacking forces could be expected to include mostly infantry supported by medium weapons (especially mortars and guided anti-tank missiles). The forces of Jabhat Fatah al-Sham or Islamic State might also contain suicide and vehicle bombers.[41]

In sum, the preferred strategy of Israel's most likely near-term opponents is to achieve the psychological exhaustion of the Israeli population by employing two complementary methods. The first is artillery bombardment, which could range in intensity from a few rockets per month aimed at military and civilian targets near the border to a medium-intensity offensive (a few hundred rockets per day over an extended period) covering most of Israel's population centres and vital national infrastructure. (It should be noted that the number of rockets in Hizbullah's arsenal would probably allow it to outlast Israel's limited anti-rocket defenses.[42]) The second method is ground raids, ranging from small, sporadic harassment raids against military and civilian targets to concerted efforts to capture population centres, including villages or towns, or the military posts and camps protecting them, located close to the country's borders. There might also be attempts to infiltrate raiders deeper into Israel.[43]

Given the current size of the hostile combat forces arrayed against Israel, this mode of operation does not pose an immediate existential threat to the country. However, it can certainly threaten and disrupt the lives of Israeli civilians: in 2006, hundreds of thousands of Israelis from the north of the country were forced to find temporary shelter in central

Israel, and a smaller number of southern Israelis became internal refugees in 2014. It also poses a threat to the lives of IDF troops deployed to defend Israeli territory. In the long run, the capabilities of the ground forces targeting Israel will only increase.

Countering the threats

Having assessed the characteristics of the most probable threats against Israel, the next task is to consider what the country's strategic, operational and tactical responses might be, as well as the role of ground forces in those responses. The similarities between the political goals, capabilities and modus operandi of Israel's most likely opponents allow for the presentation of generic scenarios, without requiring that any given enemy be considered separately.

The ground threat

Given the offensive tactics and weapons employed by Hizbullah, Islamic State and Jabhat Fatah al-Sham (and to some degree by Hamas), defending against the ground threat requires the IDF to possess both defensive and offensive regular ground-warfare capabilities. Using airpower to hold ground has repeatedly proven ineffective. The air force can provide immense support to ground troops, and can inhibit large concentrations of enemy forces from moving freely, but, as was proven during the Second World War and many times since then (including during failed attempts by the anti-Islamic State coalition in Iraq and Syria over the past year), it cannot completely prevent the enemy from gradually accumulating forces and attacking.[44]

When on the defensive, therefore, the IDF needs to be able to physically cover entire borders with contiguous observation and highly responsive fire capabilities. Because Israel's enemies are known to employ rapid massive infiltration, villages and towns near the border must be surrounded by permanent defensive forces. These forces must be well protected from light artillery and advanced anti-tank missiles, as well as from multiple attacks by large, vehicle-mounted bombs.

The defending forces must be deployed for 360-degree defence, and be capable of withstanding attacks by dozens to hundreds of attackers while waiting for reinforcements. Quick-reaction forces must be close enough to rapidly reinforce any area under attack, especially villages and towns adjacent to the border. The reaction forces must be capable of negotiating difficult terrain under light-artillery and heavy anti-tank fire while crossing small fields of improvised explosive devices (IEDs) and mines.

Carrying out such a defensive mission with light-infantry forces would be casualty-intensive for the Israelis. The casualty ratio would only improve through the prodigious use of long-range fire and well-protected armoured vehicles.[45] Precision-guided munitions (PGMs) can be used effectively only against a small number of enemy targets; area-coverage weapons are more effective against mass infantry attacks. In other words, contrary to recent statements by many senior IDF officers, what Israeli forces need are not more PGMs, cyber capabilities and special forces, but rather simple artillery, tanks, heavily armoured personnel carriers and denser infantry strong-points to make infiltration between them more difficult.

It is true that, against the enemies discussed here, the *Merkava* 4 tank is not necessary, but tank-mounted firepower, protection and mobility do offer a major advantage. The IDF could make do with older, cheaper tanks equipped with effective anti-personnel shells and the latest defences against anti-tank missiles (such as the *Trophy* system). Throughout the past 100 years, simple field artillery and mortars have proven to be the most effective anti-infantry weapons.

The artillery threat

Since 1969, Israel's preferred response to artillery bombardment has been to use its air force to attempt to simultaneously suppress the bombardment directly by attacking the enemy's artillery forces and dissuade the relevant Arab authority from continuing the bombardment by attacking targets (personnel and infrastructure) thought to be too important for that authority to risk losing them.

A comparison of the intensity of Arab artillery fire against Israel with the intensity of Israeli aerial-suppression strikes (targeting weapons, logistics and operating personnel) from the 1969–70 artillery bombardments of the War of Attrition through to the Gaza war in summer 2014 shows that the overall intensity of Arab artillery fire was rarely affected by the IDF's suppression airstrikes. The gradual improvement of Israel's strike capability over the years was more or less matched by increases in the survivability and redundancy of enemy forces. This is not to say that suppression airstrikes are irrelevant – they do have a limited cumulative effect, insofar as they gradually degrade the enemy's artillery force, especially its personnel, which might ultimately induce the enemy leadership to cease fire. However, achieving this necessarily entails a protracted period during which Israelis continue to suffer bombardment.

In the end, Israeli suppression attacks have not been the decisive factor in the numerous stand-off-fire campaigns between Israel and its enemies. Rather, casualties across the full range of the enemy's military hierarchy and damage to its infrastructure have usually created the conditions for achieving a ceasefire with terms favourable to Israel. However, this method is also time-consuming, depending on the determination of the opponent's leaders and the availability of relevant targets.

Ground operations are superior to stand-off operations in diminishing enemy artillery fire and convincing the enemy to cease fire because they lead to the capture of launch sites and storage sites, and inflict heavier casualties on the enemy much more quickly. However, they have obvious disadvantages, which is the main reason why the IDF has tended to avoid them. These include:

- Increased casualties: There is a perception among the Israeli leadership that Israeli society is casualty-sensitive, although a recent study showed that the level of sensitivity is contingent on various factors. The Israeli public can in fact be casualty-tolerant under certain circumstances.[46]
- Range: Many artillery weapons have ranges of dozens – if not hundreds – of kilometres, placing them beyond the reach of a ground operation.
- International opinion: Israel can usually expect an international diplomatic backlash whenever it defends itself aggressively.
- The difficulty of devising an exit strategy: There are situations in which Israel's exit strategy is to merely withdraw IDF forces and

let the fighting fizzle out, but other situations require some form of political arrangement, with or without international involvement.

These disadvantages create a vicious circle. IDF senior commanders know that the political leadership is hesitant to use ground forces, so they economise on investing in those forces and instead focus on other capabilities relevant to stand-off fire. This in turn further reduces the willingness to employ ground forces.

Despite these disadvantages, the Israeli government might still be compelled to order a ground-force operation to drive a threat away from Israel's borders – as was the case in Lebanon in 1982 and 2006, and in Gaza in 2008 and 2014. It might also have to do so in cases where the IDF had otherwise failed to suppress enemy artillery fire, the conflict was expected to become protracted if confined to stand-off fire by the Israeli air force, the IDF possessed only a limited number of expensive anti-rocket missiles relative to the number of rockets in enemy arsenals, or if a suitable stand-off response to some enemy tactic, such as the offensive tunnels in Gaza, could not be found.

Conducting a ground offensive

Though it is a less desirable approach from a military standpoint, Israel can, for political reasons, leave the initiative for ground combat in enemy hands, seeking only to defend itself, and perhaps to make small cross-border attacks that improve its defensive capability, while waiting for its aerial offensive to gradually convince the enemy to desist. However, as noted, the Israeli government might be compelled to order a ground offensive with either the minimalist aim of reducing enemy access to Israel's border and pushing at least its short-range rocket launchers beyond their range, or the maximalist aim of compelling the enemy to request a ceasefire.

Whatever the strategic goal, the IDF, in order to conduct an effective ground operation, needs the tactical capability to cross, clear and cover large tracts of ground, some of it hilly and wooded; capture and clear numerous built-up areas of various sizes; and search for tunnels and other hidden storage sites. It must accomplish all this while being fired at with mortars and long-range anti-tank missiles; ambushed by infantry with small arms and personal anti-tank rockets, mines, explosive booby-traps and remote-controlled explosives; counter-attacked by infantry units and suicide bombers; and confronted with a variety of natural and artificial obstacles.

The IDF was surprised in Lebanon in 2006 and in Gaza in 2014 by the intensity of enemy resistance. In future, the IDF must assume this level of resistance. Indeed, as its potential enemies continue to gain in combat experience, an even higher level of intensity and competence should be expected. Even though Israel's current enemies are not as big, well-armed or well-trained as the Egyptian and former Syrian armies, they must be considered not merely guerrillas, but trained armies. Defeating them will require the application of regular-warfare tactics adapted to the specific circumstances.

The IDF faced such a situation in 1982. The forces of the Palestine Liberation Organization (PLO) in Lebanon at the time were roughly equivalent in size to each of the separate enemy forces facing the IDF today – albeit undoubtedly less competent, technologically advanced and fortified than Hizbullah. They were deployed across southern Lebanon and along the coast up to Beirut. Defeating them in *Operation Peace for Galilee* in 1982 required the employment of three IDF divisions.[47] Though few of Israel's current enemies are significantly more competent than were PLO forces in 1982, Hizbullah certainly is, and the learning curve shown by Hamas since 2006 indicates that it is heading in the same direction.

To defeat these enemies, the IDF might not need massive numbers of the latest high-tech ground weapons, but it will need the tanks, armoured personnel carriers and artillery it has used in the past, upgraded with specific capabilities (especially protection against anti-tank missiles, artillery and IEDs). Furthermore, as recently retired IDF Major-General Gershon Hacohen stated in an interview, to simultaneously capture and clear large tracts of territory requires large quantities of such weapons – a statement with which the IDF strategy document seems to concur, given its acknowledgement of the importance of 'critical mass'.[48]

In addition to any offensive operations it might undertake, the IDF will require large forces to secure its lines of supply and to constantly survey its tactical rear to find and destroy stay-behind or infiltrating elements of enemy forces. The deeper the advance, the more forces will be required to secure supply routes.

In fact, the threat posed by current long-range (up to 5km) guided anti-tank missiles to a convoy of trucks carrying supplies (especially fuel and ammunition) to combat forces through recently taken territory can be countered only by using a large number of highly protected armoured personnel carriers to carry the supplies, or by saturating the terrain with combat forces to prevent enemy missile teams from attaining a position overlooking the supply routes. When such forces are not available, casualties among support units will be heavy.

*   *   *

Cultivating a small and highly capable ground force with the latest gadgets is important, but not enough to meet Israel's security requirements as set out in the IDF's own strategic document. Instead, Israel should seek to maintain a large, mechanised, capable and ready ground force, as it has done in the past – even if a large portion of this force is equipped with older armoured fighting vehicles and artillery that has been upgraded only in specific crucial components.

The IDF has acknowledged that it needs to maintain 'critical mass' to achieve its missions, but has not attached any specific number to this term.[49] We estimate that a scenario requiring Israel to maintain a defensive line along all fronts, while leaving the country with sufficient ground combat power to conduct simultaneous major offensives on two fronts (for example, Lebanon and Syria, or Lebanon and Gaza), would require a ground force equivalent to at least ten armoured or mechanised divisions, plus a large force of lighter rear-area security forces. Assessments suggesting that the duration of most future wars will be measured in weeks, if not months, further reinforce the need for a force of this size, so as to allow for the rotation of units in action.

Time and again, expectations that new technologies would allow wars to be won without deploying ground forces have proven to be false. Ground forces are still crucial for winning wars, even against foes that lack the tactical competence and advanced weaponry of Israel's current enemies, as the American experience in Iraq and Afghanistan has shown.[50] The lesson for the IDF is that the past and planned reductions in its ground-force units are imperilling its ability to meet its own standards and provide for Israel's security against a range of threats.

Acknowledgements

The authors would like to thank Professor Efraim Inbar for his useful comments on earlier drafts of this article. They also wish to thank Elad Erlich for his essential assistance in research. The overall study of which this article is a part was sponsored by a BESA Center research grant.

Notes

1   See Frank G. Hoffman, '"Hybrid Threats": Neither Omnipotent nor Unbeatable', *Orbis*, vol. 54, no. 3, Summer 2010, pp. 441–55; and David E. Johnson, *Hard Fighting: Israel in Lebanon and Gaza* (Santa Monica, CA: RAND Arroyo Center, 2011), pp. xxi, xxii.

2   Ground forces are flexible and perform a variety of missions. However, we refer here to ground forces primarily capable of and designed for manoeuvre and heavy mechanised combined-arms operations.

3   IDF Chief of the General Staff, *Estrategyat Zahal* [IDF Strategy], August 2015, http://www.idf.il/SIP_STORAGE/FILES/9/16919.pdf. One should bear in mind, when analysing this document, that it is the shorter, unclassified version of a comprehensive document designed as the conceptual framework for a new IDF five-year plan. Michael Herzog, 'The IDF Strategy Goes Public', Policy Watch no. 2,479, Washington Institute, 28 August 2015,

http://www.washingtoninstitute.org/policy-analysis/view/new-idf-strategy-goes-public.

4   IDF, 'IDF Strategy', pp. 1, 28.

5   *Ibid.*, p. 29.

6   *Ibid.*, p. 28. Essentially, this is still a raid, albeit a more extended one, since the political intention is to return the territory to the enemy either by withdrawing during the war when the clearing operation is deemed complete (as in summer 2014 in Gaza) or after the ceasefire (as in summer 2006 in Lebanon).

7   *Ibid.*, p. 29.

8   *Ibid.*, p. 27.

9   *Ibid.*, p. 29, paragraph 20.

10 IDF Website Board, 'Kol Mah SheRatsitem LaDa'at Al TaRaSh Gid'on' [All You Wanted to Know About the Multi-Year Plan – Gideon], 26 July 2015, http://www.idf.il/1133-22449-he/Dover.aspx. As Amir Rapaport reports: 'The truth is that the IDF has been engaged in an effort to adapt to the wars of the present and

the future for some time: since 1985, the number of tanks was reduced by 75%, the number of aircraft was reduced by 50% and the number of UAVs – Unmanned Airborne Vehicles – increased by 400%. The number of reservists was cut down by hundreds of thousands.' See Amir Rapaport, 'The New Multi-Year Plan of the IDF and the Agreement with Iran', *Israel Defense*, 9 September 2015. According to the IISS *Military Balance* between 1989 and 2015, the number of standing armoured brigades was reduced from six to four, and reserve brigades were reduced from 18 to ten. The IDF's entire remaining fleet of M-60s and *Centurions* was decommissioned, which means a decrease of 1,510 tanks, leaving 1,500 *Merkava* (Mk. 1 through 4) main battle tanks in the order of battle. According to a 2014 report by the Institute for National Security Studies in Tel Aviv, *Merkava* 1 will soon be decommissioned as well, further reducing the number of operational tanks. See Institute for National Security Studies, 'Israel', 26 November 2014, http://www.inss.org.il/upload-Images/systemFiles/Israel106082368.pdf. See also press reports announcing the disbanding of the 500th Armoured Brigade in 2003 at http://www.himush.co.il/?item=2061&section=687; a memo issued for the disbanding of the 130th Armoured Brigade in 2014 at http://www.yadlashiryon.com/vf/ib_items/7121/130.pdf; an article about the disbanding ceremony of the 11th Armoured Brigade at http://www.yadlashiryon.com/show_item.asp?levelId=63829&itemId=6328&itemType=0; and an additional

press report on the disbanding of the 600th Armoured Brigade and the 27th Armoured Brigade, and the planned decommissioning of the *Merkava* 1, at http://www.ynet.co.il/articles/0,7340,L-4512425,00.html.

11 Some statements were made by senior officers to the authors on condition of anonymity. Representative public statements were made by Brigadier-General (Reserves) Gal Hirsch, Brigadier-General (Retd) Avigdor Klein and Colonel (Retd) Shmuel Gordon at a BESA Symposium on the IDF's 2013 Build-Up Programme, Bar-Ilan University, Ramat-Gan, 30 December 2013; and by Brigadier-General (Reserves) Moni Horev at a BESA conference on the IDF Commander's Initiative, Bar-Ilan University, Ramat-Gan, 16 June 2015.

12 See Amir Rapaport's interview with Major-General Gershon HaCohen: 'HaTsava Sovel MeOdef Miktsoyoot' [The Army Suffers from Excessive Professionalism], *Israel Defense*, 31 July 2015, http://www.israeldefense.co.il/he/content/%D7%94%D7%A6%D7%91%D7%90-%D7%A1%D7%95%D7%91%D7%9C-%D7%9E%D7%A2%D7%95%D7%93%D7%A3-%D7%9E%D7%A7%D7%A6%D7%95%D7%A2%D7%99%D7%95%D7%AA.

13 See Itay Brun, 'Lean Ne'elam HaTimrun' [Where Has the Manoeuvre Disappeared?], *Maarachot*, no. 420–21, September 2008, pp. 4–14; Victor Israel, 'Kach Hishta'abed ZaHaL La Esh VeZanakh Et TaTimrun' [This is How the IDF Subjected Itself to Fire and Abandoned Manoeuvre], *Maarachot*,

no. 415, November 2007, pp. 4–9; and Ron Tira, 'HaEem Viter ZaHaL Al HaTimrun' [Has the IDF Given Up on Manoeuvre?], *Maarachot*, no. 453, February 2014, pp. 14–17.

14 Motti Golani, *Tiheeyeh Milkhamah BaKayitz…* [There Will Be War Next Summer…], Volume I (Tel Aviv: Maarachot, 1997), p. 18.

15 Images of the German aerial bombardment of Britain and the British and American aerial bombardment of Germany have left a lasting impression on Israel's political leadership.

16 IDF, 'IDF Strategy', pp. 3 and 32, paragraph 35.

17 See Amir Rapport, 'Khorim BaEstrategyah' [Holes in the Strategy], *Israel Defense*, 20 August 2015, http://www.israeldefense.co.il/he/content/%D7%97%D7%95%D7%A8%D7%99%D7%9D-%D7%91%D7%90%D7%A1%D7%98%D7%A8%D7%98%D7%92%D7%99%D7%94#comment-1593.

18 Some serving and retired officers have expressed even more extreme versions of this view both in private and in public. Examples include Haim Asa and Major-General (Retd) Yedidia Ya'ari, *LiLkhom Akheret – Tfisat Lekhima Khadasha* [Fighting Differently: A New Combat Concept] (Tel Aviv: Hemed Books – Yediot Akharonot, 2014); and Colonel (Retd) Gordon at the BESA Symposium, 30 December 2013.

19 See, for example, Brigadier-General (Reserves) Hirsch at the BESA Symposium, 30 December 2013.

20 See, for example, Ron Ben Yishai, 'Mone'a Hidavrut. Kach Mecharsem Morsi BeHeskem HaShalom' [Preventing Discussion: Thus Morsi is Eroding the Peace Treaty], Ynet News, 22 August 2012, http://www.ynet.co.il/articles/0,7340,L-4271733,00.html; Liad Porat, 'The Muslim Brotherhood in Egypt and Its True Intentions Towards Israel', BESA Center Perspective Paper no. 192, December 2012, http://besacenter.org/perspectives-papers/the-muslim-brotherhood-in-egypt-and-its-true-intentions-towards-israel/; and Liad Porat, 'The Muslim Brotherhood and Egypt–Israel Peace', Mideast Security and Policy Studies no. 102, Begin–Sadat Center for Strategic Studies, 1 August 2013, http://besacenter.org/mideast-security-and-policy-studies/the-muslim-brotherhood-and-egypt-israel-peace/.

21 See, for example, '26 Egyptian Officers Allegedly Jailed for Plotting Coup Against Sisi', Middle East Eye, 17 August 2015, http://www.middleeasteye.net/news/26-egyptian-officers-jailed-plotting-coup-against-sisi-997863448; and 'Army Officers Sentenced to Death "For Plotting Sisi's Assassination"', The New Arab, 22 December 2015, http://www.alaraby.co.uk/english/news/2015/12/22/army-officers-sentenced-to-death-for-plotting-sisis-assassination. The Egyptian government has denied these reports, but neither its own credibility, nor that of the original sources for the reports, is above suspicion.

22 Iran does not share a border with Israel, therefore all direct confrontations with Iran to date have occurred sub-conventionally with terrorist and sabotage attacks. Because of this, Iran does not figure directly in this discussion, though it is not unrealis-

tic to assume that in the future both sides might also employ air forces or surface-to-surface missiles. Indirect confrontations occur via Hizbullah, Iran's proxy in Lebanon, and might in the future occur on the Syrian front via other proxies as well. In theory, Iran could provide some reinforcements for the Syrian army itself. For further discussion see IDF Chief of the General Staff, *Estrategyat Zahal*.

23 See, for example, a comparison between Hizbullah's 2006 tactical practice and the Syrian army's pre-civil-war tactical doctrine in Amir Eshel, 'BaDerech LeKipaon BaTimrun' [En Route to Immobilising the Ability to Manoeuvre], *Maarachot*, no. 434, December 2010, pp. 17–19; Hoffman, '"Hybrid Threats": Neither Omnipotent nor Unbeatable'; and Johnson, *Hard Fighting*, pp. xxi, xxii. No detailed study of Hamas tactics during *Operation Protective Edge* has been published, but sifting through fragmentary descriptions of the ground battles reveals that Hamas was attempting to emulate Hizbullah tactics, if, for the time being, at a lower level of competence.

24 Conversation with IDF Officer, Name Withheld, Tel Aviv, 5 October 2006.

25 On the Palestinian Authority and Fatah see Adnan Abu Omer, 'Security Services Drain Palestine's Budget', Al-Monitor, 10 May 2015, http://www.al-monitor.com/pulse/originals/2015/05/palestine-gaza-security-services-annual-budget-finance-aman.html. On Hamas see Muhammad Omer, 'Hamas Growing in Military Stature, Say Analysts', Middle East Eye, 17 July 2014, http://www.middleeasteye.net/news/hamas-gains-credibility-fighting-force-analysts-say-371780262. On Islamic State see Jim Sciutto, Jamie Crawford and Chelsea J. Carter, 'Isis Can "Muster" Between 20,000 and 31,500 Fighters, CIA Says', CNN, 12 September 2014, http://edition.cnn.com/2014/09/11/world/meast/isis-syria-iraq/; Samia Nakhoul, 'Saddam's Former Army Is Secret of Baghdadi's Success', Reuters, 16 June 2015, http://www.reuters.com/article/2015/06/16/us-mideast-crisis-baghdadi-insight-idUSKBN0OW1VN20150616; and Daveed Gartenstein-Ross, 'How Many Fighters Does the Islamic State Really Have?', War on the Rocks, 9 February 2015, http://warontherocks.com/2015/02/how-many-fighters-does-the-islamic-state-really-have/. On Hizbullah see Aram Nerguizian, 'Assessing the Consequences of Hezbollah's Necessary War of Choice in Syria', CSIS, 17 June 2013, http://csis.org/publication/assessing-consequences-hezbollahs-necessary-war-choice-syria; and Dominic Evans, 'Analysis: Hezbollah Takes Syrian Centre-Stage, Yet Remains in Shadows', Reuters, 18 June 2013, http://www.reuters.com/article/2013/06/18/us-syria-crisis-hezbollah-analysis-idUSBRE95H10Y20130618.

26 See 'Iran: Senior IRGC Commander: 130,000 Trained Basij Forces Waiting to Enter Syria', National Council of Resistance of Iran, http://ncr-iran.org/en/ncri-statements/terrorism-fundamentalism/16496-iran-senior-irgc-commander-130-000-trained-basij-forces-waiting-to-enter-syria;

'Iranian Media Reports Deleted Following Publication (1): Senior IRGC Official Speaking on Iran's Military Involvement in Syria Says Iran Has Established "Second Hezbollah" There', MEMRI Special Dispatch no. 5848, 25 September 2014, http://www.memri.org/report/en/print8162.htm#_edn1; and 'The Syrian Army in the Civil War', GlobalSecurity.org, http://www.globalsecurity.org/military/world/syria/army-war.htm.

27 For an example of such an uncoordinated, simultaneous war see the various offensives being conducted concurrently against the Islamic State.

28 In *Operation Peace for Galilee* (1982), the IDF employed seven divisions, but only three against the Palestine Liberation Organization, whose forces in southern and western Lebanon were equivalent in size to two infantry divisions. The other four IDF divisions were employed against the Syrian forces in central and eastern Lebanon.

29 IDF, 'IDF Strategy', p. 27.

30 Hizbullah is estimated to have approximately 100,000 rockets and missiles; the Gazan arsenal was significantly depleted in summer 2014, but the group is working to replenish and increase it. See Shakhar Khai, 'Aviv Kochavi, "Medooyakim VeKatlaniyim: 170,00 Tilim Me'aymim"' [Aviv Kochavi: 'An Accurate and Lethal Threat: 170,000 Missiles'], Ynet News, 29 January 2014, http://www.ynet.co.il/articles/0,7340,L-4482538,00.html; 'Rocket Testing and Tunnel Reconstruction', IDF Blog, 22 December 2014, https://www.

idfblog.com/blog/2014/12/22/hamas-reconstructing-tunnels-southern-israel/; and 'Hamas Commander Says Group Rebuilding Rocket Arsenal', Al-Monitor, 3 March 2015, http://www.al-monitor.com/pulse/fr/contents/afp/2015/03/israel-palestinians-conflict-gaza-hamas.html.

31 Yoav Zeitun, 'Commando Hamas Mit'atsem; HaYa'ad: Ashkelon VeAshdod' [Hamas's Amphibious Commando Getting Stronger; The Target: Ashkelon and Ashdod], Ynet News, 20 August 2015, http://www.ynet.co.il/articles/0,7340,L-4692519,00.html.

32 Gilli Cohen, Shirley Seidler, Yaniv Kobovic and Revital Khovel, 'Atsoor MeKoach HaMinharot Shel Hamas: "Avarnu Imuney Tsnikhah BeMalaysia"' [Captured Hamas Tunnel Unit Member: 'We Received Parachute Training in Malaysia'], *Haaretz*, 31 July 2014, http://www.haaretz.co.il/news/politics/1.2392945.

33 Zeitun, 'Hamas's Amphibious Commando Getting Stronger; The Target: Ashkelon and Ashdod'.

34 Shimon Shapira, 'Tochnit Mivtsa'it Shel Hizballah LeMilkhamah Eem Yisrael: Yeri Tilim Al Tel-Aviv VeKibush HaGalil' [Hizbullah Operational Plan for War With Israel: Launching Missiles on Tel-Aviv and Conquering the Galilee], Jerusalem Center for Public Affairs, 3 November 2011, http://jcpa.org.il/2011/11/%D7%AA%D7%95%D7%9B%D7%A0%D7%99%D7%AA-%D7%9E%D7%91%D7%A6%D7%A2%D7%99%D7%AA-%D7%A9%D7%9C-%D7%97%D7%96%D7%91%D7%90%D7%9C%D7%9C%D7%94

-%D7%9C%D7%9E%D7%9C%D7%97%D7%9E%D7%94-%D7%A2%D7%9D-%D7%99%D7%A9%D7%A8/. This article is based on public speeches and interviews with Hizbullah sources published in Lebanese newspapers. Although these sources were likely exaggerating for propaganda effect, the basic premise of ground attacks into Israel, rather than merely small raids, seems to be taken seriously by the IDF: see Ron Ben Yishai, 'What the Third Lebanon War Will Look Like', Israel News, 13 September 2015, http://www.ynetnews.com/articles/0,7340,L-4700232,00.html.

35 See Or Heler, 'LeHizballah Yecholot Hetkefiyot BeShitkheynu' [Hizbullah Has an Offensive Capability in Our Territory], *Israel Defense*, 13 September 2015, http://www.israeldefense.co.il/he/content/%D7%9C%D7%97%D7%99%D7%96%D7%91%D7%90%D7%9C%D7%9C%D7%94-%D7%99%D7%9B%D7%95%D7%9C%D7%95%D7%AA-%D7%94%D7%AA%D7%A7%D7%A4%D7%99%D7%95%D7%AA-%D7%91%D7%A9%D7%98%D7%97%D7%A0%D7%95.

36 See Karam Shoumali and Anne Barnard, 'Slaughter Is Feared as ISIS Nears Turkish Border', *New York Times*, 6 October 2014, http://www.nytimes.com/2014/10/07/world/middleeast/isis-moves-into-syrian-kurdish-enclave-on-turkish-border.html?_r=1; Hannah Lucinda Smith, 'Fears of Massacre as ISIS Tanks Lead Assault on Kurdish Bastion', *The Times*, 4 October 2014, http://www.thetimes.co.uk/tto/news/world/middleeast/article4226717.ece?shareTok

en=f90094518fabc34e4ca7f4a59e7a3990#tab-5; and Gilad Shiloach, 'This Is ISIS's Favorite Drone', *The Week*, 30 January 2015, http://theweek.com/articles/536593/isiss-favorite-drone.

37 In summer 2012, for example, it was reported that Hizbullah had conducted an Iranian-mentored exercise in which 10,000 fighters practised defensive battles and attacks to capture portions of northern Israel. See N. Yahav, 'Hizballah Arach Targil BeHishtatfut 10,000 Pe'ilim' [Hizbullah Conducted 10,000-Man Exercise], Walla News, http://news.walla.co.il/item/2560837.

38 See Jeffrey White, 'The Qusayr Rules: The Syrian Regime's Changing Way of War', Washington Institute, PolicyWatch 2,082, 31 May 2013, http://www.washingtoninstitute.org/policy-analysis/view/the-qusayr-rules-the-syrian-regimes-changing-way-of-war; Complex Operational Environment and Threat Integration Directorate, 'The Battle for al Qusayr, Syria', June 2013, https://info.publicintelligence.net/USArmy-TRISA-alQusayrBattle.pdf; Nicholas Blanford, 'The Battle for Qusayr: How the Syrian Regime and Hizb Allah Tipped the Balance', Combating Terrorism Center at West Point, 27 August 2013, https://www.ctc.usma.edu/posts/the-battle-for-qusayr-how-the-syrian-regime-and-hizb-allah-tipped-the-balance; and Jeffrey White, 'Hizb Allah at War in Syria: Forces, Operations, Effects and Implications', Combating Terrorism Center at West Point, 15 January 2014, https://www.ctc.usma.edu/posts/hizb-allah-at-war-in-syria-forces-oper-

ations-effects-and-implications.

39 See Amir Bohbot, 'HaMilkhamah HaBa'ah Mool Hizballah Kvar Tiraeh Akheret LeGamrey' [The Next War Against Hizbullah Will Look Completely Different], Walla News, 23 March 2015, http://news.walla.co.il/item/2839981; Yishai, 'What the Third Lebanon War Will Look Like'; and Heler, 'Hizbullah Has an Offensive Capability In Our Territory'.

40 The Islamic State, for example, has conducted mass-sacrificial raids into towns behind enemy lines. In one such raid into Kobane in June 2015, it employed 80–100 men, two suicide vehicles and three to four suicide personnel. Two hundred and sixty Kurds were killed and 300 wounded before this force was finally destroyed. See 'ISIL on 24-Hour "Killing Rampage" in Syria's Kobane', Al-Jazeera, 27 June 2015, http://www.aljazeera.com/news/2015/06/isil-24-hour-killing-rampage-kobane-150626144824173.html; '79 IS Killed in Ein al-Arab "Kobane"', and an Egyptian Captive Reveals the Mission Details', Syrian Observatory for Human Rights, 28 June 2015, http://www.syriahr.com/en/?p=22128; and Christopher Kozak with Jennifer Cafarella, 'ISIS Counterattacks in Northern Syria', Institute for the Study of War, 25 June 2015, http://iswsyria.blogspot.co.il/2015/06/isis-counterattacks-in-northern-syria.html.

41 Both Jabhat al-Nusra and the Islamic State routinely employ suicide bombers, many driving vehicles (including armoured vehicles) carrying five to ten tons of explosives to break through enemy obstacles and fortifications in order to 'prepare' them for infan-try assault. In summer 2014, Hamas employed suicide bombers against IDF ground forces inside Gaza. There is no reason to assume they won't study and adopt Jabhat al-Nusra and Islamic State methods which have proved successful in Syria, Iraq and Sinai.

42 Hizbullah has more than ten times the number of rockets Hamas had in 2014, and can launch many more per day than Hamas. A portion of these rockets are precision weapons. Determining stockpiles is complicated and inherently imprecise, but given the statistics of the two recent bouts in Gaza (2012, 2014), to ensure total worst-case coverage, the IDF would need to stock tens of thousands of interceptors costing at least $50,000–$75,000 each, and possibly more. See Uzi Rubin, 'Israel's Air and Missile Defense During the 2014 Gaza War', BESA Center, *Mideast Security and Policy Studies*, no. 111, 11 February 2014, note 40; and Yuval Azolay, 'Kipat Barzel Hharbe Yoter Zola Mh'aadvarim Sheal'ehem Hi Megina' [Iron Dome Is Much Cheaper Than the Stuff It Protects], Globes News, 21 November 2012, http://www.globes.co.il/news/article.aspx?did=1000799542.

43 In 2014, in one offensive tunnel in Gaza, the IDF found motorcycles, suggesting a plan to reach targets much further in Israel than the adjacent border villages. Amir Bokhbot, 'Ti'ude: Ha'oFnoeim SheNoadu LeHavriakh Kchatufim BaMinhara LeAza' [Documentation: The Motorcycles Allocated to Carry Kidnapped in the Tunnel to Gaza], 3

August 2014, http://news.walla.co.il/item/2772074.

44 The few exceptions to the rule have all taken place in completely open and flat terrain against large, concentrated, mechanised forces, such as in 1991 in the Saudi desert near Kuwait. Even then, in their single offensive action of the war, the Iraqis made some gains before being forced to halt and then being beaten back by a combined air and ground force.

45 Combat experience from Israel's wars; from American fighting in Vietnam, Somalia, and Iraq; and from NATO forces in Afghanistan shows that, on average, light infantry suffer heavier casualties than tank and armoured infantry forces across the entire intensity spectrum of warfare. After repeatedly denying the utility of armoured forces in guerrilla warfare and urban combat, most armies found themselves repeatedly compelled to send in heavy armour to support their infantry in these situations. See

Clinton J. Ancker, 'Whither Armor?', *Journal of Military Operations*, vol. 1, no. 2, Fall 2012, pp. 4–8.

46 Pnina Shuker, 'Tfisat HaKhevrah KeRegishah LeAvedot VeHashpa'atah Al Nihul Milkhamah: Yisrael BeMilkhemet Levanon HaShniya (2006)' [The Perception of Societal Sensitivity to Casualties and Its Impact on War Management: Israel in the Second Lebanon War (2006)], MA Thesis, Bar-Ilan University, Ramat Gan, 2013.

47 Another four divisions were employed against the Syrian forces in central and eastern Lebanon.

48 Rapaport, 'The Army Suffers from Excessive Professionalism'; IDF, 'IDF Strategy', p. 27.

49 IDF, 'IDF Strategy', p. 27.

50 A lack of sufficient ground forces relative to the size of the contested area was a central reason for the Americans' and their allies' immediate loss of control in these conflicts.

Review Essay

Dangerous Games

Bruno Tertrais

World War Three: Inside the War Room (TV documentary)
Gabriel Range, director. First broadcast on BBC Two on 3 February 2016.

Assured Resolve: Testing Possible Challenges to Baltic Security
Julianne Smith and Jerry Hendrix. Washington DC: Center for a New American Security, 2016. 18 pp.

2017 War With Russia: An Urgent Warning from Senior Military Command
General Sir Richard Shirreff. London: Coronet, 2016. £20.00. 448 pp.

Reinforcing Deterrence on NATO's Eastern Flank: Wargaming the Defense of the Baltics
David A. Shlapak and Michael Johnson. Santa Monica, CA: The RAND Corporation, 2016. 16 pp.

In 2016, several fictional scenarios exploring the possibility of a major conflict between NATO and Russia were publicly presented in various forms.[1] With one partial exception, they all described events that would take place in the real world, involving real countries, in the near future. This is in contrast with the scenarios NATO devises for itself, which, for lack of a political consensus among its members, or a fear of giving offence, are usually based on fictitious countries.

Bruno Tertrais is a Senior Research Fellow at the Fondation pour la Recherche Stratégique, and a Contributing Editor to *Survival*.

Survival | vol. 58 no. 5 | October–November 2016 | pp. 149–158   DOI 10.1080/00396338.2016.1231536

In February 2016, the British Broadcasting Corporation (BBC) aired an hour-long 'crisis management' documentary entitled *World War Three: Inside the War Room*, featuring debates within a 'cabinet war room' in London among former UK government officials, many of them seasoned practitioners. Over a period of several days, the participants discussed the possibility of a 'hot war' in Eastern Europe without, apparently, having been told in advance of all the moves the scenario would include. That same month, the Washington-based Center for a New American Security (CNAS)

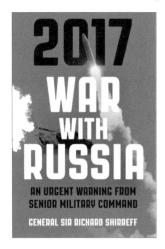

conducted a two-day table-top exercise that gathered together several dozen high-level officials, as well as experts from NATO and partner countries. Although fictitious names were used ('Grosland' and 'Baltia'), the real-world parallel was clear.

A third addition to the genre came in the form of *2017 War With Russia*, a Tom Clancy-esque work of fiction written by British General Sir Richard Shirreff, a former Deputy Supreme Allied Commander Europe (D-SACEUR). Rather pompously subtitled 'An Urgent Warning From Senior Military Command', it will remind Cold War veterans of a well-known prede-
cessor: Sir John Hackett's *The Third World War: August 1985*, published in 1978 and written by another British general and former senior NATO commander. Finally, the RAND Corporation, which had conducted a series of NATO–Russia military war games in 2014 and 2015, published the results earlier this year.

These attempts to imagine a NATO–Russia conflict do not assume an out-of-the-blue Russian military attack. Instead, they wisely proceed on the assumption that the situation would escalate after a series of incidents or provocations. Both *World War Three* and *2017 War With Russia* begin the same way: with trouble in Russian-populated areas of the Baltic states encouraged or fomented by Moscow that leads to the deaths of Russians. These deaths 'force' Russia to intervene to protect its 'fellow citizens', first with militias, then with conventional troops. Latvians and Baltic experts argued post hoc, however, that the BBC scenario was far-fetched, given that it was set in a region of Latvia where the Russian minority does not feel at all disenfranchised.[2]

The CNAS table-top exercise included particularly interesting non-traditional or complex situations involving unanticipated incidents (the downing of a European airliner; a nuclear-plant accident; a search-and-rescue operation), as well as deliberate provocations (cyber attacks; threats to cut off oil supplies; small-scale border penetrations) leading to frictions and ultimately to actual fighting between NATO and Russia. For its part, the RAND Corporation study, designed as a purely military series of war games, simply assumed a full-scale Russian operation against Estonia and Latvia, with NATO having only one week's notice.

Parsing Article V

Most of the exercises rightly drew attention to the potential difficulty of reaching a consensus among NATO allies to invoke Article V of the Washington Treaty. Any non-traditional aggression by Russia involving a slow-motion escalation could well make it difficult to determine when a clear threshold to full-scale aggression had been crossed. This would likely make NATO hesitant to act, to the point, perhaps, of losing precious time, despite the fact that the wording and legal interpretation of Article V allows for an early declaration, long before any large-scale Russian military action.[3] Yet it is easy to understand why some member states might hesitate before acquiescing to an Article V declaration, since doing so would be tantamount to accepting a state of war with a major nuclear-armed power, even if the states in question did not commit significant forces to the conflict. (Article V does not explicitly commit Washington Treaty signatories to actually fight.) During the CNAS war game, in which I participated, a former top-level NATO military commander admitted to the surprising assumption that it would be easy for the North Atlantic Council (NAC) to reach a consensus for an Article V declaration even if a Russian attack were limited and non-overt. However, as the CNAS report states:

> During *Assured Resolve*, there was a considerable variation of views as
> to what should follow initial consultations and invocations of security

agreements. Such fissures across the alliance have resulted in both differing interpretations of the meaning of Article 5 as well as alternative response plans to invoking it. (pp. 5–6)

Still, the absence of an Article V declaration need not paralyse NATO members: any of them could offer military support to the Baltic states by responding to a call for collective self-defence, a legitimate action recognised by the United Nations Charter. This is what happens in both *World War Three*, in which the United States and the United Kingdom send forces in the absence of an Alliance consensus, and *2017 War With Russia*, in which the US

president sends American troops as debates within the NAC drag on. In both cases, Germany leads the push-back against escalation. Because there is no consensus within the Alliance, the use of NATO collective assets for war-fighting purposes is not possible.

A general takes aim

Of the four scenarios considered here, *2017 War With Russia* stands out for its authorship, length and attention to detail. Sir Richard Shirreff is clearly intent on settling scores with politicians, decrying 'the posturing, the vanity, the political cynicism, and the moral cowardice' (pp. 13–14) that, according to him, characterise most of them. British leaders – both Labour and Conservative – are accused of having eviscerated the UK's military. His description of a feeble, media-obsessed prime minister is amusing but too much of a caricature, though less so than his depictions of German and Greek officials, which border on the farcical. Meanwhile, the novel's unnamed Russian president seems to be a mixture of Vladimir Putin and Dr No. The romance between a British officer and his (unavoidably ash-blonde and beautiful) Latvian liaison officer could have been dispensed with. The book is also replete with excessive references to the 1930s, which appear even on the book's dust jacket.

Much more interesting are Shirreff's comments on NATO's real-world capabilities (for instance, the much-vaunted Very High Readiness Joint Task

Force, or VJTF, created in 2014); on the limits of SACEUR's authority; and on the inter-operability problems of multinational forces. He offers valuable descriptions of lengthy intra-NATO discussions that delay critical reinforcement decisions in wartime, as well as useful remarks on the logistical difficulties that such reinforcements would face, including for a European border crossing – a current topic of interest in the Alliance.

Some of the key Western and Russian decisions in the novel are sure to raise eyebrows. Would London really send a brand new aircraft carrier into a war zone 'naked' (that is, without its aircraft) and barely protected? Would Moscow broadcast live, without so much as a few seconds' tape delay, the visit of its president to newly occupied territory, thereby giving the Allies the opportunity to humiliate him in the eyes of the world? Nevertheless, Shirreff's scenario, which assumes that Moscow creates a diversion in Ukraine to hide its real goal of bringing the Baltic states into the Russian orbit, appropriately includes accidental events induced by the fog of war. These include, for instance, the unintended sinking of two minesweepers, one British and one German, by Russian aircraft, which finally triggers collective action. The option of invading Kaliningrad also makes a logical appearance. Without spoiling the grand finale, suffice it to say that a cyber virus called *Rasputin* and nuclear-armed missiles figure prominently.

The nuclear card

In contrast with the BBC documentary and Shirreff's novel, the CNAS table-top exercise and the RAND study give scant attention to nuclear weapons, as though they might be a mere hindrance or annoyance. (To be fair, the focus of the RAND study – which only explored the force-on-force dimension – was narrow.) Surely Russia would play the nuclear card in one way or another, if only politically to divide the Alliance by making more or less specific threats? The question is whether Moscow could actually use nuclear weapons. The country's official doctrine restricts the use of such weapons to circumstances in which the survival of the Russian state is at stake. Yet it is not illegitimate to imagine that risk-prone decision-makers in the Kremlin, particularly those who did not benefit from a Cold War nuclear education, could consider the limited use of nuclear weapons to divide the Alliance, regardless of official doctrine.

This is where *World War Three*, which features a heavy emphasis on the nuclear dimension in its second half, contributes a fascinating idea: what if Russia detonated a nuclear weapon at sea (to limit collateral damage and thus escalatory pressures) but claimed that it had been a local, entirely unauthorised initiative? Although not stated in the film, such a claim would almost certainly be untrue. It is very hard to believe that contemporary Russia lacks the necessary security features to prevent such unauthorised use, *and* that a local commander would be foolish enough to risk the firing squad by taking such an enormous decision on his own. Less certain, however, is whether all NATO countries would be equally convinced that the incident was a Kremlin ploy. Moreover, instead of feeling tempted to reply, European (and global) public opinion would likely favour the immediate cessation of hostilities, even if this was not in the Alliance's interest. Unlike *2017 War With Russia*, *World War Three* ends on a sour and dramatic note, with different nuclear decisions being taken in London and Washington.

World War Three lacks any discussion of the interactions between NATO's Eastern and Southern problems, even though this is a common feature of all four scenarios presented here. Moreover, in this universe, the Islamic State (also known as ISIS or ISIL) does not exist; the problem of force allocation among various operations is almost non-existent (absent a passing reference to France's constraints); Russia is not involved in the Middle East; and Turkey is just another NATO member. A broader perspective encompassing a wider range of real-world problems would have made for more interesting, and more realistic, scenarios.

A problematic force posture

All of the scenarios detailed here were publicised before the NATO Warsaw Summit of Heads of State and Government on 8–9 July 2016. At the meeting, the Alliance decided, inter alia, to bolster its forward presence near its eastern borders to four multinational battalions, totalling about 4,000 troops, including one in each Baltic state and a fourth in Poland. (The VJTF, which could also be deployed to the area, includes one permanent brigade deployable at two to three days' notice, and two additional reinforcement brigades.) Even when one adds host-country forces, this would hardly be enough if one accepts the RAND Corporation's conclusion that a force of six or seven brigades would be needed to defeat a Russian invasion of the Baltic states. The results of the RAND study, involving a NATO force centred on 12 land-manoeuvre battalions generated on one week's notice and defending against 22 heavier and better-equipped Russian ones, were devastating for the Alliance. In every scenario, Russian forces reached the outskirts of Tallinn and Riga in no more than 60 hours. If the RAND study is correct, NATO might be unable to defeat a hypothetical full-scale invasion of the Baltic states.

Although the recommended RAND posture would have been a major commitment, NATO countries had, on paper, the manpower to do so. But in order to retain the moral high ground in its dispute with Moscow, the Alliance demurs from tearing up the unilateral commitment it made in the 1997 NATO–Russia Founding Act not to permanently station 'substantial combat forces' in the East, even though this was explicitly premised on an unchanged security environment.[4] NATO hopes that its multinational battalions – which symbolise the collective will of the Alliance to uphold Article V – will be enough of a deterrent, sufficient at least to act as a 'tripwire': a Cold War concept according to which even a symbolic deployment at the border could be a deterrent, since it would 'force' the opponent to confront it, unavoidably triggering a political reaction and escalation.

*   *   *

How does contemporary Russia view these public attempts at thinking the almost unthinkable? This is a non-trivial question, one which reflects the asymmetry between open, transparent Western societies and autocratic countries. At least two possible answers present themselves. Perhaps Moscow sees these attempts as little more than government-dictated propaganda calibrated to conceal nefarious strategic designs, an interpretation that could fuel Russian paranoia with unpredictable consequences. (Remember that in the 1980s some Soviet leaders actually feared a NATO attack, as archives have now revealed.[5]) Or perhaps it sees them as a sign of Western desperation, vindicating its own policies ('The West fears us!'). In January 2016, a television channel operated by Russia's ministry of defence published an article about *World War Three* headlined 'Britain will not reply to Russia's nuclear strike'.[6] Such thinking could encourage more aggressive behaviour, perhaps unwittingly and dangerously pushing the Alliance to its limits.

These unpleasant possibilities do not mean that we should stop thinking through such scenarios and staging war games. But perhaps Western policymakers, think-tankers and academics could take them as a warning that any real-world work of fiction they might make public could be interpreted by some parties in ways they had not anticipated, and which could run counter to Western interests.[7]

Notes

1   See also the valuable 'long read' by British–French analyst Iskander Rehman, 'Radioactive in Riga: The Latvian Nuclear Standoff of 2018', parts I, II and III, *War on the Rocks*, 27 November, 30 November and 1 December 2015, http://warontherocks.com/2015/11/radioactive-in-riga-the-latvian-nuclear-standoff-of-2018-part-i/, http://warontherocks.com/2015/11/radioactive-in-riga-the-latvian-nuclear-standoff-of-2018-part-ii/, http://warontherocks.com/2015/12/radioactive-in-riga-the-latvian-nuclear-standoff-of-2018-part-iii/. In Rehman's scenario, the Latvian president, in light of Moscow's nuclear threats, begs the US president to avoid military action and enter negotiations with the Kremlin despite the invasion of his country.

2   See, for example, Juris Viļums, 'The Phantom of Separatism in Latgale, or What BBC Did Not Show', jureits.lv, 9 February 2016, http://jureits.lv/?p=1043.

3   For my own elaboration of this point see Bruno Tertrais, 'Article 5 of the Washington Treaty: Its Origins, Meaning and Future', Research Paper no. 130, NATO Defence College, April 2016, http://www.ndc.nato.int/news/news.php?icode=934.

4   The text of the act reads: 'NATO reiterates that in the current and foreseeable security environment, the Alliance will carry out its collective defence and other missions by ensuring the necessary interoperability, integration, and capability for reinforcement rather than by additional permanent stationing of substantial combat forces.' See 'Founding Act on Mutual

Relations, Cooperation and Security between NATO and the Russian Federation signed in Paris, France', 29 May 1997, http://www.nato.int/cps/en/natohq/official_texts_25468.htm.

5 See, for example, Nate Jones (ed.), 'The 1983 War Scare: "The Last Paroxysm" of the Cold War', part I, National Security Archive Electronic Briefing Book no. 426, National Security Archive, 16 May 2013, http://nsarchive.gwu.edu/NSAEBB/NSAEBB426/.

6 'Britanija ne otvetit na jadernyj udar Rossii – Daily Mail', TV Zvezda, 31 January 2016, http://tvzvezda.ru/news/vstrane_i_mire/content/201601311618-sa53.htm. Various Russian officials have described the film as 'trash' or a 'dangerous provocation'. See Tom Batchelor, 'Kremlin Brands BBC "Trash" over World War 3 Documentary Simulating Russian Attack', *Express*, 4 February 2016, http://www.express.co.uk/news/uk/641193/Kremlin-brands-BBC-trash-World-War-3-documentary-simulating-Russian-attack.

7 After viewing *World War Three*, one commentator lamented that it had contributed to 'the general erosion of the line between news and entertainment', adding that Russian TV could offer the BBC 'a handsome royalty for the right to re-broadcast the show – and perhaps slightly edit it here and there'. Mike Collier, 'Oh! What a Lovely War Fame', lsm.lv (Public Broadcasting of Latvia), 4 February 2016, http://www.lsm.lv/en/article/culture/viewpoint-oh-what-a-lovely-war-game.a167428/.

Latin America's Invisible War

Russell Crandall and Savannah Haeger

Gangster Warlords: Drug Dollars, Killing Fields, and the New Politics of Latin America
Ioan Grillo. New York: Bloomsbury Press, 2015. $28.00. 384 pp.

The Para-State: An Ethnography of Colombia's Death Squads
Aldo Civico. Oakland, CA: University of California Press, 2015. $29.95. 264 pp.

The pageantry of death that has accompanied Mexico's ongoing war against drug cartels often features the *narcomanta,* a banner left by the assailants alongside the corpses of their victims. These banners, sometimes professionally printed but often little more than crude scribbles on bed sheets, serve as the killers' warning to authorities or rival cartels, or attempt to justify their crimes. On 19 September 2014, security forces found a *narcomanta* alongside the bodies of four men and one woman who had been gagged and shot in the head, their bodies abandoned in a remote area of Guanajuato state, allegedly for their ties to a rival organisation. According to reports, the banner, left by the group Cartel de Guanajuato Nueva Generación, read, 'There are 16 dead ones. We have money and operate with the permission of the *federales*'.[1] If the murders were not themselves alarming enough, the message

Russell Crandall is a professor of American foreign policy at Davidson College in North Carolina and a Contributing Editor to *Survival*. He served as a national-security aide to presidents George W. Bush and Barack Obama. His new book is *The Salvador Option: The United States in El Salvador, 1977–1992* (Cambridge University Press). **Savannah Haeger** is a recent graduate of Davidson College, where she was the recipient of the college's Latin American Studies prize.

Survival | vol. 58 no. 5 | October–November 2016 | pp. 159–166   DOI 10.1080/00396338.2016.1231537

highlighted a frightening truth about the evolution of the Latin American drug wars in the past decade: criminal gangs, which are more organised than ever before, have been able to take advantage, either through extortion or corruption, of weak states and their inability to control violence and criminal activity.

Compared with Pablo Escobar's drug trafficking of the 1980s, which is currently being revisited in the popular Netflix series *Narcos*, Latin America's problems with narcotics and the groups that compete over its sale and dis-

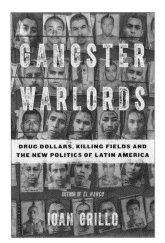

tribution have become larger, more complex and more violent in the past decade. More than 60,000 intentional homicides occurred in Mexico alone between 2006 and 2012, during the height of the Mexican government's militarised assault on drug cartels, according to the University of San Diego's Justice in Mexico Project.[2] Drug-trafficking organisations now pursue myriad other criminal activities, such as extortion and human trafficking. They are even said to have taken control of lime and avocado production through the extortion of growers.[3] Two new books, Ioan Grillo's *Gangster Warlords* and Aldo Civico's *The Para-State*, highlight the region's ongoing struggles, an under-reported and understudied issue in foreign-policy circles given its prominence and body count. *Gangster Warlords* is a must-read for anyone interested in the war on drugs. *The Para-State* is a solid and well-researched account of the evolving criminality of armed groups in Colombia, suited particularly for those with pre-existing knowledge of, and a deep interest in, Colombia's tragic political history. Although stylistically different, both books provide valuable insight into the underlying problems, each of them concluding that solutions will be difficult to achieve.

A region-wide problem

Latin America's new crime wars have left highly corruptible states struggling to enact an effective response to gangs and the violence they perpetuate. In *Gangster Warlords*, the follow-up to his enthralling 2013 release, *El Narco*,

Grillo, a talented and engaging British journalist, examines gang activity in Brazil, Jamaica and the 'Northern Triangle' of Central America (El Salvador, Honduras and Guatemala), as well as in Mexico, the subject of his previous book. Although the origins and tactics of, and even the languages spoken by, drug gangs differ from country to country, each of Grillo's case studies features a foundational narrative of narcotics trafficking and narco-capitalism; a distinctive code of conduct governing group activities; and the manipulation or defeat of weak state institutions. Together, these qualities produce the highly structured and corporatist criminal organisations plaguing Latin America today. Acknowledging 'just one god ... the green of dollar bills', these groups profit from the trade in narcotics, the most lucrative set of black-market goods in the world (p. 23), and seek to punish those who disrupt their business. To fully understand the rise of these gangs and militia groups, Grillo also emphasises the importance of Latin America's role during the Cold War, and how 'ideological conflicts' gave way to uncontrollable criminality as the region democratised (p. 53).

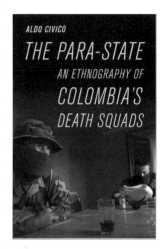

Grillo's argument rests on his presentation of his chosen case studies, beginning with urban violence in Brazil. His memorable narrative embeds the reader in the *favelas* of Rio de Janeiro, where local residents revere the gangsters for providing services in areas where the state is absent, treating them as local celebrities (p. 85). Grillo describes how Brazil's violent prison system became the cradle for Rio's infamous Comando Vermelho, or Red Commando, whose founder, William da Silva Lima (alias 'the Teacher'), is interviewed at length. The Red Commando was initially an ideologically driven group, borne out of frustration with the country's military dictatorship in the 1960s and 1970s. Grillo doubts that today's young gangsters have much knowledge of the group's original 'quasi-socialist perspective', finding that they are largely motivated by a hatred of the police and the spoils of the lucrative drug trade. In his analysis of the loosely affiliated São Paulo-based group PCC (Primeiro Comando da Capital), he notes that a 'dangerous pattern' has emerged in the state's response to such groups: 'The government is repressive, the commando uses violence, and the government gives concessions. It's a vicious circle' (p. 100). As such, the Brazilian case demonstrates a larger point about the relationship between the state and Latin America's criminal organisations, which is complex and, at times, symbiotic.

Grillo finds a similar entanglement between politics and the criminal underworld in Jamaica, where politicians once aligned themselves with gangsters to bring in votes. Eventually, the gangs became too powerful, resisting any attempt by the government to reassert control. So powerful and iconic was one gang leader (or *don*), Christopher Michael Coke (alias 'Dudus'), for example, that he was also known as the 'President' – an ironic title in a country led by a prime minister – and described as the 'real ruler of the island' (p. 110). Acknowledging that it is uncommon to link criminal activity in Jamaica to parallel problems in Latin America, Grillo believes that the 'ganja-and-gun-filled ghettos of the Afro-Caribbean' in fact play a significant role in the hemisphere's drug trade, given that the region is situated between coastal Colombia and Mexico, and between the consumers of drugs in Europe and the US (p. 114).

As it turns out, Latin America's criminal organisations wield significant power within another important state institution: prison. Grillo describes his visit to a jail located in the homicide capital of the world, San Pedro Sula, Honduras, as being like stepping into a 'prisoner-run ghetto', where criminals associate freely, receive undisrupted deliveries of prostitutes and firearms, and easily upend the authority of prison wardens (p. 207). The prisoners, Grillo concludes, are the 'real authority' within the prison system, which currently does more to perpetuate criminal activity than to prevent it (p. 207). So dire are prison conditions in the countries of the Northern Triangle that the current president of El Salvador has declared a state of emergency, hoping to end the use of penitentiaries as a home base for criminal gangs by barring visitors and containing prisoners in their cells.[4] Grillo recounts a particularly chilling exchange with a 23-year-old member of the Mara Salvatrucha (MS-13) gang in Honduras, named Montana, who committed his first murder at age 14, earning him roughly $45. 'That is the price of a life in Honduras', notes Grillo (p. 216). He reveals how MS-13, a street gang born in the US, has expanded into Central America without encountering any real check on its power or criminal activity (p. 232).

Grillo's final destination is Mexico, the country he admits to being the most familiar with because of his work there beginning in 2000. He devotes substantial space to the story of Nazario Moreno, nicknamed 'the Maddest One', the former leader of the Knights Templar cartel who has been deified by cartel members and normal citizens alike, featuring in prayers, religious statuettes and his own holy book (pp. 236–7). Contributing to his mythical persona is the allegation that he 'died twice'; he appears to have survived his first death in December 2010, an event that was trumpeted as a victory for the Mexican authorities in the war against cartels.

Once it became clear that the Mexican government could not by itself contain the violence generated by drug cartels such as the Knights Templar, incorporating civilian self-defence militias, or *autodefensas*, into the state apparatus became the strategy of choice for an otherwise desperate Mexican government. '"You have suffered too much at the hands of kidnappers, extortionists, and drug cartels"', exclaims the leader of one such militia in Michoacán, alluding to the failures of the state to protect its citizens (p. 297). '"Clearly, we have a right to do this"', says another in Guerrero, '"because the government has not attended to our needs"' (p. 300). Grillo admits that he too became 'swept up' by the promise such groups appeared to offer after so many years of unrestrained narcoviolence, travelling to Michoacán himself to investigate the new groups (p. 114). Yet despite their good intentions, the *autodefensas* were soon to disappoint: as the militias expanded, they became less selective and more easily corrupted by the cartels. While Grillo does not believe the *autodefensas* were created as part of some grand cartel-led conspiracy, they certainly did more to worsen cartel violence than to eliminate it.

If the region's security forces, prisons and politicians cannot limit the violence, what is to be done? While proposed solutions range from improving social services to legalising or decriminalising at least some drugs, Grillo underscores the fact that 'large parts of the region's security forces are fundamentally flawed and need to be reformed from the bottom up' (p. 338). Increased funding for national security, already a big ask for poorer nations

(p. 340), must be coupled with reforms that rein in uncontrollable or corruptible subgroups within the defence forces. No resolution, whatever form it takes, will come easily.

Focus on Colombia

Not all drug traffickers start out as criminals. In *The Para-State*, Italian anthropologist Aldo Civico offers an in-depth look at Colombia's right-wing paramilitaries, who transitioned to the drug trade after the government forced them to disband. Civico's work – which features lengthy interviews – benefits from unprecedented access to paramilitary figures and their victims, who normally seek to evade reporters, especially foreigners. Civico's determination to present the paramilitaries 'not as the embodiment of perverse evil' (p. 17) but as human beings adds depth to his narrative. While his decidedly academic prose requires more focus on the part of the reader – and more knowledge of the historical context – than does Grillo's less formal text, *The Para-State* contains valuable material for anyone interested in the evolving narcotics trade in Colombia.

Following a period of intense, politically motivated bloodshed in Colombia in the 1950s and 1960s known as *La Violencia*, Colombians found themselves facing a new threat: the emergence of the Revolutionary Armed Forces of Colombia, or FARC, a leftist insurgent group. In the face of bombings, attacks on military forces and high-profile kidnappings, including that of former Colombian presidential candidate Ingrid Betancourt, eradicating FARC became the main focus of a succession of presidential administrations. Unable to quell FARC directly, the Colombian government, private sector and civil society banded together to support self-defence paramilitary groups, first created in 1982, that were meant to attack FARC and re-establish stability and state control.

It wasn't long before these paramilitaries, 'supported by a justificatory counterinsurgency discourse' (p. 1), began to engage in *limpiezas* (cleansings) and extortion, leaving just as much destruction and terror in their wake as the groups they were originally meant to combat. Their targets were often private citizens thought to be in league with the leftists. According to one paramilitary leader interviewed by Civico, nicknamed Doble Cero, 'we had to temporarily transgress the rules … The army was the defense fortress [of democracy]' (p. 82).

In 2005, the Colombian government negotiated a peace settlement with the country's largest umbrella group for the *autodefensas*, the AUC (Autodefensas Unidas de Colombia), and sought to reintegrate former paramilitaries into society (p. 179). These efforts were not without controversy: human-rights advocates, for example, decried the absence of prison sentences. Between 2008 and 2010, more than 400 politicians were indicted for their ties to the AUC (p. 154). Yet demobilised paramilitaries often found more opportunity as cocaine mercenaries than as pacified citizens. Many joined Colombia's *Bacrim*, a portmanteau for 'criminal bands' in Spanish. It is widely acknowledged that many such groups retain the same structure and leadership as their paramilitary predecessors.

Paramilitaries are now active participants in narcotrafficking, acting as the *donos* in many of Colombia's drug-producing regions, including Civico's region of focus, the Middle Magdalena Basin near Medellín. Cocaine flows freely through the region's economic veins, exerting a similar appeal to the gold that originally drew Spanish conquistadores to Colombia in the sixteenth century (p. 122). In fact, this 'white gold' is so essential to the daily workings of the region's communities that wherever he went, Civico found that the drug was the true 'ruler of the town' (p. 138). In what he calls an 'ethnography of cocaine', he describes the commodity as a force of both liberation and oppression, creating financial opportunities for locals who are recruited to participate in a rigid and aggressive system of production (p. 142).

Drawing on his Italian background, Civico makes an interesting comparison between Colombia's paramilitaries and the Italian mafia. He asserts that the kind of dangerous 'intertwinement' seen in Colombia between the state's security apparatus and underworld organisations represents a phenomenon that is not limited to Latin America (p. 150). While he might have found smoother ways to transition between the various parts of his argument, each one makes a worthy contribution to his analysis of the inner workings of Colombia's paramilitaries. Civico's suggestion that 'we consider the simultaneity of barbarism and civilization as immanent to the notion of modernity and the state', as exemplified by the cooperative relationship between the Colombian state and the paramilitaries (p. 118), is a provocative one, but underscores the extreme nature of the paramilitaries' actions and their ties with the state apparatus.

*   *   *

The mostly male youths who join violent organisations in Latin America do so facing few alternatives. A desire to provide for and protect their families, as well as to achieve a sense of belonging in a group with a bigger purpose than themselves, however nefarious that purpose might be, are reasons enough for many young men in countries such as El Salvador and Brazil to join gangs.

Both *Gangster Warlords* and *The Para-State* make equally clear that state responses to narcotics trafficking and other forms of organised criminal activity are severely lacking. State weaknesses promote, either directly or indirectly, the work of gangs and criminal bands, wreaking havoc on the lives of citizens caught in the middle. If the conflicts these books depict seem distant to many readers, the narcotics that fuel the violence end up in communities around the world. There is a war going on in the Western Hemisphere, and it deserves greater attention. Grillo and Civico have done much to raise awareness of a conflict that is more urgent, and closer to home, than many people realise.

Notes

[1] '5 Templarios Executed on Border of Michoacán, Narco Message Left Attributed to New Generation', Borderland Beat, 19 September 2014, http://www.borderlandbeat.com/2014/09/5-templarios-executed-on-border-of.html.

[2] Kimberly Heinle et al., 'Drug Violence in Mexico: Data and Analysis Through 2014', Justice in Mexico Project, 29 April 2015, p. 8, https://justiceinmexico.org/wp-content/uploads/2015/04/2015-Drug-Violence-in-Mexico-final.pdf.

[3] See Benjamin Locks, 'Extortion in Mexico: Why Mexico's Pain Won't End with the War on Drugs', Yale Journal of International Affairs, 6 October 2014, http://yalejournal.org/article_post/extortion-in-mexico-why-mexicos-pain-wont-end-with-the-war-on-drugs/.

[4] Michael Lohmuller, 'El Salvador Extends Tough Prison Restrictions for One Year', InSight Crime, 19 May 2016, http://www.insightcrime.org/news-briefs/el-salvador-extends-tough-prison-restrictions-for-one-year.

Britain's Difficult War in Iraq

Ben Barry

The Report of the Iraq Inquiry
The Iraq Inquiry – A Committee of Privy Counsellors. HC 265.
London: The Stationery Office, July 2016. Approx. 6,400 pp.

Between 2003 and 2009, Britain's war in Iraq became increasingly unpopular with the British people, politicians and media. This greatly damaged the domestic standing of Tony Blair, the prime minister who had taken the country to war. Also eroded were the reputations for competence of the British government, its defence, foreign and development ministries and the United Kingdom's intelligence services and armed forces.

These perceptions greatly influenced British attitudes to the use of force. A striking example was the August 2013 parliamentary vote that rejected the government's proposed airstrikes on Syria following the use of chemical weapons by the Bashar al-Assad regime. A narrow majority of MPs were unconvinced by the government's case for military intervention. As Philip Hammond, then the defence secretary, noted, 'there is a deep well of suspicion about military involvement in the Middle East stemming largely from the experiences of Iraq'.[1]

An independent inquiry into Britain's role in the war was commissioned in 2009 by Blair's successor, former prime minister Gordon Brown. Its purpose was to consider 'the United Kingdom's involvement in Iraq, including the way decisions were made and actions taken, to establish as

Ben Barry is IISS Senior Fellow for Land Warfare.

Survival | vol. 58 no. 5 | October–November 2016 | pp. 167–178   DOI 10.1080/00396338.2016.1231538

accurately and reliably as possible what happened, and to identify the lessons that can be learned'.[2]

For reasons that have not been adequately explained, the inquiry lasted a year longer than did the British war in Iraq. Chaired by former senior civil servant John Chilcot, it reported almost seven years after it was commissioned. This was a source of considerable frustration to many. British anti-war activists, and some parents of British servicemen killed, are very disappointed that the inquiry has neither declared the war illegal nor recommended Blair's arrest on war-crimes charges.[3] The report nevertheless contains a wealth of evidence and analysis, clearly showing that, throughout the Iraq War, Britain was lacking in competent strategic leadership.

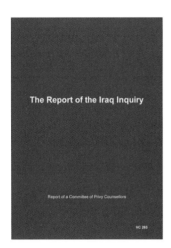

The report consists of 2.6 million words, in 12 volumes. The executive summary is over 150 pages long. But a good sense of the report can be gained from Chilcot's short statement, and pages 109–40 of the executive summary, in which lessons identified by the inquiry are listed on pages 129–40.[4] The report is clearly written and easy to read. The website is simple, clear, user-friendly and easy to navigate.[5] The large number of witness statements and 2,000 declassified official documents it contains make it an invaluable resource for analysts and historians. These are all supported by a capable search engine.

The report's centre of gravity is an exhaustive analysis of high-level government decision-making. It appears to have comprehensively tracked the paper and email trail of advice and assessments flowing into the Prime Minister's Office at Number 10 Downing Street and to the Cabinet Office (the central coordinating machinery of British government). It has identified all the relevant decisions made in Number 10, and the extent to which the decisions were implemented. It also provides much detail on the making of decisions in the key government departments: the Foreign and Commonwealth Office (FCO), the Ministry of Defence (MoD) and the Department for International Development (DfID).

A mistaken intervention

The inquiry displays single-minded concentration on analysing high-level decision-making in Number 10 Downing Street and Whitehall. This is its strength. Its most important assessment is that the British government 'failed to achieve its stated objectives'.[6] This is the core conclusion, from which all the other assessments flow.

It finds that, prior to the invasion, the British intelligence and policy communities had an 'ingrained belief' that Iraq possessed a weapons-of-mass-destruction (WMD) capability.[7] This gave rise to flawed assessments that were never adequately tested or challenged. The report particularly criticises the chairman of the Joint Intelligence Committee and head of the British Secret Intelligence Service for presenting weak intelligence concerning Iraq's WMD with excessive certainty. It assesses that 'the circumstances in which it was decided that there was a legal basis for UK military action were far from satisfactory'.[8]

The report assesses that the UK's post-conflict effort 'failed to take account of the magnitude of the task of stabilising, administering and reconstructing Iraq, and of the responsibilities which were likely to fall to the UK'.[9] This was because prime minister Blair 'did not establish clear Ministerial oversight of UK planning and preparation. He did not ensure that there was a flexible, realistic and fully resourced plan that integrated UK military and civilian contributions.'[10]

These judgements are sound. From mid-2003 onwards, British military commanders in Basra, for example, all sensed a profound lack of civil–military coordination in London, a lack of leadership from the top, and a government approach to Iraq that was under-resourced and inadequately led and coordinated.

Chilcot concludes that, by 2007, 'militia dominance in Basra, which UK military commanders were unable to challenge, led to the UK exchanging detainee releases for an end to the targeting of its forces. It was humiliating that the UK reached a position in which an agreement with a militia group which had been actively targeting UK forces was considered the best option available. The UK military role in Iraq ended a very long way from success.'[11]

On the lessons the inquiry identifies, it is worth quoting from Chilcot's public statement in full:

> Military action in Iraq might have been necessary at some point. But in March 2003:
>
> - There was no imminent threat from Saddam Hussein.
> - The strategy of containment could have been adapted and continued for some time.
> - The majority of the Security Council supported continuing UN inspections and monitoring.
>
> Mr Blair overestimated his ability to influence US decisions on Iraq. The UK's relationship with the US has proved strong enough over time to bear the weight of honest disagreement. It does not require unconditional support where our interests or judgements differ.
>
> The lessons also include:
> - The importance of collective Ministerial discussion which encourages frank and informed debate and challenge.
> - The need to assess risks, weigh options and set an achievable and realistic strategy.
> - The vital role of Ministerial leadership and co-ordination of action across Government, supported by senior officials.
> - The need to ensure that both the civilian and military arms of Government are properly equipped for their tasks.
>
> Above all, the lesson is that all aspects of any intervention need to be calculated, debated and challenged with the utmost rigour. And, when decisions have been made, they need to be implemented fully. Sadly, neither was the case in relation to the UK Government's actions in Iraq.[12]

In the dry prose of a retired mandarin, these are scathing criticisms. They are all supported by the evidence.

Providing context

In the aftermath of the 9/11 terrorist attacks on the United States, both Tony Blair and then-US president George W. Bush were under enormous pressure. Another such attack, which they feared might have included the use of WMD, would not only have been a catastrophe in its own right, but would also have been politically lethal to both governments. This is an important part of the context for the decision to go to war.

The domestic context for the UK's failures after the invasion should also be borne in mind. From mid-2003, the UK's inability to have a positive impact on the Iraqi citizens in Basra, the failure to find weapons of mass destruction and the rising toll of casualties rapidly eroded public support in both Iraq and the UK. This put the British government, as well as senior officials and officers, under ever-increasing pressure, both to reduce military casualties and, ultimately, to withdraw. This conflicted with the desire of the prime minister and the MoD to safeguard the 'special relationship' with the US by seeing the war through to its conclusion. That these key factors are hardly acknowledged is ironic, as it was the war's unpopularity that led to the commissioning of the inquiry.

While the report's executive summary provides a 100-page commentary on strategic decision-making in chronological order, it is written from the perspective of central government. This is a perspective removed from the ebb and flow of the campaign as it unfolded in Iraq in general, and in the British-occupied south in particular. The report lacks a simple, single narrative of Britain's military role in Iraq. It is not an authoritative account of the British military effort, nor of the country's diplomatic, development or intelligence work. This makes it harder for a general reader to understand than it should be.

The Iraqi domestic political context could also be better explained. From June 2004, the coalition expected Iraqi politicians to assume increasing responsibility. This did not turn out the way the coalition hoped. From January 2005, Iraqi politicians elected to local, provincial and city office in Basra and the south were united in their opposition to the British military presence.[13]

A useful account of Britain's military role in Iraq is provided in a recently published book by the journalist Tim Ripley: *Operation Telic: The British*

Campaign in Iraq 2003–2009.[14] Drawing extensively on military reports, accounts in regimental journals and interviews with key British commanders, Ripley provides the best available account of the role of British forces from the 2003 invasion to their withdrawal in 2009. He gives an excellent account, for example, of the innovative intelligence-led British operation to capture Basra without destroying it, and of the heavy fighting against Shia militias in Basra in 2006–07.

Ripley's book shows that from 2006 the UK had insufficient resources to sustain both the Iraq campaign and the increasingly difficult operations in Afghanistan. So, when the US decided to surge additional troops into Iraq in early 2007, Britain declined to do likewise, and UK and US strategies diverged. From a position of increasing weakness, the British made an 'accommodation' with Shia militias, conceding control of Basra to their malign rule, in return for a ceasefire deal that undoubtedly saved British lives. But the contradictions of British strategy in Iraq were unforgivingly exposed by the Easter 2008 Iraqi government attack into Basra, *Operation Charge of the Knights*, which initially failed. Despite the operation's eventual success, the exposure of the weaknesses of the British forces in Basra damaged the reputation of British forces with the US and the Iraqis, and inflicted a major dent in British military self-confidence.

This loss of military credibility in the eyes of the United States had serious consequences. The inquiry's focus on the passage of information in and out of Number 10, however, means that the key dynamics of *Operation Charge of the Knights* are absent from the report. This is but one of many examples of the inquiry's concentration on Number 10 and Whitehall at the expense of overlooking important contours of the conflict, especially the activity conducted on the ground, mainly by the UK military, but also by its diplomats and development officials.

As such, the report is best thought of as an inquiry into British strategic leadership of the Iraq War, rather than into Britain's overall role. For a more balanced picture of Britain's war, as well as some livelier prose, the inquiry's report is best read alongside Ripley's engaging volume.

British post-conflict stabilisation

Having accepted responsibility for the post-conflict occupation of the four provinces of southern Iraq, the UK, like the US, was taken by surprise by extensive looting and the rapid deterioration of security. The report concludes that the UK had little positive impact on the US-led Coalition Provisional Authority (CPA) that initially administered Iraq. And it had no influence over the CPA's infamous decisions to disband the Iraqi security services and exclude Ba'ath Party members from public service.

It very quickly became apparent both to British commanders in Basra and officials in London that the situation had significantly changed. The inquiry identifies a number of occasions from August 2003 onwards when changes in the situation in Iraq should have prompted strategic reassessments by the UK government.[15] No such action occurred. The report argues that the military leadership, specifically the Chief of Joint Operations and Chief of the Defence Staff, should have pressed for such reassessments.[16]

This is but one of a large number of instances identified by the inquiry of poor performance by the British governmental machinery. Pre-invasion planning in Whitehall had identified that post-conflict operations would be decisive; that a major reconstruction effort would be necessary; that the US plans for post-conflict activity were weak; and that the rapidly improvised US Office of Reconstruction and Humanitarian Assistance (ORHA) would be overwhelmed by the task.

But no one person or government department was placed in charge of pre-war planning for reconstruction. The development minister, Clare Short, displayed 'reluctance to engage in post-conflict activity other than for the immediate humanitarian response to conflict, until it was confirmed that the UN would lead the reconstruction effort' (Section 10.4, pp. 532–4). Leadership of the UK reconstruction effort was eventually given to the FCO in late March 2003. Although an ad hoc committee considered reconstruction plans, it assumed no effective role in implementation (Section 10.4, p. 531).[17]

Despite agreement by Short and foreign secretary Jack Straw that the UK should do more to support ORHA, DfID effectively opted out of doing so. After Short's resignation in May 2003, DfID assumed leadership of reconstruction, but by then the UK reconstruction effort had fallen well behind requirements, and well behind Blair's public and private rhetoric. Relations between DfID and the British military were badly damaged and took years to recover.

There were also strategic failures by the FCO. At a July 2003 cabinet meeting, for example, Blair concluded that the UK should make the CPA regional office in Basra, CPA(South), a 'model' for the coalition. In a subsequent video conference, Blair told Bush and other US leaders that the UK would do its 'level best to meet any demand for additional resources' (Section 10, pp. 95–109). A senior diplomat, Hilary Synnott (later an IISS senior fellow), was called out of retirement to head the team.

The inquiry analysed the extent to which this direction to support CPA(South) was met. It provides abundant evidence that the UK never provided the staff or resources that Synnott requested. It judges that the FCO, the department responsible, 'did not provide adequate practical support to Sir Hilary Synnott as Head of CPA(South)', and specifically attributes responsibility to the FCO permanent secretary (Section 10, pp. 536–7). What it does not explain is why inadequate implementation of a cabinet decision, which had been declared to the US government, was tolerated by the central cooordinating machinery of government, the foreign secretary or the prime minister.

In his memoirs, Synnott offered his assessment that the consistent failure of the FCO to provide sufficient personnel

> stemmed from a lack of political direction. Seen from Iraq and notwithstanding Blair's rhetoric, there was little evidence that the British Government as a whole saw itself as being at war. Management and oversight at ministerial and senior official level was essentially ad hoc and bore little resemblance to the highly organised arrangements for post-conflict reconstruction which had been put in place, for instance, some four years before the end of the Second World War. Blair put a constant public emphasis on the importance and urgency of making progress in Iraq. But seemingly little interested in the processes within Government by which this might be brought about, he proved unable to mobilise Government departments to produce the necessary results.[18]

Leadership is more than decision-making

The inquiry's accumulated analysis and judgements provide overwhelming evidence that Blair's leadership and management of the post-conflict stabilisation of Iraq was ineffective. While there is abundant evidence of decisions being made, there is equally abundant evidence that follow-up action was either absent or insufficiently coordinated, and that progress was inadequately monitored. There is considerable evidence of politicians, government departments and senior officials not only ignoring direction given by the prime minister, but also being allowed to ignore it.[19]

Following a June 2003 visit to Iraq, for example, Blair told his ministers that the British government should return to 'a war footing' to avoid 'losing the peace in Iraq'. The inquiry concludes that there were 'no indications that Mr Blair's direction led to any substantive changes in the UK's reconstruction effort' (Section 10.4, p. 535).

Reading between the inquiry's lines, it appears that Nigel Sheinwald, the prime minister's foreign-policy adviser for much of the post-conflict period, attempted to energise the UK effort in Whitehall. But he was unable to overcome bureaucratic inertia, and differing ministerial and departmental agendas.

Many of the decision-making structures used by Blair appear to have been ad hoc. This need not have been a problem, provided that implementation of strategic decisions was properly managed. It was not. The inquiry suggests that appointment of a single senior minister to lead British post-conflict stabilisation and reconstruction might have improved the formulation and implementation of strategy. This presumes both the availability of a minister with sufficient leadership abilities, and a head of government sufficiently versed in implementing strategy to both identify the need and confer the necessary political authority. Alternative options would have been to use the deputy prime minister, cabinet secretary or Blair's chief of staff, all officials in a position to use their authority to impose the necessary discipline on government ministries. But without the political direction and energy to support them, such efforts would probably have failed.

Blair had previously displayed an ability to both take strategic decisions and see them implemented. His role in the Northern Ireland peace process was a clear example. But Iraq was an even more difficult problem than Northern Ireland, and became increasingly difficult as the popularity of the war declined. The inquiry shows that, during the post-conflict phase of the war, Blair was less able to impose his will on the delivery of strategic outcomes necessary for Britain to maximise its chances of successfully stabilising southern Iraq.

Previous British governments had managed wars by using a war cabinet. In the Second World War and Falklands War these had been highly successful vehicles for prime ministers Winston Churchill and Margaret Thatcher to exercise leadership, both for making decisions and monitoring their implementation. It is not clear that this option was ever considered for Iraq.

Management of British operations in Afghanistan, by contrast, was improved in autumn 2009 by prime minister Gordon Brown setting up a specific committee for this purpose. This followed a summer of significant casualties and growing controversy over the size of the British deployment to Helmand, and the equipment and resources available to the troops. It improved coherence of British efforts in Afghanistan.

A UK National Security Council was established in May 2010. The new prime minister, David Cameron, chaired a meeting of the council on his first day in office. It became the principal forum for both the formulation of British defence, intelligence and security strategy and the monitoring of the execution of that strategy, including for the wars in Afghanistan, Libya and against the Islamic State (also known as ISIS or ISIL). While not perfect, many UK military and security officials believe that it has greatly improved both the formulation and execution of strategy.[20]

*   *   *

The Iraq inquiry reminds us that, while decision-making by leaders is important, so too is getting decisions implemented. Decisions must be converted into plans that assign roles to those responsible for implementation. Then implementation needs to be monitored to assess whether it is succeeding, or whether the situation has changed sufficiently as to require either adjustments to the plan or formulation of a new one.

Successful leaders ensure that implementation happens. As well as relying on the existing machinery, they check implementation for themselves, not only through constant communication with their principal staff, but also by visiting the front line. They can also make use of personal representatives empowered to provide unvarnished assessments not only of the facts on the ground, but also of the degree to which all subordinate organisations are both implementing the strategy and providing accurate assessments.

There is nothing new about these approaches. They have been employed by successful military, business and political leaders. But the inquiry points to their absence from Blair's leadership of post-conflict stabilisation in Iraq.

The inquiry acknowledges that the UK was a junior partner in this effort to the United States. Decisions taken, and not taken, early in the post-conflict phase of the war greatly reduced the chances of success. Perhaps inevitably, most of these decisions were made in Washington. The inquiry therefore rightly accepts that reconstruction of Iraq was always going to be extremely difficult.[21] It could not

> identify alternative approaches that would have guaranteed greater success in the circumstances of March 2003. What can be said is that a number of opportunities for the sort of candid reappraisal of policies that would have better aligned objectives and resources did not take place. There was no serious consideration of more radical options, such as an early withdrawal or else a substantial increase in effort. The Inquiry has identified a number of moments, especially during the first year of the Occupation, when it would have been possible to conduct a substantial reappraisal. None took place.[22]

> … Better planning and preparation for a post-Saddam Hussein Iraq would not necessarily have prevented the events that unfolded in Iraq between 2003 and 2009. It would not have been possible for the UK to prepare for every eventuality. Better plans and preparation could have mitigated some of the risks to which the UK and Iraq were exposed between 2003 and 2009 and increased the likelihood of achieving the outcomes desired by the UK and the Iraqi people.[23]

The implications are clear. After a successful regime-change operation, the British government failed to adequately align strategic ends with the ways and means it chose to apply. Implementation of decisions was consistently inadequate. And although many organisations, officials, military officers and ministers contributed to this failure, the Iraq inquiry makes clear that the single most important factor was Blair's inability to make his decisions stick.

Notes

1   Robert Winnett, 'Syria Crisis: No to War, Blow to Cameron', *Telegraph*, 29 August 2013.

2   John Chilcot, statement at news conference, 30 July 2009, http://www.iraqinquiry.org.uk/the-inquiry/news-archive/2009/2009-07-30-opening/statement-by-sir-john-chilcot-chairman-of-the-iraq-inquiry-at-a-news-conference-on-thursday-30-july-2009/.

3   Esther Addley, 'Iraq War Families Crowdsource for Funds to Sue Tony Blair', *Guardian*, 19 July 2016.

4   See John Chilcot, public statement , 6 July 2016, http://www.iraqinquiry.org.uk/the-inquiry/sir-john-chilcots-public-statement/; and 'Report of the Iraq Inquiry: Executive Summary', 6 July 2016, http://www.iraqinquiry.org.uk/media/246416/the-report-of-the-iraq-inquiry_executive-summary.pdf.

5   See http://www.iraqinquiry.org.uk/.

6   Chilcot, public statement. See also 'Executive Summary', pp. 109 and 134.

7   'Executive Summary', p. 12.

8   Chilcot, public statement.

9   *Ibid.*

10 *Ibid.* See also 'Executive Summary', p. 86.

11 Chilcot, public statement.

12 *Ibid.*

13 For a good account of political dynamics in Iraq in 2003–12, see Toby Dodge, *Iraq from War to a New Authoritarianism* (Abingdon: Routledge for the IISS, 2013).

14 Tim Ripley, *Operation Telic: The British Campaign in Iraq 2003–2009* (Lancaster: Telic-Herrick Publications, 2016).

15 'Executive Summary', pp. 94, 95, 124.

16 *Ibid.*, p. 94.

17 See also Executive Summary, pp. 81–2.

18 Hilary Synnott, *Bad Days in Basra: My Turbulent Time as Britain's Man in Southern Iraq* (London: I.B. Tauris & Co., 2008), p. 252.

19 'Executive Summary', pp. 134–5.

20 See Peter Ricketts, 'National Security in Practice', address to the IISS, London, 30 November 2011, http://www.iiss.org/en/events/events/archive/2011-1092/november-75d8/national-security-in-practice-the-first-18-months-of-the-national-security-council-123b; and David Richards, *Taking Command* (London: Headline, 2014), Chapter 16.

21 'Executive Summary', p. 135.

22 *Ibid.*, p. 110.

23 *Ibid.*, p. 136.

Book Reviews

Economy

Erik Jones

Busted Sanctions: Explaining Why Economic Sanctions Fail
Bryan R. Early. Stanford, CA: Stanford University Press, 2015.
$29.95. 275 pp.

Economic sanctions are the weapons of the rich and powerful. This is as true today as it was when E.H. Carr wrote *The Twenty Years' Crisis* in the 1930s. Equally true is that sanctions frequently fail to achieve the desired effect. Worse, it often seems that a sanctioning country's closest allies are among the most determined to undermine the pursuit of its foreign-policy objectives. Given that the alternative to sanctions is often a choice between impotence or violence, it is worth considering why that is the case.

Bryan Early offers a fascinating window onto sanctions busting. He focuses on two strategies. The first involves replacing the trade that sanctions are meant to embargo, while the second uses aid to mitigate the impact of any clampdown on foreign demand. Using a mixture of broad statistical analysis and detailed case studies of Iran and Cuba, Early identifies which countries are most likely to use either strategy to undermine sanctions.

The countries that replace trade do so for commercial reasons: to gain market access and to lock in economic advantages. The worst offenders are those that are both geographically close to the country being targeted and politically close to the country imposing the sanctions. In other words, governments that seek to apply sanctions should pay special attention to any wealthy friends in the area.

The governments that bust sanctions with aid are those for which the commercial advantages of trade are limited. They seek a political or ideological advantage, using financial assistance to reinforce alliances or to undermine

Survival | vol. 58 no. 5 | October–November 2016 | pp. 179–208   DOI 10.1080/00396338.2016.1231541

their adversaries. These countries need to possess some wealth, but do not need to be located close to the country they are assisting. They are less likely to be friendly to the country imposing the sanctions.

Early's argument has the advantage of being intuitive. He also demonstrates great analytical skill. Nevertheless, a few elements of his argument warrant deeper consideration. Although governments in China or Russia might be accused of busting sanctions, it is probably more useful to focus attention on firms in countries like Germany and France. Governments are certainly implicated in cases where private companies defy sanctions, but the kind of supportive action required is different. Whereas governments in China and Russia choose to grant or withhold aid to governments under sanction, governments in France and Germany choose how tightly to enforce foreign rules on domestic companies.

Moreover, Early's argument focuses on trade, with less attention paid to other types of sanction. Although he alludes to the importance of finance and financial infrastructure, particularly in the latest phase of the Iranian case, he does not highlight the unique attraction of having access to a global currency like the US dollar (and to dollar clearing), or to key financial services and infrastructure (such as SWIFT). Loss of these things is less easily mitigated or replaced. Early also overlooks stranded assets and sanctions targeted at key individuals. There is more than just trade in the sanctions toolkit. None of this undermines the insights that Early has to offer. It only suggests that he has embarked on an important – and much broader – research programme.

Fed Power: How Finance Wins
Lawrence R. Jacobs and Desmond King. New York: Oxford
University Press, 2016. $24.95. 252 pp.

The independence of central banks is under attack, particularly in the United States. When the dust began to settle on the presidential primaries in spring 2016, three of the four leading candidates – one Democrat and two Republicans – supported legislation to audit the Federal Reserve (or Fed) and to compel it to follow a rigid and transparent rule for policy changes in response to shifts in a limited range of macroeconomic variables. It is a proposal that seems to have emerged from the same populist resentment that swirls around global trade. And while the Fed has not received the attention given to the Transatlantic Trade and Investment Partnership, for example, it is arguably just as important.

Lawrence Jacobs and Desmond King do a great service by explaining why central-bank independence has become so unpopular. Their argument centres on perceptions of the links between central banking and big finance. Central bankers tend to come from the financial community and to protect (and even be 'captured' by) the interests of major institutions. They frequently champion policies with side effects that are injurious to the middle and working classes. This is a subtle argument and not a populist rant. Although the tone of the book is often strident, the analysis it contains shows considerable nuance. Moreover, Jacobs and King are impartial observers. What they see makes them angry, but they are open to reason.

The authors have uncovered a fundamental tension within the macroeconomic consensus around the virtues of central-bank independence. Economists argue that central banks should be politically independent because this best serves the public interest. So long as monetary policy remains the purview of experts, monetary policymakers will be able to send credible signals into the marketplace, and market participants will be able to use those signals to coordinate their own actions. Over the longer term, this coordination yields a better trade-off in terms of inflation and unemployment than the alternative of having more 'political' control over monetary policy.

The problem with this argument is twofold. Firstly, it privileges 'experts' over politicians. This is a problem because voters have no obvious way to hold experts to account for their actions. Secondly, the argument for central-bank independence suggests that communication between central banks and market participants is more important than communication between voters and politicians. This seems less like political independence than an attempt to swap one broad group of constituents (voters) for a much narrower group (financiers). Of course voters may be willing to ignore these points of tension so long as they are rewarded with strong performance in terms of inflation and unemployment. When macroeconomic performance goes disastrously wrong, however, they are less likely to be so supportive.

The challenge for economic policymakers is to confront these problems by holding experts to account and giving pride of place to communication between politicians and voters. This does not necessarily entail the elimination of the advantages achieved by central-bank independence. Instead, it requires recognition that the days of permissive acceptance of the virtues of central-bank independence have ended. Policymakers can choose to accept this now, while they retain some control over the institutions of government, or they can wait for pressure to build behind some more radical and populist alternative.

Priests of Prosperity: How Central Bankers Transformed the Postcommunist World

Juliet Johnson. Ithaca, NY: Cornell University Press, 2016.
$35.00. 292 pp.

The United States is not the only country in which the consensus on central-bank independence is in trouble: central bankers across the former communist world are facing sustained political challenge as well. The difference in the latter is that central-bank norms, practices and policies never sat that well within regimes in transition, and the consensus spread only weakly beyond the central banks themselves. This is the argument Juliet Johnson makes in her brilliant book on the role that central bankers played in the transformation of the post-communist world.

Johnson starts by applying the literature on epistemic communities. All central bankers use the same models and speak the same languages (English and economics), so it should not be surprising that they interact better among themselves than with politicians in the outside world. This pattern became even more pronounced once the argument for central-bank independence was accepted in the West and as communist regimes embraced the virtues of market economics in the East.

Nevertheless, it would be a mistake to assume that modern, market-based central banking diffused by osmosis from West to East. On the contrary, the spread of norms and values required substantial investment – in training and seminars, but also in dinners, retreats, phone calls and other forms of (almost constant) communication. It also relied on the establishment of the usual social conventions of hierarchy, reinforcement, persuasion and sanction. Western central bankers convinced their counterparts in the countries of Central and Eastern Europe (reaching deeply into Central Asia) that they were all part of the same club, and that club membership was worth the effort both personally and professionally.

The central bankers were quick to latch onto what was for them a new normative consensus, and to promote it within their own institutions. Since central banks are relatively hierarchical organisations, the consensus took root relatively rapidly. The same norms spread less rapidly into the wider political arena, however. Politicians in transitioning countries were willing to heed the advice of international experts, yet remained wary of many of the domestic con-sequences. Their acceptance was more reluctant than indulgent.

This reluctance has proven important in the context of the recent crisis. Although central bankers have done much to improve economic governance, certain pathologies were also transmitted from West to East, chief among them the privileging of monetary policy over financial supervision. The recent crisis revealed just how important that pathology is. Local politicians have been quick to show their frustration. Johnson highlights developments in Hungary and Russia. The long-term prognosis is unclear. Although politicians have forced central banks to adapt, they have not broken what Johnson describes as the 'wormhole' community that continues to link central bankers across countries. Indeed, there is some evidence that central bankers are taking up the reins of cross-national policy coordination. Whether that will be tolerated by national politicians remains to be seen.

Currency Politics: The Political Economy of Exchange Rate Policy
Jeffry A. Frieden. Princeton, NJ: Princeton University Press, 2015. £29.95/$39.95. 301 pp.

Currency policy is important, but that does not mean that currency politics is straightforward. On the contrary, understanding who wins and who loses from changes in the exchange rate is a complicated undertaking that depends on knowledge of a number of different factors, including how exposed different groups are to international markets; how much they compete with groups from other countries; how quickly and how broadly any changes in the exchange rate pass through to other relative prices; and whether the stability of the currency or the level of its value relative to other currencies is the focus of policy consideration.

Jeffry Frieden makes a significant contribution to our understanding of currency politics by framing an argument around these variables that builds upon and brings together seminal works that he has written over the past three decades. He demonstrates that groups which take an interest in currency policy tend to form two clusters: those who want a stable exchange rate that they can build into their business models and investment decisions, and those who want a weak currency that can be used to enhance relative price competitiveness.

Frieden does not pretend that these are the only voices in the debate about exchange-rate policy. There are others who see currency as an important prestige symbol or an anchor for monetary policy. Moreover, when a country is relatively closed to the outside world, other considerations are likely to predominate as exchange-rate policy takes a back seat to more important macroeconomic instruments.

Once a country opens up to the outside world, however, currency policy becomes more controversial. When that openness includes cross-border capital flows, currency policy begins to pull monetary policy along with it. As Frieden shows with illustrations from the United States in the nineteenth century, and more recent experiences in Europe and Latin America, currency policy is hotly contested during periods of intense globalisation. These findings are important, but do not answer a number of significant questions. At the top of the list is the question of which exchange rate matters most. Major groups in the United Kingdom, for example, are trapped between dollar and euro exposures that are roughly equal in importance. Likewise, when China increased its penetration into European markets during the aftermath of the recent crisis, Chinese policy-makers faced a similar dilemma.

The 'which exchange rate?' question also applies to Europe. Frieden argues that a monetary union is a special kind of fixed exchange rate. He has a point. But that understanding only applies to relations among participants. How the euro moves as a collective against the dollar or other external currencies is a different matter. During the early years of Europe's experiment with a common currency, exchange-rate movements were the greatest source of distress for participating countries. The multinational currency politics that resulted were altogether more complicated than anyone in Europe expected.

Currency Power: Understanding Monetary Rivalry
Benjamin J. Cohen. Princeton, NJ: Princeton University Press, 2015. $29.95. 286 pp.

The US dollar is the indispensable currency – at least for now. This is the bold suggestion that emerges from Benjamin (Jerry) Cohen's distillation of half a century of careful consideration of the relationship between currencies and power. Although rivals to the dollar have emerged in the past – the Deutschmark and the yen, and later the euro and the yuan (or renminbi) – none of these currencies have posed a serious threat to the use of the dollar as the world's currency. Moreover, none is likely to do so in the near future.

The reasoning behind this conclusion tells us a lot more about the responsibilities and obligations associated with currency leadership than about the relationship between great currencies and great powers. It is true that the United States' status as the world's greatest power lends pre-eminence to the dollar as well. As Cohen reminds us, quoting Susan Strange, it is easier to imagine a world in which Germany or Japan have been taken over by communism (or, more recently, in which Europe and China are beset by major turmoil), than one in which the United States is defeated (or self-destructs). In that sense, storing global wealth in dollars can be seen as a form of insurance.

Yet the theme that emerges time and again in *Currency Power* is how reluctant the governments of potential rivals are to accept the burdens of currency leadership. The German government feared the use of its currency would threaten the conduct of its domestic monetary policy. The Japanese government saw the internationalisation of the yen as a price to pay for American security guarantees and not as a tool for challenging Washington's global leadership. As for Europe and China, their problems are rooted in political institutions and market structures. The euro cannot seriously rival the dollar because the euro-zone lacks the necessary decision-making capacity; the yuan cannot rival the dollar because China's financial economy is not strong enough. These defects are well known domestically, and neither the Europeans nor the Chinese are sufficiently enthusiastic about the prospect of assuming the mantle of global currency leadership to engage in sweeping structural reform.

As Cohen points out, monetary power is a two-edged sword. A powerful government in monetary terms can always finance its balance of payments, and so push the costs of adjustment either into the future or onto other, weaker currencies. That is the exorbitant privilege the United States gains from global use of the dollar. But this privilege is also a form of addiction. US governments rely on their ability to delay or deflect the cost of any imbalances with the outside world. This dependence gives them a stake in the system and a reason to make sure that it does not falter. It also gives US governments a reason to bind the economies of other countries to the American one so that it can more easily prevent imbalances from spiralling out of control. Hegemonic power creates the conditions for currency leadership, but currency leadership creates incentives for governments to assume responsibility for the international monetary system.

The dollar may be the indispensable currency, but that is no cause for complacency. The effectiveness of the dollar as a global currency depends on the strength of the US economy and the country's political institutions. In turn, the US must deploy much of its strength to maintain both its leadership role and global economic stability. There is no guarantee that future US governments will want to continue to make the necessary investments. If they choose to turn inward, the world as a whole could suffer the consequences. As Cohen makes clear, no global currency lasts forever. The question is what happens during periods of transition.

War, Conflict and the Military
H.R. McMaster

Tribe: On Homecoming and Belonging
Sebastian Junger. New York: Twelve, 2016. £12.99/$22.00. 192 pp.

Dr Jonathan Shay noted in his 1995 book *Achilles in Vietnam: Combat Trauma and the Undoing of Character* that what soldiers returning from combat need most is not a mental-health professional but rather a community to which their experience matters. Sebastian Junger, a war correspondent and the best-selling author of *War*, *The Perfect Storm* and *A Death in Belmont*, agrees. He laments, however, that Western societies lack the cohesion to reintegrate returning warriors. That is why, to soldiers and others who, like Junger, have experienced the risks, hardships and sacrifice of combat, war can feel 'better than peace' (p. xvii). *Tribe* is more than a book about post-traumatic stress and the reintegration of combat veterans. It is a call to action for citizens in Western societies to restore a sense of belonging, connectedness and loyalty to one another.

Adopting an anthropological perspective, Junger draws from the history of eighteenth-century North America to highlight the appeal of Native American tribal life to white colonials. Since that time, what he describes as 'the alienating effects of wealth and modernity on the human experience' have increased individuals' susceptibility to social and psychological ills, such as immorality and depression, that communal living might otherwise prevent (p. 23).

Junger combines research with his personal experience with post-traumatic stress to debunk myths and deepen understanding. He observes that, although many soldiers lose a friend or witness harm to others, most do not experience long-term trauma. He presents evidence that soldiers' susceptibility to trauma depends on their experiences before the war, including any family history of psychological disorders, educational or cognitive deficits, or instances of childhood abuse. Moreover, cases of post-traumatic stress disorder (PTSD) are lower in combat units than in support units, a fact he attributes in part to a high degree of social and emotional cohesion in units trained to directly engage the enemy. He attributes the counter-intuitive rise of PTSD claims at a time when combat deaths are falling to improved access to benefits, a minority of veterans who seek disability payments, and especially to veterans' sense of alienation from their societies when they return home. He points out that veteran suicide, rather than the most extreme manifestation of PTSD, is actually less likely among veterans of the Afghan and Iraq wars than it is among those who have not gone to war. The book counters the widespread view of Western combat veterans as victims or traumatised human beings.

Junger is well qualified to take on this topic. He recounts his early experience as a war correspondent in Sarajevo, where he witnessed war's brutality and the attendant breakdown of society. He observes how the hardships of war can be strangely reassuring where they serve to renew human connections. While he is no advocate of war or calamity, he argues that the relative security of the modern West 'eliminates many situations that require people to demonstrate a commitment to the collective good' (p. 59). Vignettes that include instances of unity between Muslims and non-Muslims in the face of terrorist violence in Kenya and courageous leadership in the midst of a mining disaster in Nova Scotia reveal how catastrophe can generate clarity of purpose and social bonds missing in normal life. It is for this reason, Junger argues, that people are often nostalgic for hard times. It is also why many soldiers miss wartime duty.

Tribe has important implications for military effectiveness and the integration of soldiers into civilian society when they return from war. Militaries should not overlook the social dimension of combat effectiveness – what Dr Shay has called the courage-making power of solidarity. Junger urges society to make returning veterans feel necessary. He further urges all of us to rediscover the solidarity that 'is at the core of what it means to be human' (p. 133).

Blood Year: Islamic State and the Failures of the War on Terror
David Kilcullen. London: C. Hurst & Co., 2016. £9.99. 256 pp.

The debate over the war in Iraq has largely focused on the decision to invade in 2003 rather than the subsequent course of the war over the following decade. This has limited the debate's usefulness, because the consensus that the invasion was ill-conceived and based, in part, on misleading intelligence analysis is sure to prove insufficient to foreclose on future policy decisions that may also, in retrospect, appear just as unwise.

In *Blood Year*, author David Kilcullen joins others in describing George W. Bush's decision to invade as a strategic blunder, but helpfully devotes most of the book to what came next. In particular, he explores the rise of Islamic State, also known as ISIS or ISIL, and what it reveals about the broader international 'war on terror' since 2001. He criticises the US, the UK, France and other Western partners for what he sees as their failure to recognise that this fight demands sound strategy and a rational determination to compete with determined and adaptive enemies. Kilcullen highlights the risks associated with direct military intervention in Syria and Iraq, but also considers the risks of continuing the current strategy, which he describes as non-committal.

The history of ISIS's rise will be well known to those who have followed closely the course of events across the Greater Middle East over the past 15 years. Kilcullen can draw on his own personal experiences in the region to shed light on those events and how they interacted with each other and with Western policy to produce the ongoing catastrophe. His succinct interpretation is worth quoting at length:

> The war in Iraq (commencing only fifteen months after 9/11) alienated a host of potential partners and ultimately created AQI [al-Qaeda in Iraq]. The disaggregation strategy, after 2005, atomized the terrorist threat, just as social media and electronic connectivity were exploding in such a way as to spread the pathogen throughout our societies, enabling remote radicalization and leaderless resistance to an unprecedented degree. The precipitate withdrawal from Iraq in 2011 revived AQI in the nick of time after it had been reduced by 90 percent and almost annihilated during the Surge. The precipitate pullout from Iraq, the killing of Osama bin Laden, the AQ [al-Qaeda] succession crisis that followed and the failure of the Arab Spring – all in the same key year of 2011 – helped turn AQI into ISIS and gave it a global leadership role it proceeded to exploit with utter and unprecedented ruthlessness. And complacency and hubris after bin Laden's death, along with vacillation in the face of the colossal tragedy of the Syrian War, created the basis for a conflict that is now consuming the Middle East and drawing regional and global powers into a hugely dangerous, and still escalating conflict. (p. 228)

Kilcullen's prognosis is not optimistic. Even so, he argues that the West cannot 'pull up the drawbridge, disengage from the world, and somehow avoid the fight' (p. 201).

High-profile instances of mass murder in Paris, Nice, Orlando and Istanbul, along with many more examples of violence across the Middle East, Africa and South Asia, support the author's argument. Cognizant of limits on Western (and particularly US) policy associated with Russian intervention in Syria, as well as with the lack of popular support for large-scale conventional military campaigns on land, Kilcullen outlines a less-than-ideal strategy of 'active containment'. That strategy, he argues, should be informed by five 'insights' gleaned from the evolution of the conflict, and the inadequacies of the Western response, since 2001 (p. 228). Among these are the exhortation to never think 'this is as bad as its gets', and the reminder that 'you can't fight without fighting'.

If the definition of insanity is doing the same thing and expecting a different result, Kilcullen's insights may offer a sane approach to evolving policy and strategy. *Blood Year* should be read and debated by anyone concerned with the threat of transnational terrorism and the political and human catastrophe in the Middle East.

Waging War: Conflict, Culture, and Innovation in World History
Wayne E. Lee. New York: Oxford University Press, 2016. $44.95.
538 pp.

As the English theologian, writer and philosopher G.K. Chesterton observed, 'War is not the best way of settling differences, but it is the only way of preventing them being settled for you.' Understanding war is not only critical for protecting vital national interests, but also for preserving peace and promoting international security. A sound knowledge of warfare, or what Wayne Lee describes as 'how humans have sought to impose their will on each other over time and around the world' (p. 1), is particularly important if leaders are to make sound judgements concerning military policy. In democracies, it is also important that citizens have a basic understanding of warfare to maintain the fundamental requirements of military effectiveness, and to draw young men and women into military service. Ignorance of warfare, therefore, is not simply regrettable, but poses a danger.

Celebrated historian Michael Howard has sagely advised that war and warfare be studied 'in width, in depth and in context'. Yet studying warfare to gain a long historical perspective ('in width') is particularly difficult given the scarcity of comprehensive, accessible and insightful treatments of the subject that do not rely on some contrived theoretical construct. *Waging War* is a rare exception and an extraordinary book.

Lee develops a useful framework for thinking about both continuities and changes in warfare. According to him, the principal continuities of warfare have been variety and interaction; history, he observes, defies single-variable explanations. He examines change through the lens of military innovation, which for him means more than just technological invention. Rather, he 'treats technologies and ideas together' (p. 3), emphasising how technology interacts with political and social developments, as well as with ideas about institutions, organisations and methods of combat.

Waging War's 14 chapters proceed chronologically from the origins of war to the world wars of the twentieth century and the experience of guerrilla warfare, insurgency and terrorism through to 2014. To impart thematic unity on his broad and complex subject, Lee employs three concepts – capacity, calculation and culture – that are useful as well as alliterative. Defining capacity as 'the ability of any given social organization to raise or commit resources, including people, to a conflict or to a military establishment' (p. 5), he notes that access to organic energy sources was for centuries the key determinant of capacity. Today, access to the energy potential of mineral sources, as well as to the necessary capital to invest in the acquisition of weapons, is more important. 'Calculation' refers to military innovation that emerges 'from the conscious seeking of advantage' (p. 5) by leaders based on their idealised visions of victory. And culture 'represents a broadly shared set of ideas about how the world functions and how to succeed in it' (p. 6.) Such ideas can sometimes limit imagination, but cultures can also interact and learn from each other.

Few historians would take on such an ambitious project. Lee, an experienced archaeologist and historian, and chair of the Curriculum in Peace, War, and Defense at the University of North Carolina, succeeds admirably. Benefiting from adequate maps, well-chosen illustrations and simple chronologies to help keep readers oriented, *Waging War* will be the text of choice for many graduate and undergraduate courses in military history. It deserves a much broader general readership, however.

Can Science End War?
Everett Carl Dolman. Cambridge: Polity, 2015. £9.99/$12.95. 187 pp.

In this volume, Everett Carl Dolman, a professor with the School of Advanced Air and Space Studies at the US Air Force's Air University, asks what science can do to prevent war, or at least to 'mitigate or limit the destruction and duration of war' (p. 11). To explore this question, he consider a range of topics, including the use of science to expand the scope and scale of war in the modern era; the ways in which scientists have responded to the increased lethality and destructive power of weapons; the emerging technologies that threaten to make wars more frequent and destructive; and how science might ameliorate the causes of war. Ultimately, he concludes that 'science, as incredibly positive as its impact has been in a multitude of human activities, cannot fully explain, adjudicate, or … solve the problem of war on its own or from within its own logic' (p. 172). In other words, science alone cannot end war, because 'what science effectively discovers are means and ways to whatever ends politics decides to put them' (p. 6).

Dolman provides a corrective to linear thinking about technology and its influence on warfare. He uses historical examples to demonstrate that technological advantage in war is often fleeting. For example, 4,000 years ago, the Hittites were a dominant military power due to the superiority of their iron weapons. Once the secret of their iron-working was transferred to others, however, they were exterminated by that same technology. Dolman's analysis makes clear that it is rarely a single technology, but rather combinations of technologies, that deliver a military advantage. For example, gunpowder and metallurgy were needed in tandem to change the character of warfare. He highlights the importance of rapid innovation given how quickly counter-technologies can proliferate: 'Scientific reaction can have a snowball effect', he says (p. 34). The English used the longbow to dominate at Agincourt in 1415. Thirty-five years later, the French used gunpowder at Formigny to kill 3,500 archers before they could loose their arrows. In 1525, the Spanish used harquebusiers at Pavia to cut down French artillerymen before they could emplace and fire their cannons. The lesson here seems particularly germane to contemporary military modernisation efforts, considering the speed with which technology is transferred (or stolen) today.

Dolman points out that science and technology interact not only with each other, but also with political and social change. The French *levée en masse* (post-revolutionary system of military conscription) and the American patent system helped complete the transition to modern science at the end of the eighteenth century. This transition set the stage for 'increasingly sophisticated weapons at a magnitude and scale well above previous efforts', rendering war 'disturbingly novel, and horrifyingly impersonal' (p. 48).

Dolman's knowledge of the past supports his analysis of the ways in which emerging technologies – including additive manufacturing, nanotechnologies, biotechnologies, robotics, communications technologies, big-data analytics and artificial intelligence – can be expected to affect future warfare. Many of these technologies, he argues, will increase both the ability of states to control populations and the ability of individuals to resist that control. He concludes, however, that none of these technologies will alter the 'essential logic of human interaction' (p. 137). War, he believes, will remain 'violent, deadly, and destructive' (p. 110). This might seem like a gloomy conclusion to draw, but Dolman ends with the more hopeful reflection that space technologies might enable democratic peace by increasing access to resources such as clean energy and enabling a consortium of states to deter conflict with space-based weapons.

At a time when many seem determined to seek simple technological solutions to the complex political and human problem of future armed conflict, Dolman's perspective may help to correct unwise thinking about defence and international security.

Agincourt
Anne Curry. Oxford: Oxford University Press, 2015.
£18.99/$29.95. 256 pp.

What can one learn from a 600-year-old battle? Quite a bit, as it turns out. Anne Curry's telling of the Battle of Agincourt, and her analysis of English King Henry V's leadership in that battle against the French, yields new insights not just about the battle itself, but about how the memories and myths that surround it have influenced both personal and national identities. After summarising the history of the battle, Curry, a professor of Medieval History at the University of Southampton and the author of many books and articles on the Hundred Years War, reveals how current experience influences historical memory, and how reimagining the past helps impose order on the present. 'Over the centuries', she writes, 'the Battle of Agincourt has become all things to all men (and women)' (p. 212).

Curry's interpretation of the factors that allowed the numerically inferior English to triumph at Agincourt delivers another set of lessons that should be of interest to contemporary military professionals seeking victory on modern battlefields. 'Agincourt is significant', she writes,

> for the leadership which Henry gave, the discipline he instilled in his troops, and his skillful exploitation of resources. His archers and his men at arms did their duty but their effectiveness was much enhanced by Henry's adroit positioning as well as his total commitment to winning. The lesson of Agincourt is perennial – commanders should never assume easy victory against a smaller, but well-led, cohesive, and skilled, enemy army. (p. 214)

Although modern battlegrounds are exponentially larger in terms of the geographic space they occupy, with battles waged not only on land but also at sea, in the air and in cyber-electromagnetic domains, Curry's description of Henry V's ability to employ 'different kinds of troops to maximum effect', as well as her observation that 'a large army is only of value if all of its soldiers engage in the fighting', seem just as relevant to fighting today as they were at Agincourt six centuries ago (pp. 25, 32).

Agincourt will appeal not just to students of the military arts, but to students of the performing arts as well, especially those interested in how history supplies material to art and how art, in turn, confers emotion and meaning to the present. Curry provides a detailed discussion of how Shakespeare's *Henry V*, for example, has both influenced popular sentiment and echoed it down the years.

During conflicts with France in the eighteenth and early nineteenth centuries, the play inspired English nationalism – and animosity toward the French. An 1879 production influenced by the Franco-Prussian War portrayed the French as victims. Early twentieth-century performances stoked British patriotism during the Boer War and at the outset of the First World War. By the end of that conflict, however, war weariness and the status of the French as allies rendered *Henry V* less popular. As the age of film gathered pace during the Second World War, Lawrence Olivier's 1944 *Henry V* popularised Agincourt to a wide audience and bolstered British resilience. Kenneth Branagh's 1989 portrayal reflected the experience of the Vietnam War.

Agincourt may even hold lessons beyond those that the author intended to convey. Through the great trials of the twentieth century, the memory of Agincourt helped bind Britain together and give meaning to the present. In contemporary Western societies, interpretations of the past often appear fragmented along ethnic, gender and other lines. Moreover, these interpretations normally panegyrise victims rather than celebrate victors. Perhaps the memory of Agincourt and its equivalent in other Western societies can reverse trends toward increasingly exclusive sub-identities and victimhood, which threaten to shatter polities and foster despondency. Recovering this memory – and others like it – may require a revival of military history and a shift in historiography and education curricula toward an exploration of what binds Western societies together and helps them prevail in times of strife. Resources like Curry's *Agincourt* could make a valuable contribution to this effort.

South Asia
Teresita C. Schaffer

Afghan Modern: The History of a Global Nation
Robert D. Crews. Cambridge, MA: The Belknap Press of
Harvard University Press, 2015. $29.95. 381 pp.

Conventional wisdom holds that Afghanistan is a remote, inwardly focused country shaped by its deeply traditional social structure. Robert Crews, a historian from Stanford University who has written extensively on Afghanistan, Central Asia and the former Soviet Union, disputes this vision. He argues instead that the area we now know as Afghanistan has for millennia been deeply involved in the imperial competitions that criss-crossed Central Asia, and that this global character has continued since the formation of a more modern state in the late nineteenth century. *Afghan Modern* tells this story, documenting in particular the way Afghans – especially the country's elites, but also people from more modest backgrounds – moved around the world, 'from China to Africa and Australia … gaining exposure to intellectual and cultural resources that then circulated throughout the diaspora and back …. [to] what is now Afghanistan' (p. 307).

His account draws on a wide range of sources from different countries and in different languages. It is a useful corrective to a narrative that has shaped Western interventions going back at least to the Afghan Wars undertaken by Great Britain in the late nineteenth century.

Crews makes a good case for Afghanistan as a country with extensive global engagement. However, I believe his account short-changes important aspects of Afghan society. Even if one rejects the caricatures found in many familiar works on Afghan social structures, family and clan loyalty has surely been critical to the dynamic through which Afghan power figures have created their power base. But this receives little serious discussion in Crews's book.

A second omission is the impact of the country's tradition of engagement with empires near and far on the negotiating style of Afghan leaders, whether national or local. Located next door to the Mughal and Russian empires and the British Raj, and more recently caught up in the Cold War and the 'war on terror' that brought intense involvement from the United States, Afghanistan has lived by its (or its rulers') wits – and by manipulating as many as possible of these imperial and quasi-imperial actors. This is still true, both in the inter-actions among political rivals within the fractious Afghan state and in their dealings with more powerful neighbours. Afghan leaders' tactics approxi-mate the kind of tribal tactics that Crews argues have been misunderstood by generations of outsiders. I wonder: those outsiders may have over-interpreted the tribal nature of Afghan society, but 'tribal' tactics persist, and may well have become tools for Afghanistan to manage its relations with the current crop of unwelcome 'empires'.

A third dimension that Crews underplays is the role of Afghanistan's imme-diate neighbours, in particular Pakistan. (He does discuss the Durand Line, the British attempt to draw a boundary between Afghanistan and what is now Pakistan that has never been accepted by any Afghan government.) Afghanistan continues to have a difficult relationship with Pakistan, tainted by a toxic blend of Pakistani interference, Afghan designs on what Pakistan regards as its sov-ereign territory, conflicting loyalties among Pashtun tribes, Pakistani fears of Indian subversion through a friendly Afghanistan and much more. This is argu-ably the most important element in today's Afghan 'globalism', and would have been worth acknowledging more fully.

We will, I fear, have ample opportunity to discuss these issues in the future, for Afghanistan is likely to remain caught up in the clashes between Islamic extremist movements and the West. This book does not have all the answers, but it will certainly help the reader to understand a frequently overlooked element of the Afghan story.

Kashmir: The Vajpayee Years
A.S. Dulat with Aditya Sinha. New Delhi: HarperCollins, 2015.
Rp599.00. 368 pp.

A.S. Dulat joined the Indian Police Service in 1965. His fast-track career included senior positions in the Intelligence Bureau, a stint as the bureau's representative in Kashmir, and another as the head of the Research and Analysis Wing (RAW, India's external intelligence agency). Between 2001 and 2004 he served as special adviser on Kashmir in the office of then-prime minister Atal Bihari Vajpayee. *Kashmir: The Vajpayee Years* focuses primarily (but not exclusively) on his long-running involvement in the Indian government's vexed relationship with Kashmir and the Kashmiris.

Memoirs, which both reveal and conceal, are a tricky genre. Critics in India complain that Dulat's account of the hijacking of an Indian aircraft in 1999 omits any mention of the presence on board of a RAW official, a fact that the author subsequently confirmed. The book itself notes that some things do not get discussed.

What it does reveal is fascinating. Dulat highlights two vital convictions throughout the book: that dialogue – 'talking, talking, talking' to anyone willing to do so – is the prerequisite to making any headway in detoxifying the Kashmir problem; and that the most important unfinished business in Kashmir is fixing the relationship between the Kashmiris and India.

Dulat provides sensitively drawn descriptions of the many Kashmiri personalities he engaged with. His favourite was Farooq Abdullah, son of the legendary Sheikh Abdullah who dominated the region from before India's independence until his death in 1982. Dulat regarded Farooq as both a Kashmiri nationalist and an Indian loyalist. He presents a surprisingly sympathetic view of some of the separatist politicians, and argues that they could well have become the instrument of a workable reconciliation between New Delhi and Kashmir had the Indian government, especially leaders who succeeded Vajpayee, been willing to give them a bit more respect and political space. This may, however, have been more difficult than Dulat lets on. Reading his account, it is easy to see how Kashmiris might feel that the author had not just been talking to his interlocutors, but also, and perhaps especially, using them.

As for Pakistan, Dulat argues for something no government of India has been willing to do thus far: holding separate but parallel talks with Pakistan and the Kashmiris. He found Pakistan's president Pervez Musharraf astonishingly willing to depart from the position that had imprisoned his country's government for decades. Here too, Dulat faults India for not taking advantage of the opportunity this offered. In another sidelight, Dulat claims to have gotten along famously with Pakistan's General Asad Durrani, the former director-general of Inter-Services Intelligence, Pakistan's intelligence agency. The two old spooks understood each other when they met post-retirement, and apparently enjoyed sparring. Having known both men, I'm not surprised.

This is a book for readers who are already familiar with the broad outlines of India–Pakistan relations and the situation in Kashmir. Dulat's habit of reproducing snippets of conversation in the original 'Hinglish' (Hindi laced with English) will be somewhat annoying to the uninitiated, though the editor supplies enough translation to convey the gist of these passages. To those who have lived in the region, such passages will evoke memories of conversations held over a cup of chai. The book is an engaging read, with tantalising insights on the bureaucratic relationships among the different parts of India's senior officialdom.

Most importantly, Dulat's major themes are correct. If the Kashmir problem is ever to be fixed, this will require a great deal of talking, both with Kashmiris and with Pakistan. Moreover, Delhi will have to fix its relations with the Kashmiris, and the Indian government will have to be willing to give Kashmiri politicians enough space to be their own people. After another violent, bitter summer in the Kashmir Valley, these are lessons worth remembering.

To End a Civil War: Norway's Peace Engagement in Sri Lanka
Mark Salter. London: C. Hurst & Co., 2015. £25.00/$35.00. 512 pp.

Mark Salter's account of Norwegian peace diplomacy in Sri Lanka is the most comprehensive published account of the last decade of Sri Lanka's long and agonising civil war. It draws on extensive interviews with those involved, backed up by published materials. The most comprehensive interviews are with Norwegian diplomats. Salter also interviewed sources in Sri Lanka, both in and out of government, as well as in India, the United States and Europe. By the time he wrote the book, the leaders of the Liberation Tigers of Tamil Eelam (LTTE) were dead, but Norwegian diplomats and others spoke extensively of the LTTE perspective as it had been conveyed to them. The result of all this research is an important book, which any student of peacemaking or Sri Lanka needs to read.

Salter conveys skilfully the ambiguity that dogs any complex diplomatic undertaking, such as the inevitable questions about whether the Sri Lankans and the LTTE had a common interpretation of the Oslo accord that started the negotiating process. No member of Sri Lanka's dramatis personae emerges as a hero. The diplomatic campaign achieved some important interim goals, such as a ceasefire agreement, but in the end the civil war continued. If it has now ended – and that is still in doubt – it was ended by war.

And yet – this was a frustrating book to read. It contains numerous small inaccuracies: people's names are misspelled and senior officials' titles are reported incorrectly. It was bound to be difficult to keep track of the different arcs of this complex story – the multiple hostile parties in Sri Lankan politics, the legacy of decades of built-up mistrust, the differing equities of relevant third parties, including India and the United States.

Salter opted to tell his story primarily through the words of his interviewees, which appear in text boxes throughout the book. While this serves to highlight the differing perspectives of those most intimately engaged in the peacemaking effort, this approach also means that the threads of the story are never really pulled together.

In the final chapters, Salter quotes extensively from a hard-hitting Norwegian government report drawing lessons for future peacemaking from this campaign. This is the closest Salter comes to giving the reader his judgement of what went right, what went wrong, and what alternative approaches might have been better. The Norwegian report concluded correctly that Norway had both advantages and disadvantages as an outside power wielding persuasion and diplomatic talent but not much 'hard power'. It criticised Norway's meagre ability to influence Sri Lankan opinion beyond elite circles. Most interestingly, it came close to concluding that Norway should probably have pulled out, at least temporarily, when it became clear, in about 2006, that the parties were no longer serious about finding a diplomatic solution. I recall discussing this in Washington with one of the principal Norwegian diplomats involved, commenting that this would be a rather un-Norwegian thing to do. The look on his face suggested that he had been thinking the same thing.

In an interview early in the book, Erik Solheim, Norway's principal negotiator, tells Salter that his principal task was to build relationships with the parties. Knowing the history of the conflict was secondary; a negotiator can find advisers to fill that gap. Solheim has his priorities right: diplomacy is about relationships. But what ultimately doomed his effort was in part the history of the problem, and the mindset that resulted – I would say especially within the LTTE, but also in the Sri Lankan body politic. Sri Lanka and the LTTE were at war. For Norway – indeed, for all outsiders – it was self-evident that a negotiated settlement would be better than the carnage of war. But for the parties involved, a negotiated settlement was preferable only if it achieved their war aims. The task of the peacemaker, in other words, was to persuade both parties to change their war aims enough to make them negotiable. With this in mind, I think the Norwegian report was too hard on the negotiators. Recognising the enormity of their task, I conclude that the Norwegian effort, with all its limitations, was remarkably effective.

The End of Karma: Hope and Fury Among India's Young
Somini Sengupta. New York: W.W. Norton, 2016. $26.95.
244 pp.

Somini Sengupta had already given us a taste of her skill as a writer through her reporting for the *New York Times*, first from India, and then from the United Nations. *The End of Karma* stands out, even amid the rich literature on the society of a dizzily changing India. She focuses here on the hopes, aspirations and anger of India's youth, which will ultimately determine where India – and Asia – are headed.

Sengupta profiles seven people, presenting details of their families and life stories, along with some discussion about which aspect of India's changing society these stories illustrate. Anupam is a striver from a 'backward caste' family. His path through the wild byways of the Indian educational system, grippingly sketched out, leads him into the Indian Institute of Technology, where he struggles to cope. He ultimately finds his upward path through the Indian School of Mines.

Mani, whose story is perhaps the most wrenching of the book, travels from her village to be a maid in the go-go Delhi business suburb of Gurgaon, all green glass and gleaming steel – only to have her niece abducted by traffickers connected with the Maoist insurgency that plagues India's eastern half. The juxtaposition of Mani and her boss, Supriya, both depicted with sympathy, shows at once the human side and the cruelty of the social system, as well as the dark side of the Gurgaons of this world, which Sengupta sees as a kind of Xanadu of the new India. Rakhi, the commander of a Maoist group, takes the insurgency theme further. Shashi, an operative in the political machine Narendra Modi made famous in Gujarat, gives an inside view of the manipulative side of political organisation. A group of so-called 'Facebook Girls' finds itself at the junction between India's techie aspirations and its collective fear of uncontrolled popular passions: the girls' posting on Facebook about the death of Mumbai's most famous political boss, Bal Thackeray, earns them a jail sentence. Inevitably, Sengupta ends up with two stories of young people wishing to defy their parents' plans for them. One ends tragically, in an 'honour killing' by the girl's brother; the other more hopefully.

The theme that runs through Sengupta's book – one which is difficult for a Westerner to internalise – is captured by her title, *The End of Karma*, which, loosely translated, means the end of predestination. Her narrative underscores the many ways in which predetermined ideas of how one should spend one's life have created a box that young Indians struggle to get out of – even as they also strive to remain close to their parents and other relatives who define their world.

The growing ability among Indians to control their own lives is the most revolutionary aspect of the social change convulsing India. The story of Anupam underlines this point, noting that he had embraced the view that his destiny was now in his own hands and not some deity's.

No one should read this book looking for 'the answer' to India's youth. There are as many answers as there are twenty-somethings navigating their way between tradition and modernity, between family ties and the unlimited vistas of the internet, between the straitjacket of village society and the unprotected expanse of emerging India. The book *should* be read as a gripping human drama, one that will play itself out millions of times as India continues to astonish itself, both breaking and preserving age-old traditions.

Iran and Pakistan: Security, Diplomacy and American Influence
Alex Vatanka. London: I.B. Tauris, 2015. £62.00/$110.00.
307 pp.

There has been surprisingly little serious scholarship on the Iran–Pakistan relationship. Alex Vatanka's study is a welcome step toward filling this gap. *Iran and Pakistan: Security, Diplomacy and American Influence* traces this complex relationship from the time of Pakistan's independence through to the present. For both countries, it was always part of a quest for 'something strategically larger' (p. 3). But Iran and Pakistan also had discordant ideas about their strategic goals and their respective roles in the region. In the early years, Pakistan considered itself the major partner. Once Iran and Pakistan joined the US-led Cold War alliance system, both sought to reap advantages from their ties with the United States, a process that was in part competitive. After Pakistan's eastern wing broke away and became Bangladesh, Iran under Shah Mohammad Pahlavi gave greater priority to ties with India, to Pakistan's great unhappiness. The complexity of the strategic relationship during this time was rivalled by the competition between the personalities of Pahlavi and Pakistani prime minister Zulfiqar Ali Bhutto. These two men embodied what was emerging as a relationship of mutual contempt between the two countries: Pakistan viewed the Iranians as 'soft' and non-martial; Iran viewed the Pakistanis as unsophisticated peasants.

Iran's Islamic Revolution ushered in a new phase in Pakistan–Iran ties. Tehran's now toxic relationship with the United States served as a speed bump in its relationship with Pakistan, which, for all its difficulties with Washington, was unwilling to risk its security connection with the Americans. Worse, both countries meddled in each other's most painful internal conflicts – the Sunni–Shia divide in Pakistan, and dissension and discontent in the Balochistan provinces of both countries. Bilateral ties became a roller-coaster ride, aggravated by disconnects in foreign policy and strategic priorities that had been apparent earlier.

Vatanka brings to light some fascinating and little-known vignettes: the apparent fascination in some quarters of 1950s Washington for a 'federation' of Pakistan, Afghanistan and Iran, an idea that went nowhere; Pahlavi's efforts to persuade Pakistan to crack down on the Baloch people – an effort that continues to plague the Pakistani state; the contradictory views of the Central Treaty Organization (CENTO) within both Pakistan and Iran. The book is strongest in discussing Iranian goals and attitudes, somewhat weaker on Pakistan, and occasionally off base on the United States. The author understates the importance that Pakistan attaches to retaining a dominant position in Afghanistan, for example. He gets some details wrong: Henry Kissinger's big, splashy summit in Pakistan took place in October 1974, not 1976 (I was there). And, astonishingly, in discussing the US response to the Soviet invasion of Afghanistan, he omits Pakistani foreign minister Agha Shahi's January 1980 visit to Washington, which was the starting point for both the successes and the great frustrations of the second big US–Pakistan engagement.

Seen from the Pakistani perspective, what is striking about Vatanka's account is the way Pakistan dealt with Iran as if the former occupied a position of dominance. Another country that Pakistan handled in this way was the United States. In both cases, Pakistan had hoped for steadfast support against India, but this hope crashed on the rocks of divergent strategic priorities.

Despite some problems, Vatanka's is clearly the most comprehensive and best-reasoned work on Iran–Pakistan ties currently available. This relationship is likely to remain problematic – and important.

Middle East
Ray Takeyh

Nasser's Gamble: How Intervention in Yemen Caused the Six-Day War and the Decline of Egyptian Power
Jesse Ferris. Princeton, NJ: Princeton University Press, 2013.
£44.95/$60.00. 341 pp.

In the 1960s, the Arab world was immersed in its own cold war, pitting the radical republics against the conservative monarchies. The so-called Arab cold war was led by the flamboyant and cunning Gamal Abdel Nasser of Egypt, who viewed the traditional monarchies, particularly the House of Saud, as relics of a distant and discredited past. The received wisdom has long suggested that this cold war ended when Israeli armour put an end to Nasser's dreams during the 1967 war. The smouldering ruins of the Egyptian army led Nasser to reconcile with his monarchical foes, trading his transformational dreams for their petrodollars.

Jesse Ferris's *Nasser's Gamble* is a thoughtful and important diplomatic reconstruction of those heady days of Arab politics. A historian of impressive range, Ferris has consulted a large number of archives and personal memoirs to shed new light on this important period. The centrepiece of his book may be Yemen, but the context of his narrative is the turbulent Middle East of the 1960s. The Arab cold war became hot in Yemen, and Egypt found itself intervening in a conflict that it did not think would last long or require many troops. This is a familiar predicament of invaders, who often tell themselves that the cost of their involvement will be manageable and its duration short. The cause of the nascent republic in Yemen that had displaced a monarchy was too attractive for Egypt, and too threatening to Saudi Arabia, to resist. The Saudis had the advantages of geography and more dexterous tribal allies. Nasser had the disadvantages of distance and feckless allies.

Nasser's impetuous intervention cost him the possibility of a workable relationship with the United States. The Kennedy administration was intrigued by Third World revolutionaries and sensed that America could reach accommodations with them. Once Nasser became entangled in Yemen, he not only dispensed with the American aid that was critical to his country's well-being, but became inordinately dependent on the Soviet Union. Yet all the Soviets had to offer him was shoddy arms and bad advice, as became apparent in June 1967. A leader who had once championed non-alignment became just another Arab dictator bargaining for weapons in the Kremlin. Nasser's Egypt may never have become a full-blown Russian client, but it also failed to become a truly independent actor on the global stage.

Nasser's Gamble does much to expose the toxic politics of Egypt during this era. Nasser's competition for power with his army chief of staff, the extraordinarily incompetent Abd al-Hakim Amir, set the stage for an unusual dynamic. The general's disastrous performance in the Suez War of 1956 was never examined so as not to disturb the convenient narrative of a great Egyptian triumph. It would not have looked good for the supposed author of that victory to be abruptly discarded. Amir was an eager advocate of the Yemen war, knowing that a good war would divert the attention of those seeking to dismiss him. Benefiting from a powerful base of support within the army, he managed to lead a willing Nasser into a conflict that would doom them both. Nasser would lose his revolution, Amir his life.

Vanguard of the Imam: Religion, Politics, and Iran's Revolutionary Guards
Afshon Ostovar. Oxford: Oxford University Press, 2016.
£22.99/$34.95. 306 pp.

Iran's Islamic Revolutionary Guard Corps (IRGC) has emerged as a subject of particular fascination for Western commentators. As is often the case with Iran, the subject has invited much speculation but little thorough analysis. Into this vacuum steps Afshon Ostovar with his *Vanguard of the Imam*, a readable and reliable account that is sure to prove an indispensable resource for anyone wishing to understand the IRGC's evolution and functioning. Ostovar has dived deeply into archives, records, speeches and news accounts to reveal how the organisation's members have sought to define the politics of the theocratic state.

The IRGC came into existence in the aftermath of the revolution, when newly empowered clerical leaders, who distrusted the armed forces, sought to develop their own militia. This was to be the muscle of the Islamic Republic, a role the guards performed with vigour during the initial post-revolutionary days as street battles and terrorist acts threatened Ayatollah Ruhollah Khomeini's enterprise. From its inception, the IRGC has been a deeply ideological organisation whose methods of indoctrination have produced a dependable cadre willing to both shed blood and die for the theocratic state. Its members truly believe that they are defending God's vision on earth.

The IRGC would have remained an internal security militia had it not been for the Iran–Iraq War. During the eight long years of the conflict, it came to displace the conventional military as Iran's principal bulwark of resistance. Through daring operations and much sacrifice, the IRGC proved its broader utility to the state. It should be noted that its operations were often amateurish and usually devoid of sound military thinking – the organisation believed that courage and commitment alone could overcome Iraq's technological superiority, a philosophy that resulted in heavy losses for limited gains. Still, a certain aura of revolutionary valour came to permeate the organisation.

Ostovar does an impressive job of illuminating the IRGC's many facets, highlighting the fact that, in addition to being a military organisation, it has developed a sophisticated propaganda apparatus. It has made movies, produced documentaries, built libraries and published a variety of magazines and newspapers. Ironically, it was the pragmatic president Ayatollah Hashemi Rafsanjani who pressed the IRGC toward economic activity in the 1990s, as the corps' engineering skills honed during the war were seen as necessary for the task of reconstruction. Over time, its business enterprise came to absorb huge slices of Iran's economy. Today, the IRGC stands as one of the largest and most opaque business conglomerates in Iran.

During the last ten years, the IRGC has proven its worth as the enforcer of the reactionary wing of the Islamic Republic. It was instrumental in subverting the reformist presidency of Mohammad Khatami, and took the lead in brutalising the Green Movement in summer 2009. The organisation seems to have set for itself the tasks of preventing any actor from liberalising the Islamic Republic (and thus potentially undermining its own power), and of spearheading Iran's imperial surge. Its famed Quds Brigade has safeguarded the fledgling Shia regime in Baghdad and the Assad dynasty in Damascus, actions that have invited internal opprobrium and external sanctions. But as Ostovar demonstrates in this impeccable book, the organisation has never been more vital to the workings of the theocratic regime.

Saudi Arabia: A Kingdom in Peril
Paul Aarts and Carolien Roelants. London: C. Hurst & Co., 2015.
£25.00. 176 pp.

Saudi Arabia has been much in the news lately. After decades of upholding an anachronistic national compact that traded political passivity for financial dividends, the House of Saud is talking reform. The Kingdom is seeking to diversify its economy, lessen its dependence on oil and shrink its cradle-to-grave subsidies, measures that astute observers have advised for years. Yet despite frequent suggestions that Washington is best placed to press its ally toward reform, Riyadh today seems to be moving in that direction not because of American pressure, but indifference. As the United States contemplates its exit from the region, the princely class is finally getting serious about setting its house in order.

In their clear and compact book, Paul Aarts and Carolien Roelants assess the Saudi reform efforts. Despite its provocative title, this is a tempered account that makes its case in a measured way. The authors offer a reasonable survey of Saudi efforts in various fields, from petroleum policy to increasing citizen participation in the workforce. They also touch on the widespread use of social media in the Kingdom, a preoccupation that seems out of place in a society that prizes strict religious observance. A burgeoning youth culture seems to be escaping the confines of Islamic enforcement even as the educational system struggles to overcome a burdensome tradition. The monarchy seems finally to have accepted the inevitability of the massive change such trends portend, and is now attempting to guide, rather than resist, it.

Will this attempt to reform the Kingdom work? Western scholars and policy-makers are fond of the conceit that reforms deemed necessary can be expected to succeed once embarked upon. China's historic achievement in replacing its planned, Marxist economy with state capitalism has only bolstered this view. Yet most reform efforts don't succeed, and countries frequently find that they cannot complete their journey of change. The Soviet Union, for instance, was unable to reform its economy, and Iran has proven unsuccessful in changing its polity. For their part, Aarts and Roelants take a pass on predicting how the unfolding Saudi effort will turn out. Given how many previously sure-footed prognostications have come and gone, this is probably for the best.

The Fall of Heaven: The Pahlavis and the Final Days of Imperial Iran
Andrew Scott Cooper. New York: Henry Holt and Co., 2016.
$36.00. 608 pp.

In this compelling and crucial volume, Andrew Scott Cooper lays bare the inner workings of the Iranian monarchy during its final years in power. His accessible and graceful writing style, along with his skilful use of historical documents and contemporary interviews, makes *The Fall of Heaven* a stand-out contribution to the literature on one of the most misunderstood revolutions in the modern history of the Middle East.

There has always been a mystery at the heart of the Pahlavi dynasty's fall in 1979. The shah was personally brave, having survived numerous assassination attempts, and during his long tenure was acclaimed for his shrewdness. And yet, when the revolution came, he responded with passivity, merely observing the collapse of his rule. Why was a man who loved Iran, and who dreaded the prospect of reactionary clerics coming to power, so strangely incapable of using the power at his disposal to crush the revolution?

Although he is often portrayed in Western historiography as a ruthless dictator overseeing a vicious secret police, the SAVAK, Cooper demonstrates that, throughout his life, the shah recoiled from the use of violence against his subjects. Having survived many challenges to his rule, particularly the 1953 uprising led by the nationalist prime minister Mohammad Mossadegh, the shah took it upon himself to transform his country from a backward agricultural nation into a modern state. He laid the foundations of modern industry, distributed land to the peasants, liberated women, expanded the educational sector and made Iran the envy of the developing world. There were mistakes along the way: corruption was endemic, and the country's once vibrant elite politics characterised by independent-minded politicians and self-assertive parliaments came to an end. The shah perceived that his modernisation drive required a strongman at the helm unencumbered by parliaments and politicians. This proved his most crucial mistake, as he stood to be blamed for everything that went wrong. And much did go wrong in the 1970s, as the economy cooled and alienation set in, particularly among Iran's youth.

Even as the revolution unfolded, the shah persisted with a liberalisation programme designed to restore the constitutional order. Indeed, his determination to revive Iran's democratic culture predated the advent of the Carter administration and its disdain for right-wing dictators. A cancer-stricken monarch wished to bequeath to his son a regime that rested its legitimacy not on monarchical whim but checks and balances. As demonstrations engulfed the streets, the shah continued to dismantle his security apparatus. The army was ordered into the streets, but instructed not to harm the protesters. The Iranians seemed to relish revolting against a crestfallen monarch who was promising them democracy in favour of a reactionary cleric who abhorred Enlightenment values. Of course, self-delusion was not limited to the Iranian crowds: the Carter White House, and America's disastrous ambassador to Iran, William Sullivan, also persuaded themselves that Ayatollah Khomeini would fade from the scene, handing power to the so-called moderates.

Cooper does a brilliant job of restoring to life all the Iranian and American players in Iran's revolutionary tragedy: scheming Iranian elites, who vanished at the first sign of trouble; confused Westerners seeking pragmatic voices in the midst of revolutionary turmoil; military leaders who were hampered by the shah's indecision and who would soon perish at the hands of vengeful revolutionaries; and, finally, the shah himself, who seemed to retreat at the crucial moment.

In the end, Cooper skilfully demolishes the popular view of the shah as a hardened autocrat and reveals him to be a decent man who died in exile with many regrets.

**Us Versus Them: The United States, Radical Islam, and the
Rise of the Green Threat**
Douglas Little. Chapel Hill, NC: The University of North
Carolina Press, 2016. $30.00. 314 pp.

Douglas Little begins his survey of America's post-Cold War misadventures in the Middle East by positing the simple thesis that Washington functions only when it conjures up an enemy to confront. There is something to this argument, given how often US politicians have used inflated language to gain support for their policies in a country at ease with its isolationist torpor. But it is also an argument that can be taken too far. After all, the Soviet Union was an empire that sought to subjugate as much of the world as it could, and Islamist terrorism is a real threat to the stability of the global order. Despite their obvious differences, neither threat is the product of an overeager political imagination.

Much in this book will prove familiar to even careless readers of daily newspapers. Little advances no novel arguments, offers no compelling new evidence and charts no real explanatory paradigm. Even his 'us versus them' thesis gets lost along the way as the author treads the familiar terrain of the elder George Bush's liberation of Kuwait and Bill Clinton's plunge into the morass of Israeli–Palestinian peacemaking. Little, as with most members of the professoriate, holds a special grudge against George W. Bush. Yet by now the Bush presidency and its headlong rush into the Iraq War has few defenders, even within the Republican Party, whose presidential nominee has denounced Bush in terms familiar to readers of *The Nation*. Thus, even in his enmities, Little is behind the curve. Still, the Bush years come closest to conforming to Little's picture of an overeager America that needs to summon threats to justify its errant policies. The Obama years receive a light touch as a presidency that has sought to transcend the usual conventions of American diplomacy. However, given the collapse of the Arab order, the tragedy of the Syrian civil war and the rise of the Islamic State, it may be that some of those conventions were abandoned a bit too hastily.

As the Soviet–American confrontation becomes a distant memory, the post-Cold War years are offering new ground for historians. Little should be commended for entering this territory, as the lack of primary sources and a slew of unreliable memoirs might have deterred a less adventurous academician. Still, the end result does little to enrich our understanding of events or to offer us a means of comprehending America's motivations. To be sure, American policy since the end of the Cold War has seemed improvisational and has lacked the consistency that a predictable Cold War adversary once furnished. But the sheer difficulty of formulating policy in a region that is full of surprises should have received a nod or two. There may yet come a day when a look back on the post-Cold War years yields a judgement long denied to the Cold War years themselves: that America did not do that badly after all.

Life Among Mafias

Rossella De Falco

I

The A29 is a four-lane coastal highway crossing northern Sicily. It is the fastest way to reach Palermo from Sicily's main airport, as the Mafia godfather Salvatore 'Totò' Riina knew very well. Riina also knew that the Sicilian judge Giovanni Falcone drove down that road, usually every two weeks, to visit his wife.[1] In February 1991, Falcone had moved to Rome, where he became director-general of criminal affairs at the Ministry of Justice. His aim was to launch a nationwide fight against the Italian Mafia through the establishment of national bodies such as the Anti-Mafia Investigation Department (Direzione Investigativa Anti-Mafia, or DIA).[2] In January 1992, the Supreme Court delivered its first devastating blow to the heart of Cosa Nostra, handing down 338 convictions, including 19 life sentences.[3] This so-called Maxi Trial was a huge victory for Falcone, who was among its main architects.[4] It also provided judicial confirmation of the long-rumoured existence of the *Cupola,* a sort of Mafia central government.

Riina wished for Falcone's assassination to be spectacular. The Mafia chief met several times with Cosa Nostra's Corleonesi bosses before agreeing on the particulars.[5] On 8 May 1992, Giovanni Brusca and five accomplices hid a half-ton of TNT and ammonium nitrate in a small drainpipe that ran under the A29.[6] The pipe, only 20 inches wide, would serve as a compressor, increasing the force of the blast.[7] The mouth of the pipe

Rossella De Falco is a recent graduate in International Affairs at the Johns Hopkins University, School of Advanced International Studies (SAIS).

Survival | vol. 58 no. 5 | October–November 2016 | pp. 209–216   DOI 10.1080/00396338.2016.1231543

was covered with rubbish, weeds and other debris.[8] Francesca Morvillo, herself a judge, was accompanying her husband back to the airport on 23 May 1992 when Falcone's white armoured Fiat Croma blew up at 17.58.[9] The explosion also killed Falcone's escort, and wrecked the stretch of highway close to the junction for the town of Capaci. The Mafia had declared war on the Italian state.

Judge Paolo Borsellino hastened to the hospital as soon as he learned of the attack. He had grown up with Falcone in an impoverished neighbour-hood in the heart of Palermo's old city. As Falcone once recalled, he and Borsellino used to play ping-pong with some of the boys who later became members of the Mafia.[10] Although the two friends had opposite political temperaments – soft-spoken Borsellino was a conservative, while the sardonic Falcone leaned to the left – they deeply trusted each other.

The death of Falcone placed Borsellino, one of Falcone's closest collaborators, next on the Mafia hit list. He was killed 57 days after his friend, on 19 July 1992. In his final days, Borsellino had been trying to find out why Falcone had been killed, and to discern trends in the Mafia's terrorist strategy. Aware he was running out of time, he had begun to hold his three children at arm's length. He wanted them to get used to his absence.

Borsellino recorded all of his secret speculations in a red police diary. He carried the book with him at all times, even in bed. When he went to visit his sick mother at her apartment in Palermo, he placed the diary in a brown leather briefcase. As he rang the bell, a car bomb killed him and every member of his five-person police escort. Borsellino's briefcase was found on the back seat of his car, where the judge had left it. The red diary was not inside it, and has yet to be found. The missing book has become one of the symbols of the anti-Mafia struggle in Italy.

II

The era of Mafia massacres, or *stragi mafiose*, began when Pio La Torre, a member of the Italian parliament, proposed to introduce a new crime, mafia conspiracy, to the Italian legal system. Pio La Torre was assassinated on 30 April 1980, but the law was introduced all the same, a few months later. As Italian institutions joined the battle against Sicilian organised crime, the Mafia responded by killing officials ranging from magistrates to mayors to police colonels, including General Carlo Alberto Dalla Chiesa and his wife, Elisabetta Setti Carraro; Judge Rocco Chinnici, the founder of the anti-mafia magistrates' group; Giangiacomo Ciaccio Montalto, a judge in Trapani who was given neither escort nor armoured car; Mario d'Aleo, chief of the Italian police (the Carabinieri); and, finally, judges Falcone and Borsellino. The escalating violence culminated in the bombing in 1993 of some of the most important art centres in Italy. There were seven attacks targeting Florence, Rome and Milan. Ten people perished, and many historical buildings were badly damaged. Then-prime minister Carlo Azeglio Ciampi said that he feared a *coup d'état*.[11]

The Mafia massacres were the epilogue to one of the bleakest chapters in Italian history. This does not mean, however, that subsequent chapters were much better. The killings of Falcone and Borsellino did galvanise public outrage and calls for justice, and Riina was arrested in 1993, as were many other Mafia chiefs. This weakened Cosa Nostra, and several *mafiosi* started to collaborate with the Italian state. Nonetheless, the Sicilian Mafia quickly adapted to the new situation. The bosses kept a low profile, carefully avoiding the use of violence against politicians, officials and judges. This seems to have allowed the Sicilian Mafia to survive. Moreover, in 2013, a trial began in Palermo in which prosecutors accused ministers, police chiefs and the Mafia of colluding to end violence in the 1990s.[12] It is alleged that government officials sought to make a deal with the Mafia, promising less harsh jail conditions in exchange for an end to the bombing campaign.[13]

Whether or not this is true, the Sicilian Mafia is sticking with its low-profile strategy.[14] At the same time, it has increased cooperation with other organised crime groups in Italy.[15] The Camorra, based in Naples, comprises more than 100 clans and 7,000 members.[16] The Calabrian 'Ndrangheta is among the richest criminal organisations in the world, and has a dominant position in the European cocaine market.[17] The Apulian organised crime group, based in Puglia and Basilicata in Italy, is also present in the Netherlands, Germany, Switzerland and Albania.[18] Although these groups differ in their interests, behavioural codes and businesses, they all began in southern Italy, where they continue to dominate entire areas and take advantage of impoverished local communities.[19]

III

In the small town of Africo, Calabria, the unemployment rate is 40% and the average gross income of those who do have a job is €14,000 per year.[20] There are few shops, no taxis or hotels, and the tiny railway station is filthy and derelict. Despite the town's untainted coastline and white-sand beaches on the Ionian Sea, there is very little tourism. Yet neither are there beggars or street crime, and the 3,200 inhabitants of Africo own 1,783 cars.[21] These contradictions, which are common in many other semi-abandoned areas of southern Italy, exemplify the Mafia's power better than violence. Socially excluded youngsters work for local clans as drug couriers in exchange for easy money.[22] Many become Mafia affiliates in order to provide a stable source of income to their families.[23] As a state within a state, the Mafia offers its own alternative to unemployment, poverty and lack of opportunities.

In the decaying neighbourhoods of Naples, the city where I grew up, it is common to see children playing at being drug dealers working for the Camorra. This is understandable. Even semi-central areas such as Secondigliano and Scampia are perceived as marginal suburbs by other Neapolitans. In such areas, there is no middle class. With their barren streets and dirty buildings, they are considered extremely dangerous, and those who live there are usually viewed with suspicion. In the absence of alternative models of masculinity and success, some young boys in these areas see Camorra's members as idols. Yet I know many honest people who live there. The main difference between us is that they have far fewer opportunities than I do.

Foreign and Italian newspapers usually depict Naples and Campania as a war zone. They print lengthy articles about infighting among Camorra clans, youth gangs and daylight shootings, and the burden on local enterprises that feel compelled to pay the *pizzo*, or protection money, to mobsters. Some areas of Naples seem to be completely under the control of drug traffickers, smugglers and killers.

During my high-school years, at weekends, I used to walk down the seafront of Mergellina, next to the Port of Naples. I enjoyed the bright skies and the beauty of Ovo Castle, the oldest standing fortification in Naples, with Vesuvius on the horizon. The port itself is not only a delight for tourists and Neapolitans, however – it lies at the heart of the Camorra's counterfeiting business. Through the Port of Naples, counterfeited goods such as luxury clothing and software are smuggled to international markets via a criminal network that links the US, Europe and Australia.[24] For the Neapolitan Mafia, counterfeiting is both a source of profit and a way of laundering the money earned through other illegal businesses: drug trafficking, extortion, robbery, illicit lottery and football pools, and illegal toxic-waste dumping.

The black market is not the only source of revenue for the Camorra. Camorra clans can be described as criminal family-owned enterprises, which compete both in the licit and illicit marketplace. Dissolving people in vats of acid, burning them alive and blackmailing them gains respect and spreads fear, but also helps clans build economic monopolies, both in southern and northern Italy. Perhaps the most famous example of this is the construction-sector monopoly built by the Casalesi clan in the area of Caserta. Camorra clans enter the legal market through a grey zone, in which the line between licit and illicit is blurred. White-collar criminals, such as accountants and corrupt politicians, are as fundamental to Camorra's affairs as illiterate killers and ruthless bosses.

The Camorra developed in Naples during the nineteenth century, under the Bourbon Kingdom; the origins of its name are uncertain. Some historians make a connection with the biblical city of Gomorrah, said to have been destroyed by God for its sinfulness along with Sodom. The Neapolitans, in any case, have a perfect word to describe the criminal association plaguing their city: o' *Sistema*, which means 'the System'. In effect, the Camorra is a fluid, horizontal and anarchic system, in which clans constantly compete for power, enrichment, impunity and respect. As a criminal version of the Hobbesian state of nature, this system is highly dangerous. In contrast with the Sicilian Mafia's hierarchical structure, no boss has ever succeeded at unifying Camorra's clans. Alliances are only based on interest.

Despite growing up in the city that gave rise to the largest criminal association in Italy, I have lived a perfectly safe life. I have never knowingly met a Camorra member or affiliate. I simply took care to avoid certain areas. When I bought my lunch, however, it is possible that I was financing an illegal business. Likewise, I might have contributed to counterfeiting networks by buying implausibly inexpensive goods. Through the anonymous channels of money, I probably interacted with the underworld on a regular basis. The members of this world are never far away, as numerous local stories demonstrate. Take, for example, the experience of entrepreneurs who find that, just as their businesses take off, a member of the Camorra suddenly shows up, looking for profitable deals and refusing to take no for an answer. Doctors face the possibility of being asked by a well-known boss for a false health certificate to justify an absence at trial. Some simply date the wrong people without knowing of their criminal connections, as did Gelsomina Verde, aged 22, who was kidnapped and murdered after enduring hours of torture when rivals of her ex-boyfriend came looking for him. Similarly, there are those who are killed by mistake during shootings, or through slower methods, such as the inhabitants of the so-called 'Land of Fires', an area which is experiencing increasing rates of cancer and leukaemia due to illegal toxic-waste dumping by the Camorra.

Many people claim that the Mafia is part of southern Italy's culture. It is fairly common to hear people in the north claiming that the south is little more than a drag on the country's economic development and a breeding ground for criminal groups. The Northern League, a populist far-right party, sought to exploit such anti-southern prejudice for a long time, before switching to migrants as a more profitable target. These accusations are bewildering. One cannot choose one's birthplace. Am I, according to this perspective, inherently more prone to criminal activity because I was born in Naples? This same logic would condemn the entrepreneur who pays the *pizzo* to the Camorra without reporting the criminals to the police. Yet doing so would clearly place not only his own life, but the lives of his relatives, at risk. How can we ask for such a sacrifice? It is not up to defenceless and isolated citizens to oppose organised crime, which is the product of historical and socioeconomic factors. This is a problem that can only be eradicated by the collective and organised effort of the state.

Today, Borsellino and Falcone are Italian national heroes. Yet these anti-Mafia advocates were simply honest men who wished to do their jobs. If we call them heroes, we are perhaps refusing to believe in the cause for which they died: a normal society in southern Italy, in which people support anti-Mafia magistrates and share their battles, fearing and deploring the *mafiosi* at the same time.

Lucia Borsellino, the daughter of Paolo, has a law degree from the University of Palermo. The day the Mafia murdered her father, she helped to dress what remained of his body. A few hours later, she attended an oral exam before some incredulous professors.[25] She was determined to go on.

Notes

1 John Follain, *Vendetta, The Mafia, Judge Falcone and the Quest for Justice* (London: Hachette, 2012), pp. 68, 76–7, ebook version.

2 John Dickie, *Cosa Nostra: A History of the Sicilian Mafia* (London: Hodder and Stroughton, 2007 edition), p. 341.

3 Roberto Suro, '338 Guilty in Sicily in a Mafia Trial; 19 Get Life Terms', *New York Times*, 17 December 1987, http://www.nytimes.com/1987/12/17/world/338-guilty-in-sicily-in-a-mafia-trial-19-get-life-terms.html.

4 Follain, *Vendetta*, p. 74.

5 *Ibid.*, pp. 76, 78.

6 *Ibid.*, pp. 87, 93–4.

7 *Ibid.*, p. 87.

8 *Ibid.*, p. 95.

9 Attilio Bolozni, 'Strage a Capaci povero Falcone', *La Repubblica*, 24 May 1992, http://www.repubblica.it/online/album/novantadue/bolzoni/bolzoni.html.

10 Wolfgang Achtner, 'Obituary: Paolo Borsellino', 20 July 1992, *Independent*, http://www.independent.co.uk/news/people/obituary-paolo-borsellino-1534572.html.

11 Massimo Giannini, 'Ciampi: "La notte del '93 con la paura del Golpe"', 20 May 2010, *La Repubblica*, http://www.repubblica.it/politica/2010/05/29/news/notte-golpe-4418306/.

12 'Italy President Napolitano Denies Knowing of Mafia Deal', BBC News, 28 October 2014, http://www.bbc.com/news/world-europe-29797887?ocid=socialflow_twitter.

13 EUROPOL, 'Italian Organised Crime – Threat Assessment', The Hague, June 2013, p. 3.

14 *Ibid.*

15 *Ibid.*

16 FBI, 'Italian Organized Crime', https://www.fbi.gov/investigate/organized-crime.

17 EUROPOL, 'Italian Organised Crime – Threat Assessment', p. 3.

18 *Ibid.*

19 *Ibid.*

20 Nicholas Farrell, 'In Italy's Poorest Town, There's Little Left to Do but Join the Mafia', *Newsweek*, 9 April 2015, http://europe.newsweek.com/people-italys-poorest-town-africo-have-little-left-do-join-mafia-321151?rm=eu.

21 *Ibid.*

22 Roberto Saviano, *Gomorra* (Milano: Oscar Mondadori, 2016 ed.), pp. 39–43.

23 *Ibid.*

24 Italian Ministry for Economic Development (MISE), Dipartimento per l'impresa e l'internazionalizzazione Direzione Generale per la Lotta alla Contraffazione – Uibm, 'La Contraffazione come Attività Gestita dalla Criminalità Organizzata Transnazionale', 2012, p. 15.

25 Manfredi Borsellino, 'La mia vita tra due stragi a Capaci morì anche mio padre', *La Repubblica*, 22 May 2010, http://palermo.repubblica.it/cronaca/2010/05/22/news/la_mia_vita_tra_due_stragi_a_capaci_mor_anche_mio_padre-4255159/.